TAXES IN AMERICA

WHAT EVERYONE NEEDS TO KNOW®

TAXES IN AMERICA

WHAT EVERYONE NEEDS TO KNOW®

Second Edition

LEONARD E. BURMAN
and
JOEL SLEMROD

OXFORD
UNIVERSITY PRESS

Oxford University Press is a department of the University of Oxford. It furthers
the University's objective of excellence in research, scholarship, and education
by publishing worldwide. Oxford is a registered trade mark of Oxford University
Press in the UK and certain other countries.

"What Everyone Needs to Know" is a registered trademark of
Oxford University Press

Published in the United States of America by Oxford University Press
198 Madison Avenue, New York, NY 10016, United States of America.

Library of Congress Cataloging-in-Publication Data
ISBN 978–0–19–092085–2 (pbk.)
ISBN 978–0–19–092086–9 (hbk.)

To our wives, our most valued friends and trusted advisors

CONTENTS

2 Personal Income Taxes   23

3 Business Income Taxes   64

4 Taxing Spending 99

PART II THE COSTS AND BENEFITS OF TAXATION

6 Taxes and the Economy   **149**

11 The Behavioral Economics of Tax Policy (or Tax Policy for Imperfect Humans)   229

PART III A TOUR OF THE SAUSAGE FACTORY

12 Misperceptions and Reality in the Policy Process 239

PREFACE

Who are we?

Leonard E. Burman is the Paul Volcker Professor of Behavioral Economics and Professor of Public Administration and International Affairs at the Maxwell School of Syracuse University and Institute Fellow at the Urban Institute. He co-founded the Tax Policy Center (TPC), a nonpartisan joint venture of the Urban Institute and Brookings Institution. The TPC is widely respected in Washington policy circles for the quality, objectivity, and clarity of its analysis of complex subjects. Burman previously served as Deputy Assistant Secretary for Tax Analysis at the Treasury Department and senior economist at the Congressional Budget Office. He was president of the National Tax Association (NTA), the leading American organization of experts in the theory and practice of taxation, from 2010 to 2011, and received the NTA's Davie-Davis Award for Public Service in 2016. He often testifies before Congress on tax and budget policy issues, and his commentaries have been published in top newspapers and aired on public radio. He is the author of a book, *The Labyrinth of Capital Gains Tax Policy: A Guide for the Perplexed*.

Joel Slemrod is the Paul W. McCracken Collegiate Professor of Business Economics and Public Policy at the Stephen M. Ross School of Business, and Professor in the Department of Economics, at the University of Michigan. He also serves as Director of the Office of Tax Policy Research, an inter-disciplinary research center housed at the Ross School of Business. He has served as the senior economist for tax policy at the President's Council of Economic Advisers, has been a member of the Congressional Budget Office Panel of Economic Advisers, and has testified before Congress on domestic and international taxation issues. From 1992 to 1998 Slemrod was editor of the *National Tax Journal* and from 2006 to 2010 was a co-editor of the *Journal of Public Economics*. From 2005 to 2006, he was president of the National Tax Association. He is co-author with Jon Bakija of *Taxing Ourselves: A Citizen's Guide to the Debate over Taxes*, whose fifth edition was published in 2017. In 2012 he received the prestigious Daniel M. Holland Medal from the National Tax Association for distinguished lifetime contributions to the study and practice of public finance.

Why did we team up to write this book?

Mostly because we're old friends and like working together. We go way back. Indeed, Len was Joel's first Ph.D. student when we both were at the University of Minnesota. Since then we have kept in close touch through the ups and downs of tax policy and have shared a commitment to educating the public about sometimes opaque tax issues, even while acknowledging that we don't have all the answers and sometimes even have differing views. Once before we took a shot at something like this, co-authoring in 2003 an article for *The Milken Institute Review* entitled "My Weekend with Nick and Adam: Tax Policy and Other Willful Misunderstandings." Some traces of that article, available at http://www.urban.org/UploadedPDF/1000554.pdf, survive in this book. Slemrod has co-authored a book (*Taxing Ourselves*) with a former University of Michigan Ph.D. student, Jon Bakija, who is Professor of Economics at Williams College. That book is used in many undergraduate and master's level classes on public finance and taxation.

We highly recommend it to readers who want to delve more deeply into tax policy.

After talking for years about doing this, we finally did it, publishing the first edition of this book in 2013.

What's the book about?

Taxes have always been an incendiary topic in the United States. A tax revolt launched the nation and the modern-day Tea Party invoked the mantle of the early revolutionaries to support the call for low taxes and limited government.

And yet, despite the passion and the fury, most Americans are remarkably clueless about how our tax system works. Surveys indicate that they have no idea about how they are taxed, much less about the overall contours of federal and state tax systems. For instance, a poll found that two-thirds of Americans say they only know a little bit or nothing at all about U.S. tax policy. Half think that 75 percent of federal revenue comes from personal income taxes, whereas less than half of federal revenues actually comes from personal income taxes.[1] The book focuses on U.S. tax policy, but includes information about other countries where it is enlightening. For example, we talk about U.S. tax burdens compared with the rest of the world and discuss the value-added tax (VAT), which is not currently part of the U.S. tax arsenal, but is ubiquitous elsewhere and often proposed for the United States by would-be reformers. We offer an overview of state and local taxation in the United States, but our main focus is on federal taxes.

The book has three main sections. Part I discusses how we are taxed in the United States. It starts with a broad overview and then more detailed discussion of personal and business taxes, taxes on spending (such as the VAT), and other taxes (such as the estate tax). Part II discusses the costs and benefits of taxation. We begin by discussing how taxes affect the economy, the trillion-plus dollars of spending that are channeled through the tax system (sometimes called the hidden welfare state), the

burden of taxation and notions of fairness, how the Internal
Revenue Service (IRS) runs the U.S. tax system and how complex the process is, and, finally, whether taxpayers always deal
with the tax system in a rational manner. Part III ("A Tour of
the Sausage Factory") covers tax politics and tax reform.

Although taxes can be mind-numbing, we hope to key our
discussion to issues that are likely to be on the mind of the
average taxpayer and be in the news, as well as supply interesting information that many readers might not know about
(such as how the IRS decides whom to audit). We have tried to
employ a light touch, interjecting tax humor and political cartoons where appropriate and illustrating key data with very
simple graphics.

Why did we write a second edition?

As we note in the book, the tax system changes. Since the first
edition, Congress passed the Tax Cuts and Jobs Act of 2017,
the biggest modification in the U.S. tax system since the Tax
Reform Act of 1986. The policy debate that led to TCJA raised
a number of important issues that weren't on anybody's radar
screen in 2013. For example: The destination-based cash flow
tax (DBCFT) is a mouthful. What is it? (p. 114). And it's made
other issues that we did discuss in the first edition a lot more
salient (e.g., territorial taxation, p. 86). In addition, the political
process leading up to TCJA has revealed much about how tax
legislation gets made in the United States that is worth exam-
ining. And the run-up to the 2020 presidential election raises
even more issues, such as, Should the United States adopt a
wealth tax? (p. 137).

This is a major update. We have revised and updated nearly
every topic in the first edition. We have added more than 40
new entries, including a new chapter on behavioral economics.

We have been heartened by the reception of the first edition,
in terms of sales, text adoption, favorable reviews, and compli-
ments. The second edition is even better.

Who provided invaluable assistance on this project?

Joe Jackson and Terry Vaughn at Oxford University Press first pitched the project to us and have provided encouragement and granted deadline extensions with a generosity that the IRS does not typically offer taxpayers. David Pervin has been similarly competent and patient in guiding the second edition to completion.

At Syracuse University, Burman's Tax Policy and Politics class cheerfully served as human subjects in all stages of the development of this book. Heather Ruby provided invaluable research assistance for the first edition, and Victoria Wright and Dan Hiller have done the same for the second edition. All three read and provided helpful comments on early drafts. And Dan has done yeoman's work in getting the second edition ready for publication, with support from Katrina Fiacchi.

At the University of Michigan, Ph.D. student Sutirtha Bagchi read carefully and researched the chapters that Slemrod drafted initially, and Katie Lim helped with compiling many tables. For both editions, Mary Ceccanese, who celebrated her 30th anniversary as Coordinator of the Office of Tax Policy Research in 2018, spearheaded the arduous process of turning a draft into a polished final product, and did so in her usual meticulous, efficient, and good-natured way.

Mary Ceccanese, Maureen Downes, Bob Mull, and Allison Paciorka offered invaluable comments and suggestions on early drafts of the first edition. Kim Clausing, Jacob Goldin, Tatiana Homonoff, and Kendra Robbins provided superb feedback and advice for the second edition.

Finally, we are grateful to Frank Sammartino and Bob Williams of the Tax Policy Center for allowing us to adapt its excellent glossary for this volume.

PART I

HOW ARE WE TAXED?

1

THE VIEW FROM 30,000 FEET

Why is everyone always so worked up about taxation?

Taxes in America amount to about 30 percent of national income, or roughly $15,000 per man, woman, and child. That's a lot of money that could otherwise be spent on goods and services that people value and enjoy, so it's no surprise that Americans pay very close attention to whether we are getting our money's worth and whether our own tax bill is too high.

Legendary Supreme Court Justice Oliver Wendell Holmes Jr. once said that "[t]axes are what we pay for civilized society."[1] This is true in the sense that tax dollars fund the basic architecture of a free society: a court system, fire and police departments, national defense. But governments now do much more than that. They support large social insurance programs that provide income and medical care to the elderly and low-income non-elderly, as well as schools, highways, bridges, dams, national parks, public housing, and so on.

Although Justice Holmes equated taxes with a price, taxes differ from prices in some essential dimensions. With most goods and services, paying more entitles you to more stuff or better-quality stuff or both. But, with one exception, that is not true of what you "get" from government. You can't bring your 1040 to Yosemite and demand VIP treatment because your tax bill is higher than most other Americans'. (You could try, but we doubt you'd get very far with the park ranger.) Also, unlike other goods and services, you don't get to choose what you spend your tax liability on. This is decided through a political process, and probably no one ends up completely happy with how much, and on what, the government spends the money. Some want a bigger military and less aid to education, while others would prefer more spending on education and less on foreign aid, and so on. And, unlike deciding whether to buy a Starbucks latte or rent a fancy condominium, you do not have a choice—evasion aside—about whether to remit taxes.

The income tax is the most common point of contact between people and the government. The filing deadline of April 15 is as well known a date as April Fool's Day, and not many events bring on more stress than a tax audit. It's really no surprise that, according to public opinion polls, the Internal Revenue Service (IRS) ranks near the bottom of American government institutions in popularity,[2] while the Social Security Administration (SSA) tops the list: for most Americans the IRS cashes your checks, while the SSA sends checks out. This image persists even though the IRS disperses billions of payments related to, for example, the Earned Income Tax Credit and stimulus programs. Nonetheless, the process of calculating what is owed is often complex, time-consuming, intrusive, expensive, and ultimately mysterious. As the noted humorist Will Rogers said decades ago, "The income tax has made more liars out of the American people than golf has. Even when you make a tax form out on the level, you don't know when it's through if you are a crook or a martyr." Many taxpayers suspect that they are suckers—while others find loopholes to escape their tax liability, they're left holding the bag.

Taxes can impose a substantial cost on people over and above the purchasing power they redirect to public purposes because they can blunt the incentives to work, save, and invest and can also attract resources into tax-favored but socially wasteful activities such as tax-sheltered orange orchards or construction of "see-through" office buildings (which could be profitable in the early 1980s because of tax benefits despite a dearth of tenants).

Tax policy affects the rewards or costs of nearly everything you can think of. It increases the price of cigarettes and alcohol, lowers the cost of giving to charity, may increase or reduce the reward to working, increases the cost of owning property or transferring wealth to your children, lowers the cost of home-ownership, and subsidizes research and development. For this reason, tax policy is really about everything, or at least everything with an economic or financial angle. Some want to extend the reach of tax policy even further, supporting proposals for a tax on fattening or sugary foods (the fat tax, not to be confused with the flat tax). Denmark and Ireland have periodically proposed to tax cattle owners (over $300 per cow per year in Denmark's latest proposal), in an effort to reduce cow flatulence, a key source of the greenhouse gas methane (the fart tax should not be confused with the fat tax or the flat tax).[3]

Why was everyone especially worked up in 2018?
(Hint: a lot has changed)

Everyone is especially worked up because in 2017 Congress passed the biggest overhaul of the income tax system in over 30 years. The new law nearly doubled the standard deduction, cut individual and corporate tax rates, doubled the child tax credit, limited the deduction for state and local taxes, provided a new 20 percent deduction for some business income, completely transformed the taxation of international income, and made numerous other smaller changes. (We discuss the big changes in some detail in a later chapter.)

There was furious debate and rhetoric in the last half of 2017, as the president and congressional committees floated various trial balloons. (See, for example, "What is the destination-based cash flow tax?") Some supporters and opponents even occasionally put forward economic arguments for or against. Once the general shape of the legislation became clear, news articles offered taxpayers advice about year-end strategies to take advantage of the coming changes.

Once January 1, 2018, arrived and the changes in what is known as the Tax Cuts and Jobs Act (TCJA) became the new tax law, people and businesses had to deal with it. (Even though it's commonly called TCJA, that isn't its official name because of an epic act of senatorial mischief. See page 267, "How did the Tax Cuts and Jobs Act become the law that must not be named?") Some decisions that made sense under the previous tax law no longer do, and some new tax avoidance strategies now become attractive.

What is a tax?

We might as well start at the beginning, by defining our subject. A tax is a compulsory transfer of resources from the private sector to government that generally does not entitle the taxed person or entity to a quid pro quo (that's why it has to be compulsory). Tax liability—what is owed to the government—may be triggered by a wide variety of things, such as receiving income, purchasing certain goods or services, or owning property.

Although the tax liability is not voluntary, the amount of any given tax that is due generally depends on voluntary choices made by people or corporations. Thus, in principle, one can legally avoid income tax by not earning any income (or have income below the taxation threshold), avoid retail sales tax by not buying anything, and avoid property tax by not owning any residential or commercial property. Of course, earning no income at all is not advisable even though it lowers tax liability; our point is that the *amount* of tax due depends on what you do and how you arrange your financial affairs. What's more, taxes are often borne by people other than those who write the check—so you may bear a burden from a tax even if you never file a return. (See page 24, "Who really bears the burden of tax?")

What are the major kinds of taxes?

Taxes can be classified on a number of dimensions. One important distinction is between impersonal and personal taxes. With the impersonal kind, how much tax is triggered is the same regardless of *who* undertakes whatever action triggers the tax. The usual retail sales tax is an impersonal tax, because any consumer (not a business—more on that later) buying a $20 hammer in a state with a 5 percent sales tax triggers a $1 tax liability regardless of who sold it or who bought it. If Warren Buffett buys it, $1 in tax is due and if one of us buys it, it is still $1. The impersonality certainly simplifies the tax collection process, as the retail business need not verify anything about the buyer such as his or her income, wealth, age, marital status, and so on. On the other hand, as we'll discuss later, this aspect of a sales tax limits the extent to which tax liability can be linked to people's ability to pay, which bothers many who are concerned with the fairness of the distribution of tax burdens.

A graduated income tax is a personal tax because the tax due per dollar of income earned depends on characteristics of the household. It depends on income—higher-income households are usually subject to higher tax liabilities and higher tax liabilities per dollar of income—and also may depend on other characteristics such as their marital status, charitable contributions, and medical expenses.

How are taxes like ducks?

What is, and isn't, called a tax sometimes becomes a high-stakes political game. Because of the heightened political resistance to anything called a tax, sometimes governments try to call taxes something else. The Reagan administration euphemistically referred to "revenue enhancement" when it proposed to raise taxes in the early 1980s.

At the 1988 Republican National Convention, George H. W. Bush famously promised, "Read my lips—no new taxes." Once elected, Bush's designated budget director, Richard G. Darman, said he would recommend that President Bush reject any tax increase. At his confirmation hearing before the Senate Governmental Affairs Committee, Darman indicated that he would not hide behind semantic niceties. He would apply the "duck test" to determine if a proposal could be perceived as a tax increase: "If it looks like a duck, walks like a duck and quacks like a duck, then it is a duck."

The distinction between a tax increase and a spending cut is not at all clear because our income tax code includes many items that may be better characterized as spending programs that just happen to be delivered through the tax system. Indeed, one of the largest antipoverty programs in the United States, the Earned Income Tax Credit, is delivered through the tax code (more on this later).

Is cutting back on subsidies a duck? Prominent conservatives disagree on that question. In early 2011, antitax crusader Grover Norquist accused conservative Senator Tom Coburn (R-OK) of breaking his no-tax-increase pledge by proposing an amendment to end a tax credit for ethanol. Norquist objected to the elimination of the credit because he viewed it as a (bad) tax increase, while Senator Coburn considered it to be a (good) spending cut.[4]

Are there "hidden" taxes?

Some taxes are more visible, or salient, than others. Hidden taxes, like hidden fees, operate under the radar of at least some of those affected. Most retail stores (at least the ones we shop at) don't remind us of the sales tax until we arrive at the cash register—the tax is not included in the shelf price of the item. On many e-tailing sites, the sales tax (and often other taxes) is added only at the very end of the transaction. Some conservatives object to this because they fear that it makes consumers,

" First, there will be NO NEW TAXES . . or I'm not six feet tall. "

Source: www.CartoonStock.com.

who are often also voters, underestimate the cost of government and therefore soften their vigilance regarding big government. Of course, the retailers are aware of the tax because
they have to remit the amount owed regardless of how visible
the tax is to the consumer.

This discussion helps sort out what it means when a retail
store—for some reason usually a furniture store—advertises
that "we pay your sales tax!" as part of a sales promotion. The
truth is that the store *always* must remit "your" sales tax, which
means that their prices are higher than otherwise. The sales-
tax claim is just another—apparently appealing—way to claim
that they are offering a special low price. As always, a purchase subject to a 6 percent off sale, or any price discount, is
only as attractive as the price before the discount.

REGARDING THE PROMISED TAX CUT... IT WILL DEPEND ON HOW YOU DEFINE 'TAX' AND 'CUT'...

Source: www.CartoonStock.com.

Hidden tax burdens are a bigger issue. The tax law specifies which person or business entity is legally obligated to remit taxes. But who must remit the tax does not pin down who ends up bearing the burden—the burden may be shifted. That burdens can be shifted is well known. Any parent knows that the burden of a school science project that is nominally the child's responsibility ends up costing the parent long hours. High parking meter charges not only increase shoppers' costs, but end up burdening local business owners through decreased sales.

Shifting of tax burdens is common, and it is almost never the case that the individual or business that remits the tax is the only one who is made worse off. At first glance, taxes on the income of a corporation appear to decrease the income of its owners, the shareholders. However, ultimately, these taxes may also lead to higher prices of what the business sells, burdening consumers; they may also reduce wages, burdening workers as well.

"Could you make it a dollar and four cents, sir? —
The Government says I have to collect sales tax."

Source: www.CartoonStock.com.

Are there ways to raise revenue other than taxes?

Yes, but these days, non-tax revenue sources play a relatively small role in the U.S. tax system.

Some non-tax revenue-raising schemes probably should be called taxes. Think about state-owned liquor stores that charge a markup far in excess of their costs; from the consumer's point of view, this is not much different from allowing private retailers to sell liquor subject to an excise tax.

Cash-strapped cities sometimes beef up police activities to raise more revenue from fines and civil asset forfeitures (confiscating valuable assets that police claim are related to a criminal activity). One study found that in North Carolina, a 1 percentage point decline in county revenues led to a 0.38 percentage point increase in traffic tickets the following year. (Increases in revenue, however, did not lead to a corresponding decline in tickets.)[5] Washington, D.C., raises about 1 percent of revenue from speed cameras, which effectively levy a tax in exchange for the privilege of exceeding the speed limit. Unlike a speeding ticket, there are no civil or criminal consequences other than the fine if it is paid on time. Critics have pointed out that these levies and forfeitures are especially burdensome for low-income residents.

There are also important ways for governments to get control over resources that don't involve raising money directly. Take the military draft. Until 1973 the United States required (and nearly 100 countries still do require) that many citizens of a certain age serve in the military.[6] A military draft has many of the features of a tax—it is compulsory and there is no quid pro quo, aside from a usually minimal salary. Just like a tax, many draftees would prefer not to bear the burden of service. Centuries ago it was common for governments to require compulsory labor service for other purposes. In Egypt, the use of forced labor on public works projects was used from the time of the pyramids until the mid-1800s. Forced labor was common in medieval Europe, when peasants were required to work for feudal lords, and it even occurred in the U.S. colonies.

The federal government could get resources by printing money and buying things with it, an option that is not available to state or municipal governments. Compared to, say, a personal income tax, this practice (called "seigniorage") obscures who bears the burden, but there is a burden nevertheless. Printing money causes inflation, which erodes the value of dollar-denominated assets such as government bonds or cash. Thus, the government gets resources at the expense of those who hold these assets. People understand this, and so when future inflation looks likely, people will not voluntarily lend to the government unless they are compensated with higher interest rates. Sometimes governments require financial institutions to hold public bonds at below-market interest rates—a practice called "financial repression"—which is another way to effectively obtain wealth from the private sector.

The United States does not typically print money to fund a substantial fraction of its operations. But in the past century several countries in desperate fiscal situations have resorted to the printing press, causing hyperinflation and disastrous consequences for the economy. Between 1914 and 1923, the Weimar Republic of Germany saw its price level increase by the mind-boggling factor of 1 trillion.[7] The printing presses ran all night and issued notes of larger and larger denomination, while workers immediately purchased goods with their paychecks as the currency depreciated by the minute. In the spring of 2006, the *New York Times* reported that in hyperinflating Zimbabwe, toilet paper cost 417 Zimbabwean dollars—not per roll, but per single two-ply sheet—a roll cost $145,750, and Zimbabwe printed $100,000,000,000,000 ($100 trillion) banknotes![8]

Why not just borrow the money instead of raising taxes?

The federal government can borrow money to fund its operations, and in recent years has been doing this to an unprecedented degree. But borrowing is fundamentally different from raising money through tax, or tax-like, means. For one thing, no one coerces anyone to lend to the government. They do so voluntarily because they find the interest rate attractive given the minimal default risk. Thus, government borrowing does not eliminate, or even reduce, the burden of government spending, but rather just postpones the reckoning of this burden, which will be felt through some combination of higher taxes in the future and cutbacks in future government spending or the inflation tax just discussed. (See page 163, "Why not run deficits forever?")

How can taxes be like regulations?

In most cases taxes are designed to raise revenue, and the changes in behavior they induce are unintended, undesirable byproducts. No policymaker intends to deter an automaker from building a plant in Michigan, but the corporate income tax may do that. Likewise, most politicians do not want to discourage spouses from entering or staying in the workforce, but the individual income tax can do that.

Some taxes, though, are intended to change behavior. One reason for taxing gasoline is to induce people to use less energy. Carbon taxes are designed to reduce emission of greenhouse gases that scientists believe contribute to global warming. Instead of using tax policy to achieve these aims, one can imagine regulations that restrict, limit, or proscribe the activities. For example, a cap-and-trade system can have effects similar to a carbon tax. Under this system the government sets a limit on total emissions and then allocates or auctions a number of permits equal to that amount. The permits can then be bought and sold, which establishes a market price. This market price has the same effect as a tax—making the polluting activity more costly. If the explicit tax, or the implicit tax due to the market price of the permits, is equal to the social cost of the polluting activity, then decision-makers are induced to take heed of the social cost of their actions. (See page 106, "What is a Pigouvian tax?")

How can regulations and spending programs be like taxes?

Some regulations have tax-like consequences because they affect prices, incomes, and behavior. For example, environmental and safety regulations add to the price of automobiles, and eligibility rules for spending programs can effectively increase or decrease households' spendable income. Eligibility for cash assistance programs is tied to income. A single parent with two young children working full time earning $8 per hour would have qualified for $87 per month in Temporary Assistance for Needy Families (TANF) and $370 in Supplemental Nutrition Assistance Program (SNAP) benefits in the District of Columbia in 2012.[9] If her wage increased by $1 per hour, her gross income would increase by $173 per month, but she'd lose $58 in TANF and $25 in SNAP benefits—a total of $83 per month. Thus, almost half of her pay increase would be offset by benefit cuts, equivalent to an effective tax rate of 48 percent. She'd also lose $28 in Earned Income Tax Credits and owe $10 in payroll taxes on the additional income. In total, the extra $173 in income would cost her $121 in lost benefits and increased taxes—an implicit tax rate of 70 percent (121 / 173).

High-income households can also face substantial implicit taxes attributable to spending programs. For example, individuals aged 65 and over pay income-tested premiums for Medicare Part B (medical insurance). In 2018, annual premiums totaled $1,608 for single people with income of $85,000 or less, $2,250 for incomes between $85,000 and $107,000, and more at higher incomes. A Medicare recipient whose income rose from $85,000 to $86,000 would owe $642 in additional Medicare premiums, for an implicit tax rate of 64.2 percent. At higher income thresholds, the effective tax rate can be as high as 96.5 percent for a $1,000 increase in income. Including the effect of Part D (prescription drugs), which is also means-tested at the same thresholds, the implicit tax rate can be over 120 percent.

There is one important difference between the implicit taxes created by spending programs and explicit taxes embodied in the Internal Revenue Code: participation in spending programs is voluntary, whereas taxes are compulsory. But for people who choose to participate in the government programs (more than 90 percent of eligible people participate in Medicare Part B),[10] the effects of the implicit taxes on economic incentives and family budgets are the same as under an explicit tax.

How have taxes changed over time?

Beginning about a century ago, the role of government began to expand all over the world, and the United States was no exception. Before World War I taxes levied by all levels of government comprised less than 3 percent of national income. Now they are over 25 percent. So, as a share of the economy, taxes are about 10 times as high as they were in 1912. But nearly all of that phenomenal growth occurred from 1912 to 1962. Since that time, federal taxes as a percentage of national income have gone up and down quite a lot, but have not trended upward or downward, while state and local taxes have drifted upward.

How do state and local taxes vary?

The Tax Foundation calculated, for each state, taxes paid (including fees) to state and local governments as a percentage of income in 2012. The ratio varies from a maximum of 12.7 percent in New York to a low of 6.5 percent in Alaska. More than three-quarters of states' tax ratios lie between 7.6 and 10.9 percent.[11]

How does the composition of tax vary across federal, state, and local governments?

The federal government's revenue comes predominantly from individual income taxes (47.9 percent in 2017) and social insurance and retirement receipts (35.0 percent), while only 9.0 percent comes from corporate income taxes, 2.5 percent from excise taxes, and 0.7 percent from estate and gift taxes.[12] In contrast, excluding intergovernmental grants and fees and charges, state and local governments get about two-thirds of their tax revenue from sources hardly used at all by the federal government: 34.8 percent from sales taxes and 31.1 percent from property taxes, while only 23.5 percent of their tax revenue derived from the individual income tax in 2015 (figure 1.1).[13]

Is the United States really the highest taxed country in the world?

President Donald Trump liked to say at campaign rallies that the United States is the highest taxed country in the world. In fact, compared to other rich countries, we are a low-tax

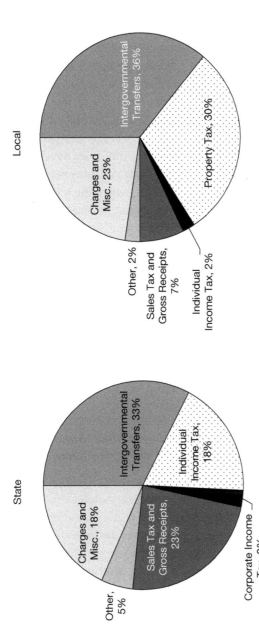

Figure 1.1 Percentage Distribution of State and Local General Revenue by Source, 2015

Source: State & Local Government Finance Data Query System. http://slfdqs.taxpolicycenter.org/pages.cfm. The Urban Institute-Brookings Institution Tax Policy Center. Data from U.S. Census Bureau, Annual Survey of State and Local Government Finances, Government Finances, Volume 4, and Census of Governments (1977–2015). Date of Access: (16-Oct-2017).

country. In 2016, our average federal, state, and local tax burdens amounted to 26 percent of GDP, well below the OECD average of 34.3 percent. (See figure 1.2.) The ratio of taxes to national output varied from 45.9 percent in Denmark to 17.2 percent in Mexico.[14] And our tax burden is even lower after the 2017 passage of the Tax Cuts and Jobs Act.

Closer examination reveals that, among developed countries, the United States raises about the average share of GDP from income taxes. What sets us apart from other developed economies is how little we collect from consumption taxes such as retail sales taxes or excise taxes, where the total tax is determined by the amount of spending, not income or wealth. Most other countries in the world raise a substantial share of revenue from a type of consumption tax called a value-added tax, or VAT, which the United States does not have, and which we discuss on page 107.

In those countries with higher taxes, governments provide services we have to pay for out of our own pockets here. Free health care is the developed-world norm, heavily subsidized childcare is common, generous childbearing and child-raising benefits are usually provided, and unemployment benefits are high and long-lasting.

Federal taxes in the United States have been at about 18 percent of GDP for 50 years. Does that mean that this is the natural rate of taxation?

Not in any meaningful economic sense. Economies can thrive with much different levels of tax. But 18 percent may represent a sort of political equilibrium that reflects the level of private consumption Americans have been willing to give up for what the federal government provides. When revenues have risen significantly above the historical norm, policymakers have chosen to cut taxes.

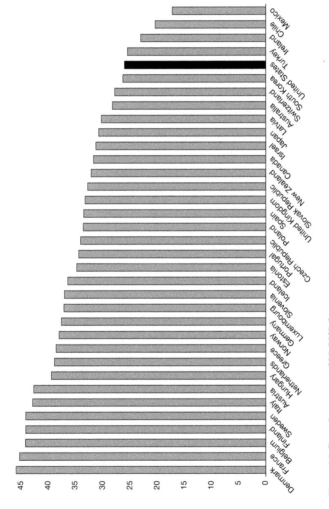

Figure 1.2 Tax as Percentage of GDP, OECD Countries, 2016

Note: Data for Australia and Japan are for 2015.

Source: OECD, tax statistics, 2018, http://stats.oecd.org/Index.aspx?DataSetCode=REV.

Why is the long-term fiscal outlook so dire?

Critics complained that the TCJA reduced revenues by almost $2 trillion over its first decade, which they viewed as especially irresponsible in light of the government's deteriorating fiscal situation. There is a huge mismatch between the promises we have made regarding Social Security, Medicare, and Medicaid benefits and the taxes we have in place to fund them. The so-called entitlement programs are projected to grow much faster than the economy (and tax revenues), because (1) Americans are living longer, so that the ratio of benefit recipients to working taxpaying Americans is rising, and (2) health care costs continue to grow faster than other prices. Medicare pays for acute care for the elderly and Medicaid pays for about half of nursing home care. By one reputable calculation, the gap between promised Social Security and Medicare benefits and the taxes, fees, and premiums that fund them amounts to over $53 trillion (yes, trillion!) over the next 75 years.[15] Given this mismatch, benefits will need to be cut, taxes increased, or both.

Can taxes be discussed without getting into government spending?

In the rest of this book, we will try our best to focus on the tax side of government budgets. But inevitably at several points along the way, we will have to talk about spending.

One reason is that, as already mentioned, sometimes the distinction between taxing less and spending more, or between taxing more and spending less, is arbitrary, reflecting semantic distinctions that are inconsequential from an economics perspective. Sometimes these inconsequential distinctions are reflected in official government accounting, so that of two programs that are effectively the same, one looks to be a tax cut and the other a spending increase. Later we will address the notion of *tax expenditures*, which are spending programs embedded within the income tax system. (See page 171, "What exactly is a tax expenditure?")

The appropriate level of taxes should reflect a comparison of the benefits of what government spending provides—be it national security, social insurance, fire departments, or national parks—with the cost of taxes. When comparing the benefits to the costs, we need to bear in mind that the cost of taxes should also reflect the disincentives and misallocations that taxes inevitably cause. For this reason a bridge that costs $500 million to build should promise benefits quite a bit higher than that. (See page 150, "Why do economists think that raising funds costs much more than the tax sticker price?")

The link between what government provides and what it collects shows up repeatedly in public opinion polls. Forty-five percent of Americans say that the amount of tax they pay is too high, according to a 2018 Gallup poll, and only 3 percent say it is too low. But when asked whether the federal government should spend more, less, or the same on Social Security, Medicare, education, or defense, the antitax sentiment dims: more than eight in 10 oppose cuts in these programs.[16] This pattern of answers does not dispose of the issues, because one should inquire into how much such programs would have to be cut back. But pairing the tax question and the spending question is the right way to think about fiscal issues. Spending without taxing does not provide free services. But the underlying benefit-cost analysis gets blurred because the federal government can borrow. When it does, the immediate, visible signal of the cost of government—taxes due—understates the true cost of government spending. *The cost of government is measured much more accurately by what it spends than by what it collects in taxes.*

Thus, a claim that taxes are too high is either a statement that (1) the government should just borrow more or (2) the government spends too much. The first is often bad economics or wishful thinking, because borrowing does not lower the cost of government and in most cases increases it by directing private saving into government bonds rather than productive capital. As to the second, we should always inquire exactly what government programs should be axed or slimmed down.

Many Americans care little about the abstract question of whether overall taxes are too high, too low, or just about right. They care much more about *their* taxes, and their own tax liability. That's a whole different matter, because whether my tax burden is $25,000 a year or $50,000 a year has absolutely no effect on the strength of our national defense, the viability of the Medicare system, or whether the local park is well manicured. At the macro level, determining the right allocation of tax burdens depends on resolving what is fair—always a contentious issue—and how alternative tax systems that assign tax burdens affect economic growth. We will do our best to answer these—and other—questions in the rest of this book.

2

PERSONAL INCOME TAXES

What's the difference between personal taxes and business taxes?

Some taxes are levied on people and some are levied on businesses. This distinction is less important than you might think. The fact is the person or business entity that writes the check doesn't necessarily bear the burden of the tax. Consider the corporate income tax. Many people like the corporate income tax because they think businesses should pay taxes, not people. But the fact that the business remits the tax doesn't really tell you whose bottom line is affected by it. It could be the company's shareholders. It could be the workers. The tax could be passed through to consumers in the form of higher prices. Or it could be some combination of all of the above. The fact that the corporation "pays" the tax doesn't tell you much. In fact, we avoid using the term "pays tax" because it is uninformative. It could mean one of two things: who writes the check (i.e., *remits* the tax) or who bears the burden of a tax.

Most people know what the individual income tax is. It's the tax that has made April 15 as iconic as the Super Bowl, without the parties or the popcorn. It's probably the most salient tax for most people, even though these days most people owe more in payroll taxes than income taxes.

The federal payroll tax is earmarked to fund Social Security retirement, survivors, and disability insurance as well as

Medicare. Sometimes it's called the FICA tax after the legislation that enacted it (the Federal Insurance Contributions Act). For self-employed people, it's called the SECA tax (the Self-Employment Contributions Act). We have no idea why there are two names for basically the same tax, but it's a fun fact that will impress your friends at cocktail parties.

Sales taxes and property taxes are mostly collected by state and local governments. Indeed, those are two of the three most important taxes collected at that level. Most states also levy income taxes.

Taxes nominally leveled on businesses include federal and state corporate taxes, a portion of payroll taxes (including taxes administered by state governments to cover unemployment and disability insurance), and excise taxes. Businesses also remit the value-added tax (VAT), which is common throughout the world, but is not levied in the United States. The VAT is a kind of sales tax. (See page 107, "What is a VAT?")

Some taxes are remitted by other entities. For example, the estate tax is remitted by the fiduciary of the estate of somebody who has died (typically somebody fairly wealthy). Fiduciaries of trusts also remit taxes. Those are effectively personal taxes, but the entity that writes the check is the trust that manages the assets, not the person on whose behalf the trust is administered. And nonprofit organizations may have to remit tax if they engage in certain profit-making activities.

But, as a practical matter, these distinctions are not particularly important because, as noted, who writes the check may have very little effect on who actually bears the burden of the tax.

Who really bears the burden of tax?

The answer is often more complicated than you might think. Let's get back to the example of the corporate income tax. As we've discussed, somebody bears the burden of the tax, but it's not obvious who. For a long time, the conventional wisdom among economists was that owners of capital, and not just owners of corporations, bore the tax burden because it pushed business activity into noncorporate activities, driving down the rate of return. But more recent research suggests that workers bear part of the tax burden because their wages are lower than they would be if the corporate tax weren't imposed. This could have a big effect on people's assessment of the tax. If you think the tax translates into lower wages, you might be less enthusiastic about it than if relatively rich shareholders are worse off because of it. We'll talk more about this later.

Let's take another example: the payroll tax. Half of FICA taxes are levied on employers and half on employees. What does that mean? For almost all employees both halves are remitted by their employer to the government. Would it make much difference if we called it all an employer tax or all an employee tax? No. Employers decide to hire workers based on what it costs to employ them. They don't really care whether the cost comes in the form of wages or payroll taxes or, for that matter, health insurance. All that matters is the total compensation cost, including taxes and fringe benefits. So if employers' payroll taxes fell, they would be willing to pay higher wages. If payroll taxes increased, they would cut cash wages. Probably not instantaneously, because workers think wage cuts are unfair and that can hurt morale, but wage increases would be slower than they would otherwise be until compensation was back in line with worker

---

SIDEBAR 2.1 **Taxing the "Rich" and Jobs**

President Obama proposed raising income tax rates on couples making over $250,000 per year (and singles making over $200,000). This is roughly the top 2 percent of households. The president argued that he was just asking the well-off to pay their fair share. Critics countered that such a tax would hurt workers because a lot of the top 2 percent are entrepreneurs who would cut jobs if their income tax went up. In other words, the critics were arguing that a significant part of the incidence of the millionaires' tax would fall on labor—ordinary folk.

---

productivity. Although it's conceivable that consumers or capital owners could bear part or all of the tax burden, statistical studies have almost uniformly concluded that workers bear the entire burden of both the employer and employee portions of the payroll tax.

The economic incidence of other taxes is less clear.[1] For example, it's commonly assumed that households bear the cost of the individual income tax, but there's little reason to think that this is so, especially when the individual income tax has all sorts of credits and deductions intended to subsidize particular activities. For example, one tax credit is designed to encourage purchase of fuel-efficient hybrid vehicles. The extra demand due to the subsidized price almost surely pushes up the price of such cars. This might be a good thing if the purpose is to encourage more carmakers to produce green vehicles, but it means that part of the benefit of the tax credit goes to producers, not consumers. There are, however, no good empirical estimates of how much of the individual income tax is borne by households and how much by others.

The bottom line is this: the person who ends up bearing the tax may be very different from the person (or entity) that writes the check to the government or the person or business entity that the tax law proclaims that the tax is "on."

Are there cases in practice where it does matter who writes the check?

Yes. For one thing, who writes the check can matter when not everyone is scrupulously honest. For example, the IRS collects a much, much larger share of what is owed from withholding taxes remitted by employers than from income tax owed by self-employed people, even though the formula for calculating liability is exactly the same. If your employer is responsible for remitting the tax, it usually makes it to the IRS. If you have to self-report, on average you're much less likely to send in all of what you owe.

Another example is sales and use taxes. If you live in a state with a sales tax, you owe the tax whether you buy something at the corner store or order it over the Internet from an out-of-state merchant. The store owner remits the tax in the first case, whereas the purchaser often has to remit a "use tax" in the second. Do you send in all the use tax you owe on your Internet purchases? If so, you're in very exclusive company. The entity that writes the check matters.[2]

We'll talk more about this in the chapter about compliance and enforcement.

Can taxes affect asset prices?

Yes. A tax on the return an asset provides generally reduces its value, while a subsidy increases its value. This effect, known as capitalization of the tax into the asset's value, is more likely to occur in cases where the total supply of the asset is not easily adjusted. The tax change can produce a penalty or a windfall for current asset owners, but it has little or no effect on the affordability for future buyers.

An important example of capitalization that troubles some economists (including us) is the mortgage interest deduction. Many middle-class homeowners think of this as their big tax break—if they itemize their deductions, they get to deduct some or all of the interest from taxable income—and it's one of the biggest tax breaks in the code. But suppose it makes people want to live on bigger properties? In places where land is scarce, that would just bid up land prices because you can't make more land, and so some of the tax break is dissipated in higher property prices. This is a boon to property owners at the time the tax break is enacted, or expanded, but means that the average new homeowner may not benefit much. People in top brackets who get the biggest tax breaks probably come out ahead. People with lower incomes, who because they don't itemize deductions or are in a low tax bracket, might get little or no benefit from the deduction, might be worse off than they would be if mortgage interest wasn't deductible. And if it also pushes up the market price of rental housing because land is more expensive, renters are unambiguously worse off.

What is the personal income tax?

Pretty simple: it's a tax on individual income collected by the federal government and most states.

The federal tax is progressive, which means the tax rate rises with income. (More on this later.) Defining income, however, is not as straightforward as you might think. The standard economist's definition of income is the sum of what you spend and what you save. Spending is straightforward. But measuring saving is more complicated. It includes what we put in the bank, mutual funds, retirement accounts, and other kinds of investments. But increases in wealth that we don't spend also add to savings (and hence to income). In many cases this unfamiliar definition lines up with the more familiar meaning—what you are paid if you are employed plus what you make from owning a business and from investments—but in some cases that we'll expand on later, it differs in important ways.

The income tax is much more than a tax on income. While some deductions account for the cost of earning income—for example, prior to passage of the TCJA, you could deduct the cost of uniforms that you had to wear to work—many deductions, exemptions, and tax credits are intended to provide subsidies of some sort or another. They often have little to do with the measurement of income.

Isn't the income tax a fraud?

Some tax protesters argue that the 16th Amendment to the Constitution, which authorized the personal income tax in 1913, was improperly ratified or otherwise invalid. You can find many of these people in jail. Courts have repeatedly concluded that the income tax is indeed constitutional and excoriated those who question its validity as frivolous, ridiculous, or worse.[3]

You may not like the income tax, but it is legal and valid (box 2.1).

BOX 2.1   **How Is Federal Income Tax Calculated in the United States?**

Adjusted gross income (AGI) =
  wages and salaries
  + self-employment income
  + capital income (taxable interest, rents, royalties, capital gains, dividends)
  + income from pensions and retirement accounts
  + a portion of Social Security benefits (for higher-income people)
  + random other stuff (like some alimony payments on divorces concluded before 2019)
  − "above-the-line" deductions for things like contributions to retirement accounts, some educational expenses, and health insurance premiums if self-employed
Itemized Deductions =
  state and local taxes (up to $10,000)
  + mortgage interest
  + charitable contributions
  + casualty and theft losses from a federally declared disaster
  + some medical expenses
Taxable Income =
  AGI
  − itemized deductions or the standard deduction (whichever is greater)
  − qualified business income deduction
Income Tax =
  Tax from tax tables
  + alternative minimum tax (if applicable)
  − nonrefundable tax credits (can be no more than total tax liability before credits)
  − refundable tax credits

What are exclusions, deductions, exemptions, and credits?

They all reduce tax liability, but in different ways.

An exclusion is a kind of income that doesn't count in the measurement of gross income for income tax purposes. For example, if your employer provides you with health insurance, that's part of your compensation, but its value is excluded from income for tax purposes.

A deduction is an expense that you get to subtract from gross income. Some deductions are available to all taxpayers who meet eligibility requirements, like contributions to Individual Retirement Accounts (IRAs). Others are only available to those who elect to itemize deductions rather than claim a standard deduction—an amount that doesn't require documentation to claim. In 2018, the standard deduction was $12,000 for single filers, $24,000 for married couples who file a joint return, and $18,000 for single parents who file as head of household.[4]

Prior to the TCJA, taxpayers were allowed to deduct a personal exemption—a fixed dollar amount for themselves, their spouses, and any dependents. The new law replaced personal exemptions with tax credits through 2025.

Exclusions, deductions, and exemptions reduce taxable income. They reduce tax liability, too, but how much depends on your tax bracket. For example, a $100 deduction reduces tax liability by $10 for someone in the 10 percent bracket, but it reduces tax liability by $35 for a high-income person in the 35 percent bracket.

Tax credits are different. A tax credit offsets tax liability dollar for dollar. For example, the tax code includes a Child Tax Credit, a maximum of $2,000 per child. If you have two qualifying children, you could get $4,000 off your taxes. There are tax credits to help pay for childcare, encourage people to buy fuel-efficient vehicles, induce people to weatherproof their house, and do all sorts of other stuff. Sometimes, like the Child Tax Credit, the credit is a fixed dollar amount. Sometimes the credit is a percentage of what you spend on a qualifying activity. But the common characteristic is that credits are effectively vouchers that are run through the tax system. They're like cash payments except that, in most cases, the cash can only be used to reduce your taxes.

"THE INCREASED CHILD TAX CREDIT IS SUPPOSED TO STIMULATE THE ECONOMY... SO HOW ABOUT A RAISE IN MY ALLOWANCE?"

Source: www.CartoonStock.com.

An exception to the last statement is a special class of tax credits called refundable tax credits. Refundable tax credits can be claimed even if you have no tax liability. The Earned Income Tax Credit, or EITC, was the first refundable credit, enacted in 1975 (table 2.1). Eligible filers may claim the credit and get its full value even if they don't have any income tax liability. The credit is substantial for families with children— worth up to $6,431 in 2018 to a family with three or more qualifying children.

The Child Tax Credit and the American Opportunity Tax Credit (which subsidizes higher education expenses) are both

Table 2.1 Earned Income Tax Credit Parameters, 2018

Number of children	Credit rate (percent)	Minimum income for maximum credit	Maximum credit	Phaseout rate (percent)	Phaseout range	
					Beginning income	Ending income
0	7.65	$6,780	$519	7.65	$8,490	$15,270
1	34	$10,180	$3,461	15.98	$18,660	$40,320
2	40	$14,290	$5,716	21.06	$18,660	$45,802
3 or more	45	$14,290	$6,431	21.06	$18,660	$49,194

Note: The beginning and end of the phaseout range is $5,690 higher for married couples filing joint returns.

*Source:*https://www.taxpolicycenter.org/statistics/eitc-parameters and https://www.irs.gov/credits-deductions/individuals/earned-income-tax-credit/eitc-income-limits-maximum-credit-amounts-next-year

partially refundable—meaning that low-income families may get a portion of the credit even if they do not have tax liability. The premium subsidies for Obamacare health insurance are also implemented as refundable tax credits.

What is the standard deduction?

Income tax filers have the choice of totaling up their deductible expenses or taking a standard deduction that varies only by marital status. The option to claim a standard deduction is intended to simplify tax preparation. Most people do not have to keep track of their charitable contributions, state and local taxes, or mortgage interest because the standard deduction is greater than their itemizable deductions.

The 2017 tax bill nearly doubled the standard deduction, from $6,350 for single filers in 2017 to $12,000 in 2018. The standard deduction is $24,000 for married filing joint returns and $18,000 for heads of household. Like most other tax parameters, the standard deduction is adjusted every year for inflation. The higher standard deduction plus other changes (especially the limit on state and local tax [SALT] deductions) vastly reduced the number of people itemizing their deductions—from 47 million to 19 million in 2018, or from 26 percent of tax units to 11 percent.[5]

Why are there itemized deductions? Isn't it unfair that most people don't benefit from them?

Policymakers could eliminate the standard deduction and require that all deductions be itemized. Because their itemizable deductions add up to less than the standard deduction (that's why they've chosen the latter option, after all), this would increase taxes on most of the 89 percent of households who do not itemize. They might feel better that they could take a charitable deduction like their richer neighbors, but the warm glow would wear off when they saw their taxes increase. Also, those who do not itemize have no record-keeping requirement to verify their deductions. In a sense, the first $24,000 of deductions for a couple is a freebie. You get them even if you have no deductible expenses.

So people who take the standard deduction actually are not disadvantaged, but some taxpayers think it is unfair that most people don't benefit from itemized deductions: "Why can't I take a deduction for the contribution to my church?" This perception may help explain why some tax reform plans would eliminate the whole concept of itemized deductions. In these plans, some deductions, like that for state and local taxes, would simply disappear, while other deductions like charitable contributions would be allowed for everyone—not just for itemizers.

Who benefits from the itemized deduction for state and local taxes (SALT)?

Prior to enactment of the TCJA, itemizers could deduct all of their property taxes plus state income or sales taxes. The 2017 legislation limited the itemized deduction for state and local taxes to $10,000. The version passed by the House would have eliminated the deduction altogether. Republican leaders argued that the SALT deduction is an unwarranted subsidy to high-income filers in high-tax states (which also happen to be mostly represented by Democrats). Further, they believe that the SALT deduction encourages states to spend more because the federal deduction lowers the net cost to taxpayers of state and local taxes. In their view, the SALT deduction is effectively a subsidy for wasteful programs; capping the deduction could thus make state and local governments leaner and more efficient. Supporters of the deduction counter that state and local taxes reduce households' ability to pay federal tax and are appropriately deducted from taxable income. They also argue that the SALT deduction indirectly helps low- and middle-income households because it reduces taxpayers' resistance to paying property taxes to finance schools, for example.

So at least part of the debate about the SALT deduction has to do with its economic incidence: is it a windfall for high-income itemizers or a boon to households who benefit from more and better state and local government services? The evidence is murky on this point. The Tax Reform Act of 1986 eliminated the deduction for state sales taxes. If deductibility was an important aspect in states' taxation policies, one would have expected them to rely more on income taxes, which remained fully deductible. In fact, the relative reliance on sales taxes *increased* after the TRA became law. After a sales tax deduction was reintroduced in 2004, the states increased their reliance on sales taxes even more.[6]

There's also a question about whether, in the absence of a subsidy via the SALT deduction, state and local governments would provide too little public goods (worse schools and roads and too little police protection, for example). Evidence on this question is scant, but economist John Hatfield has argued, in a simplified model of federal and local governments (there are no states in this alternate reality), that too little local public goods are produced when local income taxes are not deductible.[7]

Hatfield also concluded that the best policy would be for the federal government to make grants to localities rather than subsidize local income taxes via a deduction. Real-world governors and mayors, however, are skeptical that the federal government would be as benign or omniscient as this argument presumes. Many would prefer the automatic subsidy via the SALT deduction, even if it is not the most efficient option.

Why could raising the standard deduction and limiting the SALT deduction depress home prices and charitable giving?

Itemized deductions for charitable giving, mortgage interest, and property taxes lower the cost of donating to charity and owning a home. Because the changes enacted in 2017 significantly reduces the number of people who itemize deductions, the law increases the after-tax cost of homeownership and philanthropy. The Tax Policy Center estimated that the number of households who claim a deduction for charitable contributions would fall from 37 million to 16 million in 2018, or from 21 percent of tax units to 9 percent. They estimated that the higher after-tax cost of giving would reduce individual philanthropy by about 5 percent (roughly $15 billion per year).[8]

The number of people who claim the mortgage interest deduction is also estimated to fall from 37 million to 16 million, and many of those who continue to itemize only get a partial benefit from the deduction. In addition, the SALT deduction limit means that many itemizers get little or no benefit from the property tax deduction because their state and local income taxes use up all or most of the $10,000 deduction limit. All of these changes raise the after-tax cost of homeownership, reducing overall demand for residences, and putting downward pressure on house prices. However, fears of a housing market crash beginning in 2018 were unwarranted. The Tax Reform Act of 1986 also cut the tax benefits of homeownership dramatically by cutting income tax rates, raising the standard deduction, and capping the mortgage interest deduction, and the housing market showed no obvious ill effects. Because tax benefits do not figure into eligibility calculations for home mortgages, it is likely that factors such as interest rates (which were very low when the TCJA was enacted) and pre-tax incomes are much more important determinants of housing demand.

At what income level do people start owing income tax?

It depends on your marital status, whether you have children eligible for tax credits, and your age. In 2018, taxpayers with simple returns started owing income tax net of credits at an income of $13,420 for a single filer with no children, but at an income of $60,510 for married filers with two children (table 2.2). Although few senior citizens qualify for the EITC or Child Tax Credit because they don't have child dependents and often don't have earned income, most are exempt from income tax because there is an additional standard deduction for filers age 65 and over, and most Social Security benefits are exempt from the income tax.

For people who really take advantage of tax breaks, the threshold can be much higher. For example, a filer can receive millions of dollars of interest from tax-exempt municipal bonds and not owe any federal income tax if that is her only source of income.

Table 2.2 Income Tax Thresholds before and after Tax Credits, 2018

	Single		Married	
	No children	1 child	No children	2 children
Before credits	$12,000	$18,000	$24,000	$24,000
After credits	$13,420	$38,865	$24,000	$60,510

Note: Assumes filer is a wage earner under age 65 with no other income who claims the standard deduction and EITC (if eligible); children (assumed under 17) qualify for the EITC and Child Tax Credit.

Source: Elaine Maag, Tax Policy Center.

Is it true that half of households owe no income taxes?

The Tax Policy Center estimates that about 44 percent of tax units (for the most part, households) did not owe federal income tax in 2018. That sounds bad—like all the burden of government is being dumped on a little more than half of households. But that statistic is somewhat misleading for a couple of reasons.

The vast majority of working families are indeed subject to taxes, many taxes in fact. Most Americans owe more in payroll taxes than income taxes (and that is even before considering the employers' share, which economists think workers ultimately bear). State and local taxes take a much bigger chunk of lower-income families' incomes than federal income taxes (figure 2.1).

About 16 percent of households were subject to neither income tax nor payroll tax in 2018. Most of these are elderly people who are exempt because they have little or no earnings and most of their Social Security benefits aren't subject to

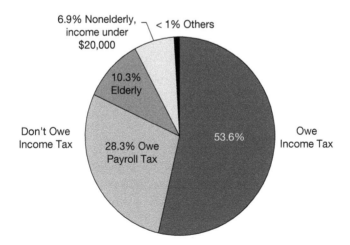

Figure 2.1 Characteristics of Households That Did Not Owe Income Tax in 2013

Source: Tax Policy Center, https://www.taxpolicycenter.org/resources/video-who-doesnt-pay-federal-taxes.

tax. (Higher-income households do owe income tax on up to 85 percent of their Social Security benefits.) Among the non-elderly, the vast majority of this untaxed group is not taxed because they're poor. President Ronald Reagan made the decision that, as part of the 1986 tax reform, families living below the poverty level should be exempt from the federal income tax, and that is still largely true.

In addition, the large fraction of Americans who owe no federal income tax reflects in part the decision of policymakers to run big pieces of the social safety net through the income tax. For example, the refundable Child Tax Credit and Earned Income Tax Credit together are much bigger than any other cash assistance program for low-income working families. There are good reasons to run these programs through the tax system rather than through welfare offices, but the consequence is that it looks like a lot of people owe no income tax. Another perspective is that they get more in benefits than they owe in tax.

The Tax Policy Center calculated back in 2010 that if all of those tax subsidy programs were eliminated, or became explicit expenditures, only 20 percent of households—mostly those with very low incomes—would have avoided income tax, compared to the 46 percent who did under 2010 tax law. Only 2 percent of households with incomes over $20,000 would have owed no income tax.[9]

Is this bad for democracy?

It could be bad if a large portion of the population thought that government was "free," and therefore supported any spending program that benefited them to any extent. However, it's not clear if that is true, or what to do about it if it were. Do we really want to impose more tax liability on seniors or people with incomes below the poverty level?

One thing that might help clarify matters would be separating the revenue-raising function of the income tax from the subsidy-providing function. If subsidies were treated as spending, which they essentially are, the fact that many people get more in tax subsidies than they owe in tax might not seem so alarming. Lots of people benefit more from government programs than they owe in tax, including a lot of senior citizens.

Taxes? They're a penalty for doing well.

Source: www.CartoonStock.com.

Do we tax capital income the same as labor income?

No. Labor income (wages, salaries, and self-employment income) is generally subject to both income taxes and payroll taxes, whereas capital income (interest, dividends, capital gains, rent, and royalties) is generally subject only to income tax. Capital gains and dividends are taxed at lower personal income tax rates than other income; interest on municipal bonds is generally exempt from tax. Savings in the form of pensions, 401(k) plans, and IRAs are also effectively tax-free, as we explain later.

A pure income tax would tax consumption and saving (income equals consumption + saving + taxes). Our "income tax" is a hybrid—part consumption tax (in which the return to all savings is tax-free) and part income tax (in which the return to savings is fully taxed). It represents a compromise between two competing objectives. On the one hand, we want to encourage people to save. As we explain in chapter 4, an income tax penalizes saving, while a consumption tax does not. (See box 4.1.) On the other hand, because capital income comprises on average a larger share of income for the wealthy, exempting it from tax would provide a relatively large tax cut for the rich. Most Americans believe that the wealthy should bear proportionately higher, not lower, tax burdens than those with more modest means. In part, how we tax capital income represents a compromise between those competing goals. (We'll talk about others later.)

What is economic income?

Economic income is a very broad measure of income intended to accurately reflect a household's economic status. In contrast, most ordinary humans' concept of income is sometimes a poor measure of economic status. For example, suppose you're lucky enough to have owned a million shares of Facebook stock in 2017. At the end of the year, your nest egg was worth about $176 million. Not only that, but your wealth increased in value by over $60 million during the year. If you didn't sell any shares, you wouldn't have any "income" as conventionally defined, and as defined by the income tax code, because Facebook has never paid a dividend. Common sense suggests that you're a lot better off, because your Facebook shares have soared in value. Facebook share prices fell in 2018, but that loss isn't reflected in conventional income measures either unless you sell the stock. Economic income would include the annual increase or decrease in value in your shares whether or not you sell them.

Economic income also includes other noncash sources of compensation, like the value of fringe benefits you receive from your employer. Health insurance is typically the biggest of these. It can be worth over $10,000 per year for a family, but it is not reflected in your paycheck or in taxable income.

Why do economists think my home earns me rent?

Funny story about that. One of us (Burman) used to work as deputy assistant secretary for tax analysis at the U.S. Treasury. It's a great job for a public finance economist because every proposal for a new credit or deduction comes through that office for review. He got to meet the president. He got to hang out with Treasury secretary Larry Summers before the movie *The Social Network* made him famous. All very cool.

But he'd also get crank calls at night from people who were outraged that the Treasury wanted to tax the rent on their home (box 2.2). "I'm a homeowner, not a renter! I don't pay rent. That's the whole point of being a homeowner. And I'm not a landlord. Nobody pays me rent. What are you crazy bureaucrats thinking?"

Here's the backstory. During the Reagan administration, in order to get a more accurate picture of how the tax burden varied across households of different levels of well-being,

---

BOX 2.2 Bill Archer Thinks "Economic Rent" Is Crazy Talk

"Imputed rent? That's the rent a person would pay for his house if he didn't own it," Scholz said.

"This is incredible," responded Archer. "Americans will never accept all that as part of their annual income."

Source: Fred Barnes, "Every Man a King," *Weekly Standard*, July 21, 1997, available at https://www.washingtonexaminer.com/weekly-standard/every-man-a-king (relating the story of Treasury deputy assistant secretary John Karl Scholz's exchange with House Ways and Means Committee chairman Bill Archer).

Treasury economists decided they'd calculate (but not *tax*) economic income. Economic income includes all those noncash forms of income mentioned earlier and "imputed rent." The idea is that your home is an investment and part of the return it provides is the rent you save. Imputed rent is basically the tax-free income your home generates.

A simpler way to put it is that a homeowner is clearly better off than a renter, all else equal, because the homeowner has a valuable asset that allows her to live rent-free. But Treasury never proposed to tax "imputed rent," in part because the concept is impossible to explain to real (i.e., noneconomist) humans. But the concept is perfectly valid.

Why don't we tax economic income?

Some economists think this is a terrific idea. If it could be measured properly, economic income would better measure taxpayers' ability to pay, and so be a more equitable basis for determining tax liability. But there are two practical problems (as well as a giant, insuperable political one). One is that economic income can be difficult to measure accurately. For example, a good measure of imputed rent on owner-occupied housing would require a comprehensive annual survey of rents for comparable properties. For some kinds of properties that are rarely rented out, accurate estimates would be very hard to come by. And even for easier-to-evaluate properties, it would be very costly to estimate rental values every year. Imputed rent could be estimated based on property assessments made by local governments to collect property taxes, but those estimates would be very imprecise.

Unrealized capital gains and losses would be easy to measure for shares of publicly traded companies, like Facebook, but much harder to come by for privately held businesses. And even the value of employer-provided health insurance and pensions is difficult to estimate and allocate among employees. Further, consider the difficulty of valuing extremely rare art, intangible assets, or other items that are not commonly sold, and for which no up-to-date market price may exist. It's also problematic to collect tax when people don't necessarily have cash on hand to pay it. For example, if we counted as taxable income the $61 million of capital gains that the lucky Facebook stockholder accrued, that would entail more than $10 million in additional income taxes. Some of that stock might have to be sold to meet the tax obligation, if it could not be used as collateral for a loan. That might not be considered a tragedy, but for a closely held business, forcing liquidation of the business to pay the tax could seem unfair and counterproductive.

SIDEBAR 2.2 **The Simplest Tax Shelter**

- Borrow $10 million at 5 percent interest.
- Invest $10 million that will pay a 5 percent return, making the investment worth $10,500,000 after a year. The return comes in the form of a capital gain.
- Borrowing generates a $500,000 interest deduction. At a 37 percent tax rate, that reduces your federal income tax by $185,000. (There may also be state tax benefits.)
- The $500,000 capital gain is taxed at 20 percent. That adds $100,000 to your tax bill.
- On net, you save $85,000.
- Because of the tax savings, this deal would be worthwhile even if the investment paid less than $500,000 (even though, absent taxes, it would make no sense).

NB: this scheme is so obvious that it is not permitted. However, a whole industry is devoted to finding economically equivalent deals.

"[A] tax shelter is a deal done by very smart people that, absent tax considerations, would be very stupid."—Michael J. Graetz, *100 Million Unnecessary Returns* (New Haven: Yale University Press, 2010), 116.

So economic income is a helpful analytic tool for understanding the effects of tax policies, but not very practical as a tax base.

How do we tax capital gains and dividends?

Long-term capital gains (those on assets held at least one year) and qualifying dividends are taxed at a top statutory rate of 20 percent. High-income taxpayers are also subject to a 3.8 percent surtax. By comparison, the top tax rate on other income is 37 percent (plus payroll taxes and a 0.9 percent high-income surtax on high earners).

While long-term capital gains have been taxed at lower rates than other income for most of the history of the income tax, dividends have been taxed at a lower rate only since 2003. The argument for a lower dividend tax rate is that corporation income is already taxed at the company level, so taxing the dividends as well corresponds to double taxation. A similar argument is often made to justify lower capital gains tax rates. However, the lower rate is a very imperfect offset. While some corporations remit a lot of tax, some are able to use tax breaks to significantly reduce their effective corporate tax rate. And assets other than corporate stock have capital gains, so this double taxation argument does not apply to them.

A better fix for the issue of corporate double taxation would be to "integrate" the individual and corporate taxes. Under such a system, corporate income would be allocated to shareholders and taxed at individual rates, much as the tax system works for partnerships. For technical reasons, however, this is much easier said than done.

What are the arguments for and against lower capital gains tax rates?

While avoiding excessive double taxation is a fairly convincing rationale for tax breaks on stock gains and dividends, the lower tax rate also applies to noncorporate capital gains. This is harder to justify. Proponents argue that capital gains tax breaks are desirable for various reasons: (1) a significant portion of capital gains simply represents inflation and we shouldn't tax that; (2) a lower tax rate on capital gains encourages investment, risk-taking, and entrepreneurship; (3) capital loss deductions are limited, so it's unfair and punitive to tax gains in full; and (4) high capital gains tax rates create an inefficient "lock-in effect."

These arguments are less compelling than they appear at first blush. While it is true that, when prices are rising, a significant fraction of capital gains may represent inflation, that is also true of other forms of capital income. For example, at a 3 percent inflation rate, the first $3 of interest on a $100 savings account simply offsets inflation, but it is taxable nonetheless. For the same reason, interest expense is also understated due to inflation. Now, two wrongs (taxing illusory capital income and deducting illusory costs of borrowing) don't make a right, but if capital gains are taxed at lower rates, then either interest expense should be deductible at lower rates or else you create large incentives for tax sheltering.

It is probably true that a lower capital gains tax rate encourages risk-taking (although MIT economist James Poterba found that much of the capital that finances new investments is not subject to capital gains taxes and, thus, is unaffected by capital gains tax breaks). The question is whether such encouragement is warranted. Investments of "sweat equity" are already treated very favorably by the income tax. As an entrepreneur, you don't have to pay tax on the value of your labor until it produces income. This is a very valuable tax break.

A more persuasive argument is that, while positive capital gains are taxed (at a preferential rate), there is a strict limit on the amount of losses that can be deducted against other income. Capital loss deductions must be limited to prevent wealthy taxpayers with large diversified portfolios from selectively realizing (i.e., selling) assets with losses and indefinitely deferring gains. The losses could offset tax due on other income—such as wages—while tax liability on the assets with gains could be avoided entirely by holding them until death (see the "Angel of Death" loophole discussed in the next section) or donating them to charity. However, the loss limit can put a real burden on someone who holds a single asset—such as a business—that suffers a loss. If the loss is quite large, it might take many years to fully deduct it. However, such situations are rare. The vast majority of taxpayers with losses can fully utilize them within a few years.[10]

Finally, consider the lock-in effect, which means that people will avoid selling their stocks so as not to trigger capital gains taxes. It is certainly true that a capital gains tax discourages people from selling assets, and therefore acts as a barrier to achieving one's desired portfolio. You can postpone the tax indefinitely simply by holding on to the appreciated asset. However, our research and the research of most other scholars generally conclude that the lock-in effect is relatively modest, at least in the range of tax rates we've recently had.

The argument against providing capital gains tax breaks is twofold: first, lower capital gains tax rates encourage tax shelters, which are inefficient. Second, the vast majority of capital gains are realized by people with very high incomes. Tax breaks on capital gains disproportionately benefit the rich and undermine the progressivity of the tax system.

What is the "Angel of Death" loophole?

One way to avoid capital gains tax is to die. Yes, it's an extreme measure, but it happens to all of us eventually. Columnist Michael Kinsley dubbed this the "Angel of Death" loophole. When you die, the tax "basis" for your appreciated assets becomes the value at time of death. Thus, for your heirs, it's as if they bought the Facebook stock at its price when they inherited it; your heirs owe no tax on the gains that accrued during your life due to your clever stock-picking.

This is surely an important factor in the lock-in effect discussed above. Postponing a tax is good, but avoiding it altogether is the ultimate tax shelter, so, especially late in life, selling assets with capital gains is usually a tax-inefficient way to raise funds.

Another way to avoid paying capital gains tax is to donate appreciated assets to charity. Although there are limits, donors can generally deduct the full value of contributions of property without owing any tax on the accrued gains. This makes contributions of highly appreciated property much more attractive than contributions of cash—and explains why nonprofit organizations with wealthy donors spend a lot of time selling things that donors have given them.

Source: Cartoon © Mark Parisi. Permission granted for use, www.offthemark.com.

What is carried interest?

Carried interest is a share of investment profits awarded to the general partner in a private equity firm (and some other businesses). Typically, private equity partnerships purchase businesses, reorganize them, and sell them at a profit. The carried interest is taxed as a capital gain, and is subject to lower long-term capital gains rates if the business is held at least a year.

The general partners are often quite wealthy—former Massachusetts governor and presidential candidate Mitt Romney made a fortune in carried interest as a managing partner of Bain Capital—and some think it unfair that a large share of their income is taxed at low capital gains tax rates. (Private equity firms also receive a managing fee that is taxed as ordinary income.) Critics of this provision argue that it is unfair because private equity managers' income is taxed at a fraction of the rate applied to the income of other more conventional investment managers. It also makes the tax code less progressive because some very high-income people may face low effective tax rates.

However, the issue is not so clear cut. People who start a successful business are taxed the same way on their sweat equity—the human capital they invest—when it is sold. If private equity profits are considered equivalent to labor income, then perhaps profits on founders' stock should be taxed the same way. Congress is reluctant to raise taxes on entrepreneurs ("job creators"), so it might not be surprising that the taxation of private equity has been stubbornly resistant to change.[11]

If we want to favor capital gains and dividends, does it make sense to do it via lower rates?

Not really. The alternate rate schedule for capital gains is really complicated. Look at the 45-line worksheet in the instructions for Schedule D (where capital gains are reported) to see how mind-numbing the calculation really is.

Source: Dan Wasserman, Editorial Cartoon / *Boston Globe* / TNS.

There is an alternative. A portion of capital gains and dividends could be excluded from taxable income. For example, if 45 percent of long-term capital gains were excluded, the effective tax rate on capital gains for people in the top bracket would be 20.4 percent (55 percent of 37 percent, or 24.2 percent including the effect of the 3.8 percent investment income surtax). And the calculation would be pretty straightforward: 55 percent of capital gains would be included in income and the other 45 percent would be disregarded. Capital gains were taxed this way before 1987.

You might wonder why Congress decided to cap the tax rate on long-term capital gains in 1987. The Tax Reform Act of 1986 lowered ordinary income tax rates and fully taxed capital gains as part of a grand compromise. However, conservatives were concerned that income tax rates would creep up from the 28 percent rate that applied to high-income people and they did not want the tax on capital gains to rise as well. So the rate on capital gains was capped at the then-applicable maximum rate of 28 percent. Of course, income tax rates did increase, first in 1990 (when President George W. H. Bush fatefully broke his "no new taxes" pledge) and again in 1993, but the tax rate on capital gains remained capped at 28 percent. Legislation in 1997 cut the top rate to 20 percent and the rate was cut further to 15 percent in 2003, only to be increased back to 20 percent in 2013 (23.8 percent including the surtax).

What is the AMT?

AMT stands for alternative minimum tax. It is an addition to regular income tax that was designed to ensure that, in spite of the proliferation of what might be called loopholes in the tax law, millionaires owed at least some tax. Originally, it was a small additional tax, but it morphed over time into a substantial alternative tax system with its own definition of income and its own rate schedule. Technically, the AMT is the excess, if any, of tax calculated under the alternative system over the tax calculated under the regular tax rules.

Here's how it works. First you calculate your regular taxable income and income tax liability. Then you start over, and add back a bunch of tax breaks to taxable income, deduct a flat AMT exemption amount ($109,400 for couples and $70,300 for singles in 2018) and calculate the tax at rates of 26 or 28 percent. The AMT exemption amount phases out for taxpayers with very high incomes. If the tax under this alternative calculation is more than tax owed under the regular income tax rules, you must add the difference to your tax bill; this is equivalent to owing the higher of the two tax liability calculations. Hence, the logic behind the name "alternative minimum" tax.

This surtax has been around in various forms since 1969, when Treasury Secretary Joseph Barr testified to Congress that 155 high-income tax filers owed absolutely no income tax in 1967. This provoked a firestorm of protest. According to law professor Michael Graetz, in 1969 Congress got more letters about this tax issue than about the Vietnam War—and the war was certainly agitating people that year. People thought it was really unfair that folks earning over $200,000 (the equivalent of over $1 million in today's dollars) could totally avoid income tax liability.

Before enactment of the Tax Cuts and Jobs Act, the AMT was the bane of many upper-middle-income families, especially those who lived in high-tax states. The biggest AMT adjustments had nothing to do with anyone's idea of a tax loophole. The deduction for state and local income and property taxes accounted for 68 percent of all AMT adjustments in 2008. Personal exemptions accounted for another 19 percent of AMT add-backs, and so-called miscellaneous itemized deductions, such as employee business expenses, made up 12 percent of the total.

The TCJA slashed the number of AMT taxpayers in two ways: by substantially raising the AMT exemption and by eliminating or curtailing many middle-class AMT preferences. The state and local tax deduction is limited to $10,000, and personal exemptions and miscellaneous itemized deductions are gone. As a result, the Tax Policy Center estimated that the percentage of taxpayers affected by the AMT would fall from 5.2 percent in 2017 to just 0.2 percent in 2018, with the vast majority of those affected having incomes of $500,000 or more.[12] The tax isn't quite dead yet—Howard Gleckman calls it a zombie tax.[13] Just as in 1986, it survived a major tax overhaul because lawmakers wanted the revenue, and the AMT makes the distribution of the liability across income tax groups more progressive. But it's been substantially defanged, at least until 2026, when it is scheduled to roar back to life.

What is the "Buffett Rule"?

President Obama invented the "Buffett Rule." It is the principle that millionaires should pay at least as high an average tax rate as ordinary folk. Warren Buffett, the billionaire investor and chairman of Berkshire-Hathaway, inspired the eponymous rule when he pointed out that he faced a lower average income tax rate than his assistant. Most of Mr. Buffett's income comes from capital gains and dividends, which are taxed at a top effective tax rate of 23.8 percent and not subject to payroll taxes. Mr. Buffett's assistant probably owes at least a 15 percent income tax rate on her Berkshire-Hathaway salary and another 15.3 percent in payroll taxes. Assuming that is most of her income, she probably faces a combined income and payroll tax rate of 30 percent or more. There are no details on how much this person actually earns or owes in taxes, or even which of Mr. Buffett's several assistants he had in mind, but her boss and President Obama made Warren Buffett's "secretary" the poster child for tax inequity.[14]

President Obama said that the Buffett Rule was not a legislative proposal, but a principle for tax reform. Senator Sheldon Whitehouse (D-RI) proposed legislation inspired by the Buffett Rule that would require millionaires to owe income plus payroll taxes equal to at least 30 percent of income. (The tax phases in between $1 and $2 million of income, so the rule would not apply with full force until income is at least $2 million.)

Critics (including one of us) have pointed out that the proposal would be tantamount to a second AMT, adding new complexity and inequity to the tax code.[15] A better approach would be to deal with the underlying aspects of the tax code that allow millionaires to avoid income tax. For example, capital gains and dividends could be taxed the same as other income, eliminating the source of inequity in the Buffett anecdote. (See page 272, "Are there some sensible tax reform ideas?")

Senator Whitehouse's bill did include a "sense of the Senate" resolution calling for tax reform and saying that the new minimum tax is an interim step. But given that the AMT has already survived two major tax overhauls, the Buffett Rule might well become another permanent blemish on the tax code if enacted.

What are hidden tax brackets?

Whenever a tax break phases out with income—which is very common—it increases the tax triggered by earning an additional dollar. For example, the Child Tax Credit of $2,000 per child phases out at a rate of $5 per $100 of income once a couple earns $400,000. So if your income increases from $400,000 to $401,000, you lose $50 of child tax credits; your tax bill goes up by 5 percent of your additional income. It is just like a 5 percent surtax added to your regular income tax.

The AMT features a very large surtax of this kind. The AMT exemption phases out at a rate of 25 percent of income over $1 million for couples. If income increases from $1 million to $1.1 million, the AMT exemption falls by $25,000. Because AMT taxable income is the difference between income as defined under the AMT rules and the exemption, taxable income increases by $125,000, so AMT taxpayers pay 25 percent more tax on the additional income than they would without the phantom tax. Those taxpayers see their 28 percent statutory AMT rate increase to a 35 percent effective rate (125 percent of 28 percent).

Does Uncle Sam really want you to live in sin?

Probably not, but the tax code treats married couples differently than single people. When you marry, even if your incomes don't change, your total taxes may go up, down, or stay the same. Marriage can affect your tax bill because we have a progressive income tax and we tax families rather than individuals. If your taxes go up when you get married, you face a "marriage penalty"; if they fall, you get a "marriage bonus."[16] The Bush tax cuts eliminated marriage penalties for most middle-income families, so you're more likely to pay less tax than more when you tie the knot. That is, "singles penalties" are more common than marriage penalties. The tax code is far from neutral with respect to marital status (box 2.3).

BOX 2.3   Vivien Kellems's Tea Party Revolt and the Origins
of the Marriage Penalty

Until 1948, married taxpayers in the United States filed as separate individuals (as they still do in most of the world). High-income couples
attempted to game this system by allocating capital income to the lower-
earning spouse who was subject to lower tax rates, but that couldn't be
done in community property states such as California. In those states,
capital income had to be allocated equally to the two spouses, resulting
in a higher total tax bill. In response to complaints about the resulting
inequities depending on one's state of residence, the United States insti-
tuted joint filing in 1948. At first couples owed twice the tax that a single
person would owe if that person had half the couple's income. This
scheme eliminated marriage penalties altogether, but it also maximized
marriage bonuses—single penalties. A married couple would owe less
tax than would an unmarried person with the same income.

   The presence of single penalties was not lost on Vivien Kellems, a
successful and outspoken single businesswoman. It galled her that
she owed much more tax than a man with similar income and a stay-
at-home spouse would. She organized a group called War Widows of
America complaining that the tax system was unfair to women who,
through no fault of their own, lost their spouses and the valuable tax
savings that would accompany them. The fact that Kellems and many
others in her group had never been married was not mentioned. She
campaigned tirelessly through the 1960s to eliminate tax penalties on
single adults.

   In 1969, her campaign was partially successful. Congress cut taxes
on single filers while leaving taxes on joint filers unchanged, creating
the first marriage penalties while cutting the extent of single penalties.
(With a graduated tax schedule, there's no way to eliminate one without
creating the other.) Ironically, those marriage penalties became a ral-
lying cry for later generations of tax protesters as married women entered the workforce in droves, creating many more penalized couples.

Source: Michael Graetz, *The Decline (and Fall?) of the Income Tax*
(New York: Norton, 1997).

The easiest way to see why marriage penalties and bonuses arise is to imagine a simple (and therefore hypothet-
ical!) flat-rate income tax where the first $10,000 of income
is untaxed and income above that threshold is taxed at a

25 percent rate. This tax scheme is slightly progressive because the tax rate as a share of income rises with income; for example, it's zero for people earning $10,000 or less and 20 percent ($10,000) for a taxpayer earning $50,000. Now suppose the same schedule applied to couples and singles. Two people with each spouse earning $10,000 would be tax-free if single, but the couple would owe $2,500 in tax on their $20,000 in household income if they married. That $2,500 in extra tax is the marriage penalty.

To eliminate this marriage penalty, the exemption threshold could be doubled for couples to $20,000. But that creates the possibility of marriage bonuses, or looked at differently, penalties for singles. If someone earning $20,000 married someone who doesn't work, her tax bill would fall by the same $2,500—a hefty marriage bonus. The government could split the difference—say, setting the exempt threshold at $15,000 for couples. In this case the first couple would still pay a penalty and the second receive a bonus, but penalties and bonuses would be cut in half.

Our tax system is way more complicated than this simple example, and the Bush tax cuts made it resemble the very marriage-friendly second example for all but very high- and low-income couples. But it's still true that couples where each spouse has similar income are more likely to pay penalties than couples with very unequal incomes.

Source: www.CartoonStock.com.

A lot of provisions can create marriage penalties, and they're not just in the income tax. In 2004, the U.S. General Accounting Office (now known as the Government Accountability Office) counted 1,049 laws "in which benefits, rights, and privileges are contingent on marital status" (although not all convey penalties or bonuses).[17] For example, Social Security provides benefits for spouses even if they have contributed little or no payroll taxes, a substantial marriage bonus. The estate tax has an unlimited exemption for bequests made to a surviving spouse—a potentially huge marriage bonus that is not available to unmarried partners. The AMT can create big penalties and bonuses depending on circumstances. The EITC—like traditional welfare programs—can also create marriage penalties (because a spouse's earnings can raise the couple's earnings into the range where the EITC is reduced or eliminated).

How does inflation affect the income tax?

Part of your income simply reflects inflation. For example, if you earned $50,000 in 2016 and $50,650 in 2017, your income, as measured by purchasing power, didn't really change because prices on average went up by the same 1.3 percent between the two years. If the tax tables stayed the same, however, your tax would grow by more than 1.3 percent because all of that $650 in additional income would be taxed at the rate of your tax bracket. Back in the 1970s and 1980s, high inflation would often push up people's incomes so much that they'd get bumped into higher tax brackets even if they had little or no increase in their "real" income. This so-called bracket creep was extraordinarily unpopular. Starting in 1985, tax brackets were automatically adjusted for inflation so people would not pay higher average tax rates simply because of inflation.

One group liked bracket creep: incumbent politicians. Inflation generated automatic real tax increases year after year, which allowed Congress to convey "tax cuts" on a regular basis—giving back part of the tax bonanza generated by inflation. Once brackets were indexed, this golden era for incumbents ended. Although real income growth also tended to increase revenues, it wasn't anywhere near as fast as during the rampant inflation of the 1970s. In that environment, tax cuts required real spending cuts or higher deficits, a much less pleasant trade-off for politicians.

Even though many income tax parameters, including the tax bracket thresholds of the regular income tax, are automatically adjusted for inflation, the tax system is far from inflation-neutral. Some parameters affecting eligibility for credits, deductions, and exclusions are fixed in dollar terms. And some key tax parameters were explicitly fixed in nominal terms as a way to purposely phase in a tax increase (albeit very slowly at current low inflation rates). The income level at which Social Security benefits become subject to tax hasn't changed since 1984.[18] Because the revenue raised is dedicated to the Social Security and Medicare trust funds, this slowly growing source of revenue helps to prop up the finances of these underfunded programs.

Inflation causes a potentially more significant problem for the income tax because capital income and expense are not adjusted for inflation. This can result in a large overstatement of income and expense. For example, if the interest rate is 6 percent but inflation is running at 3 percent, half of interest simply compensates for inflation, and does not represent real income. But the tax code includes the whole 6 percent in taxable income, effectively doubling the tax burden on interest income. For example, someone who has $1,000 in the bank earning 6 percent interest would report $60 of income. At a 25 percent tax bracket, that generates $15 in tax. But the *real* interest is only $30 (half was simply offsetting inflation), so the $15 in tax corresponds to a 50 percent tax rate on real income. A similar problem occurs with other kinds of capital income— dividends, capital gains, rents, royalties, and so on.

By the same token, inflation also causes interest expense to be overstated. Thus, when there's inflation, the tax system subsidizes debt and penalizes saving. When inflation is substantial, this can cause havoc in financial markets, severely distorting the incentives to save, lend, and borrow. Some countries with persistent, high inflation have tried to adjust taxable capital income and tax-deductible expense to include in taxable income only the parts not reflecting inflation, but these adjustments can get very complicated, and are probably not worth the trouble as long as inflation stays as low as it has recently been in the United States. But if higher inflation returns, this might again become an important tax policy issue.

Why did TCJA change the inflation index for adjusting tax brackets and other parameters?

The TCJA changed the inflation index from the traditional Consumer Price Index (CPI) to the "chain-weighted" CPI. The old measure calculated inflation by measuring the change in the cost of a fixed basket of goods and services that people buy. Basically, it answers the question, "If people don't change their consumption patterns at all, how much more will it cost them to buy this basket of goods and services?" The chain-weighted CPI reflects the fact that people change their consumption patterns when relative prices change. For example, if the price of butter increases, some people will switch to margarine or vegetable oil to mitigate the impact of the price change. Price increases for goods with many close substitutes will increase the cost of living less than price increases for goods with fewer alternatives. Thus, except when all prices are increasing in lockstep, the chain-weighted CPI will show a smaller inflation rate than the old CPI.

Switching to the chain-weighted CPI will raise revenue because tax bracket thresholds will increase more slowly (meaning that more income is taxed at higher rates) and other indexed deductions and credits will also grow more slowly. The JCT estimates that the change would raise revenues by about $100 billion over the 10-year budget period, and the revenue gain grows over time as the effects compound.

What are payroll taxes and how are they different from income taxes?

Payroll taxes are taxes on wages and salaries. The largest payroll taxes are the 12.4 percent tax (technically, but not substantively, 6.2 percent collected from employers and employees) to fund Social Security and the 2.9 percent tax (half collected from each) to fund Medicare. States also levy smaller taxes to fund unemployment insurance and sometimes other programs. Some local governments (notably New York City and Philadelphia) impose a wage tax to collect revenue from workers who live outside the city. This kind of tax is sometimes called a commuter tax.

The earnings base for Social Security tax was capped at $128,400 in 2018. That cap is adjusted every year for increases in average wages. Because of the cap, the Social Security tax is a much smaller share of earnings at the top than for low- and middle-income earners. However, in contrast to the income tax (where higher tax liability does not earn free passes to national parks or personalized platinum-grade anti-missile defense), Social Security benefits are tied to payroll taxes remitted during one's working life. Because these benefits are also capped and the benefit formula is highly progressive, the program overall—taxes and benefits together—is not especially onerous for the poor.

Social Security and Medicare taxes are examples of *earmarked* taxes. The funds raised are dedicated to providing benefits under these two programs. To the extent that revenues exceed benefit payments, as they have for the past several decades, the surplus is invested in a special Treasury account and earns interest. In principle, the money set aside in the trust fund will allow benefits to be paid long after benefits exceed revenues, which due to demographic changes will soon be the case. Economists would say that such earmarking is purely symbolic because money is fungible—revenue from other taxes could fund these programs—but many advocates for the programs believe that the earmarking is an essential factor in the programs' political success. People support spending money on Social Security and Medicare because they think they have earned the benefits by contributing payroll taxes.

Another difference between payroll taxes and the income tax is that payroll taxes have traditionally applied only to wages plus earnings from self-employment. Income from capital had been exempt. Also there are no deductions and there's only a single tax rate, as compared with the deductions and graduated tax rate schedule in the income tax.

Aren't other taxes also dedicated to Medicare and Social Security?

Yes. To help secure Social Security's finances in 1983, a portion of Social Security benefits was included in taxable income for higher-income recipients and the revenue collected dedicated to the trust fund. In 1993, a second tier of tax was added and the additional income tax revenue earmarked for Medicare.[19] As mentioned earlier, the thresholds are not adjusted for inflation—a deliberate choice intended to phase in the taxation of a larger and larger share of benefits over time.

" DO AWAY WITH ALL THE TAX LOOPHOLES YOU WANT, BUT DON'T MESS WITH MY ENTITLEMENTS! "

Source: www.CartoonStock.com.

In 2013, a provision in the Patient Protection and Affordable Care Act of 2010 (health care reform) began to apply a 0.9 percent "additional Medicare tax" on wages and self-employment income for individuals with income (actually AGI with some slight modifications) of over $200,000 and couples with income greater than $250,000, earmarked to bolster Medicare's finances.[20] And in 2011 and 2012, the individual portion of the Social Security tax was reduced by 2 percentage points (out of 6.2 percent) in an effort to stimulate the economy. However, the revenue lost from this temporary provision was made up from general revenues (that is, other taxes or borrowing). In 2018, individuals and employers each owe 6.2 percent toward Social Security.

Over time, payroll taxes have comprised a smaller share of Social Security and Medicare's finances. This trend concerns those program advocates who think a large part of their political popularity comes from the perception that recipients have earned their benefits by virtue of their payroll tax liability. If the connection between payroll taxes and benefits becomes attenuated, the programs might come to seem more like welfare and less like insurance.

Is it true that most taxpayers owe more payroll than income tax?

Yes. The Tax Policy Center estimates that 66 percent of tax units with earnings owe more payroll tax than income tax, even when counting only the half of payroll tax technically levied on the employee.[21] Economists believe that the employer share is also borne by employees in the form of lower wages. Counting both the employee and employer share, 86 percent of taxpayers owe more payroll tax than personal income tax. Only within the top 10 percent of taxpaying households do a majority of households owe more income tax (figure 2.2).

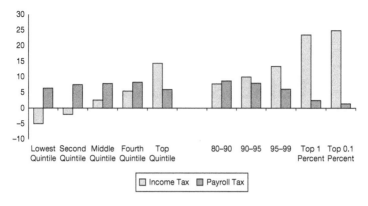

Figure 2.2 Average Income and Payroll Tax Burden as Percentage of Income, by Income Group, 2018

Source: Tax Policy Center, table T18-054, available at https://www.taxpolicycenter.org/model-estimates/distribution-federal-payroll-and-income-taxes-may-2018/t18-0054-distribution-federal.

3

BUSINESS INCOME TAXES

How do we tax corporations' income?

In principle, under an income tax all income is subject to taxation. Moreover, no kinds of income are subject to exceptionally high tax and no kinds are subject to exceptionally low tax. This principle applies to labor income, the income from savings (i.e., capital income), and business income. In reality, the U.S. income tax diverges from this ideal in many important ways. For just one example, capital income can be shielded from tax if it is earned within a retirement account.

The taxation of business income earned by corporations also deviates from this principle because, except for those mostly small corporations that can opt out (more on this later), corporate income is subject to a separate tax. Net income is calculated the same way as it would be for any other business, receipts minus the costs of doing business—that's not the issue. But corporate income is taxed according to its own separate tax schedule that, as of 2018, is a flat rate of 21 percent. Thus, the tax rate has nothing to do with the tax bracket of the company's owners, even if the owners are nontaxable pension funds.

But this is not the end of the story. Not only does corporate income trigger corporate income tax, it may also generate a tax liability for the owners of the corporation—the shareholders—on their personal income tax. The amount of personal tax liability depends on what the corporation does with its money. If it pays it out in the form of dividends, the dividends are taxed as income of the shareholders. However, as mentioned earlier, since 2003 dividends have been taxed at substantially lower rates than other income—now no higher than 23.8 percent (including the net investment income tax)—but before that, dividends were usually taxed like other income.

What if the corporation keeps the profits in the company and uses them to make further investments? To the extent that these investments look to be profitable, this will increase the value of the corporation, so its stock price rises. If a shareholder sells any of these shares, the appreciation in value since the time the stock was purchased is also subject to tax as a capital gain. If the shares sold had been owned for at least a year, they are classified as long-term capital gains and, like dividends, are subject to a lower tax rate than other income, a maximum of 23.8 percent.

Why do economists say that we "double-tax" corporations' income?

Double taxation in this context refers to the fact that the income earned by corporations may be taxed at the business level by the corporate income tax, and also at the shareholder level by the tax on dividends and capital gains (or both).

There are, however, a couple of problems with this characterization. First, while individual income taxpayers do face two levels of tax on the shares of corporate stock they hold in taxable accounts, most corporate shares are held by entities immune from the individual income tax. About 70 percent of corporate equity is held in retirement accounts, pensions, life insurance, nonprofits, and by foreigners, none of which is subject to U.S. tax on dividends or capital gains.[1]

Second, despite two layers of tax, the label of double taxation is misleading, especially now that the corporate income tax rate has been cut to 21 percent, because it suggests the tax rate levied on corporate income is "twice as big" as the tax levied on other income. But this is simply not true. It is not the *number* of separate taxes that matters, but rather the combined effective tax rate. To see that point, consider a retail sales tax. Say you had a choice of being subject to one of two sales tax regimes. Under the first, there is a single retail sales tax levied at a rate of 6 percent. In the other, retail sales trigger two separate taxes—say a regular tax and a surtax—but both the regular tax and surtax rates were 1 percent. You would, of course, prefer the "double tax" regime, because the total tax of 2 percent is lower than the single tax of 6 percent. The same reasoning applies to the double taxation of corporate income; we need to inquire into the total rate of tax and the consequences of the two layers of tax and how they operate, rather than fixate on the fact that there are two layers rather than one layer of tax.

What are the other ways business income is taxed?

Most businesses, especially smaller ones, do not operate as corporations. Most small businesses are sole proprietorships, with one owner. Others are partnerships, which have explicit rules about how the profits of the business are split among the partners. In fiscal year 2017, there were 4.0 million partnership tax returns, 4.8 million returns of "S corporations" (defined later), and 2.1 million (regular, or C) corporations. In addition, in tax year 2015, 25.2 million individual tax returns reported receiving income from nonfarm sole proprietorship businesses.[2]

In the first three cases, no tax applies to the business per se. Instead the owners, or part owners in the case of partnerships and S corporations, must include their business income as part of their individual taxable income. Sole proprietor income must be reported on Schedule C of the Form 1040, and the partners' shares of partnerships' income shows up on Schedule E. Thus, for noncorporate business income there is just one layer of tax at the owner's personal level, and the applicable tax rate depends on the owner's total taxable income—not the amount of profits of any one business. For tax purposes these businesses are called *pass-through* entities, because there is no business-level tax at all, but instead the business income is subject to the owner's personal taxable income. This means that the losses of pass-through entities are also passed through to the owners and are subtracted from any other income the owners have. In contrast, if a business subject to corporate tax has negative taxable income, the loss cannot be subtracted from other income of its owners. Instead, as of 2018 it may be carried forward (without interest) to offset future profits. Because of the disparate treatment of losses, many businesses operate as pass-through entities in their start-up phase, when losses are common, and then switch to C corporation status later.

"First the good news -- we don't have to pay any corporate taxes this year."

Source: www.CartoonStock.com.

For two reasons, the line between the tax rules that apply to corporate and noncorporate businesses is not as hard and fast as the previous discussion suggests. Many businesses that are legal corporations can elect to be exempt from the corporate tax and be taxed much like partnerships, where each owner's share of the corporation's income becomes part of that person's taxable income. These businesses are known as S corporations, or S corps, because their tax treatment is spelled out in Subchapter S of Chapter 1 of the Internal Revenue Code (and not because S corporations are usually Small). Several restrictions limit which corporations qualify for this election, the most important of which is that there may be no more than 100 shareholders. This eligibility restriction makes S corporation status infeasible for the big, public corporations that have millions of distinct shareholders. In fact, most S corporations have only a few shareholders. In 2013, there were 4.3 million S corporation returns, with a total of only 7.1 million shareholders. Only 4,501 S corporations had more than 30 shareholders, while 2.7 million had only 1 shareholder and another 1.2 million had just 2.[3]

The dividing line is also not clear-cut because of the growth of hybrid forms of business organization, in particular the limited liability company, or LLC. An LLC is not a corporation but does, like a corporation, provide the owners with limited liability—no matter how badly the business does, the owners' assets not invested in the business are safe from creditors. For tax purposes, an LLC gets pass-through treatment—it escapes the corporate income tax and instead each owner's share of the business profits adds to the owner's individual taxable income. When business owners are deciding on the type of business entity, they look at both the legal ramifications and the tax treatment.

Why tax corporations?

To many people, taxing corporations is a no-brainer. Moreover, most Americans say corporations pay less than their fair share of taxes. A 2017 survey by Gallup found that 67 percent of people think that corporations pay too little in tax.[4] To these people, the reason is obvious—corporations are big, rich, and maybe even evil. Are these things true, and if so, do they justify taxing them as separate entities?[5]

Let's start with big. Corporations as a whole are certainly a big part of the U.S. economy.[6] In 2017, nonfarm corporate businesses accounted for about 76 percent of the economy's net output.[7] So how we tax corporations and their profits affects a major chunk of the U.S. economy.

Are corporations rich? Some corporations are huge, and in good times make enormous profits. In 2017, Walmart was the world's biggest company, with profits of $13.6 billion and worldwide revenues of $485 billion, and was the world's largest private employer, with 2.3 million workers.[8] Apple had over $45 billion in profits in 2016.[9]

Corporations make lots of money when times are good. But corporate profits are quite cyclical, and in recessions corporate profits tumble, as do corporate tax collections. Federal corporation income tax receipts dipped from $370.2 billion in fiscal year 2007 to just $138.2 billion in 2009 in the depths of the Great Recession, only to bounce back to $343.8 billion by 2015.[10]

Not all corporations are huge, though, and not all huge businesses are corporations. For example, despite each having over 200,000 employees, the accounting firms PricewaterhouseCoopers and Ernst & Young are both partnerships (and therefore not subject to the corporate income tax). Are the people who own corporations rich? Certainly well-to-do people own the lion's share of corporations. Taking into account indirect holdings through mutual funds, trusts, and retirement accounts, the wealthiest 10 percent of households own 81 percent of stock; the same percentage is owned by households who earn $100,000 per year or more. Nevertheless, many people who own shares in corporations, directly or indirectly through their pension funds, have modest incomes.[11]

So the corporate sector is hugely important, and some— but not most—corporations are enormous. Are they bad?

Ascribing an ethical judgment to a legal entity is tricky. The overriding objective of corporations is to maximize the profits earned by their owners. It was Adam Smith who over 200 years ago clarified the connection between, on the one hand, people and businesses seeking their own private interests and, on the other hand, the greater good of society. Smith argued that, in the appropriate setting, society's goals would be served by harnessing the talents, energy, and information of people and businesses, who seem guided by an "invisible hand" to enrich society. He was right, for the most part. Corporations seeking profit is generally a good thing. Market forces encourages them to be innovative and efficient. At the same time, corporations (and people, too) may take actions that harm others and, to address this, such actions often need to be regulated.

Some people believe that big corporations have acquired too much political power and financial resources, using these resources to influence legislation they favor at the expense of consumers and workers, bargaining for favorable tax treatment and other policy favors. These concerns were intensified after the 2010 Supreme Court ruling in *Citizens United v. Federal Election Commission* that held that political spending is a form of protected speech under the First Amendment, and the government may not keep corporations (or unions) from spending money to support or denounce individual candidates in elections. Some worry that giant businesses can become "too big to fail," which make them prone to take inappropriate risks, believing that taxpayers will bail them out if things go badly. We don't mean to diminish these issues, but we don't think the corporate income tax is the appropriate policy instrument for dealing with them.

Another reason why lots of people think taxing corporations is a good idea is that they think that the burden is borne by somebody else, and not them. It's a tax on rich CEOs and shareholders. Are they right?

Which people bear the burden of the corporate income tax?

As we discussed in chapter 2, the fact that money is transferred to the IRS from the corporation's bank accounts to settle a corporation's tax liability gives no clue as to who ultimately bears the tax burden. Because who actually bears the burden is not apparent, the corporation income tax is in a sense a hidden tax.[12]

Economists are sharply divided on who bears the corporation income tax—and who benefits when it is cut as it was in the TCJA. In the short run, an unanticipated decrease in the corporate income tax rate would raise expected after-tax profits and thereby increase share prices, and thus benefit stockholders. But most economists also believe that, over time, the benefit will be spread beyond the shareholders. Some economists maintain that in the long run the corporate income tax falls mainly on labor, rather than on the somewhat wealthier owners of shares, because the tax reduces capital investment and lowers workers' productivity—and ultimately their wages. Other economists believe that the burden of the corporate tax ultimately rests mainly on the owners of capital, but not just shareholders. When the corporate tax is cut, corporations' after-tax rate of return increases, which makes them more attractive to investors. Investment will shift from the noncorporate sector into the corporate sector until the after-tax rates of return are equalized. When the dust settles, rates of return in both sectors increase. The corporate tax cut helps all investors, not just corporate shareholders. This has been the operative assumption of the Congressional Budget Office, the Treasury, and the Joint Committee on Taxation—the three key tax shops in DC—when they analyze the distributional impact of changes in the corporate income tax.[13] Based on slightly different economic models, they all conclude that the benefit of a corporate tax cut would accrue about 60 percent to shareholders, 20 percent to other wealth holders, and 20 percent to workers.

Just because the excellent economists in these agencies agree on something doesn't make it right, of course, nor does it end all controversy. Indeed, no question was more hotly debated in 2017, preceding the passage of the TCJA, than who would benefit from the corporate tax rate cut. Supporters argued that this was not just a tax cut for rich stock-owners, and stressed the role of capital accumulation, as follows. A lower tax rate would induce businesses to invest more, which would make workers more productive, which in turn would drive up wages as businesses bid to attract these workers.[14] This line of economic reasoning is unassailable, but the magnitude of the effect is difficult to pin down. How much would the tax cut reduce the cost of capital? For any given reduction in the cost of capital, how much more would businesses invest? For any increase in investment and ultimately the stock of productive capital, how much would the prevailing wage react? Although no consensus on the answers to these questions exists, that did not stop some supporters of a cut in corporate taxes to make some pretty stunning claims. In the midst of the 2017 debate, the Council of Economic Advisers speculated that a big corporate tax cut could eventually increase average wages by as much as $9,000 per year, equal to about 20 percent of current median wage earnings. In the aggregate, such wage gains would far exceed the size of the corporate tax cut. Most economists scoffed at this, including the authors of this book.[15]

The bottom line is that, alas, we simply do not know for sure exactly who will benefit from cutting the corporate tax rate. Eventually workers may be better off because of it, but in the meantime most of the benefit will probably accrue to business owners. And, as we discuss later, when tax cuts are financed by government borrowing, the result may be higher interest rates, which can negate some or all of the salutary effects of cutting businesses' tax rates that would occur because of increased business investment.

What are the impacts of double-taxing corporate income?

This system causes inefficient incentives for corporations to raise capital by borrowing and thus to become excessively leveraged and susceptible to bankruptcy in bad times. This happens because, although interest payments are generally deductible as a business expense (and are taxable income to the lender), corporations cannot deduct anything in recognition of the cost of attracting equity financing, even though the equity providers (i.e., the shareholders) are taxed to some degree on the income they receive.

What would happen if we just eliminated the corporate income tax?

Simply eliminating the corporate tax without other changes is a bad idea. It would make the effective tax rate on the income earned by corporations less than on other income, so it would provide an artificial, purely tax-driven preference for corporate business activity. It would also make operating a corporation a tremendous tax avoidance opportunity. People like us would find it tremendously attractive to incorporate ourselves; the corporation would owe no tax, and our accountants would devise ways for us to enjoy the fruits of any profits in untaxed, or lightly taxed, ways, such as driving a company car for our weekend errands. This would apply not only to existing businesses but also to new "businesses" because it would now become attractive for people to incorporate themselves and thereby make their labor exempt from income tax. If the corporation tax were abolished, taxpayers could shift what is essentially labor income to the corporate sector and receive it free of tax, while financing their consumption via loans from their companies. Policymakers could (and would) try to write laws to stem this kind of abuse, but that would just add to complexity (and create more jobs for smart tax lawyers and accountants). Thus, one function of the corporate income tax is a "backstop" to the individual income tax because in part it applies to the labor income of corporations' principals.

Finally, as we noted earlier, individuals subject to income tax hold only about 30 percent of corporate shares in taxable accounts. The rest is held in untaxed pension and retirement accounts, by tax-exempt organizations, and by foreigners. So, if the corporate income tax did not exist, that income would never be subject to any tax in the United States.

How can some companies get away with paying no income tax despite billions in profits?

It's not surprising, or troubling, that when a company has a bad year and no profits, it owes no income tax. More troubling is the case of a corporation that reports to the world in its financial statements that it is phenomenally profitable and still remits no income tax. This happens. For example, the *New York Times* reported that General Electric, one of the largest companies in the world, paid no income tax in 2010 despite worldwide profits of over $14.2 billion and U.S. profits of $5.1 billion.[16] (GE has since fallen on hard times.) A 2017 report found that 18 consistently profitable Fortune 500 companies, including General Electric, paid no federal income tax over the period 2008 to 2015.[17] How can that happen?

For one thing, the IRS definition of corporate income subject to tax differs from the definition of income for public financial statements. The rules have different objectives. Generally Accepted Accounting Principles, known by the acronym GAAP, are designed to constrain corporations from painting too optimistic a picture of how well the company is doing in an effort to attract investors. The accounting rules governing taxable income, on the other hand, should, in principle, be designed to keep corporations from lowballing their income to minimize their tax liability.[18]

Based on this logic, you might think that taxable income is generally higher than earnings on financial statements. You'd be wrong—very wrong. Academic researchers have estimated

Source: Dan Wasserman, Editorial Cartoon / Boston Globe / TNS

that in the late 1990s the total book income of firms with more than $250 million of assets was consistently higher than their total taxable income, as much as 60 percent higher in 1998.[19] While the aggregate "book-tax" difference has continued to rise since then, the relative magnitude has stayed about the same.[20]

In the last half century, Congress has often altered how business taxable income, and business tax liability, is calculated in an attempt to stimulate business investment. Between 1962 and 1986, investment tax credits (ITCs) were the preferred policy instrument. Under an investment tax credit, a business could get a credit of usually between 7 and 10 percent of the purchase price of qualifying capital goods. The 1986 tax reform eliminated the ITC, and it has not returned. But the idea of defining income more generously for tax purposes (i.e., reducing taxable income) as a way to make investment more attractive did not perish. Since 1981 the most popular approach has been to accelerate how quickly depreciation allowances, used to allocate the cost of long-lived capital goods over their useful life, can be taken for particular investments. These accelerated depreciation allowances explain much of the difference between taxable income and income calculated under GAAP. Other items that intentionally have different accounting treatment for GAAP and tax purposes (such as stock options) also explain why corporations may have higher book income than taxable income. In any given year, taxable income may fall short of accounting income for corporations that in previous years suffered big losses, because the losses may be carried forward to offset the tax on profits earned later.

Why is it troublesome that some companies view their tax departments as profit centers?

Surveys of corporate tax departments document that they are often evaluated by—and compensated on the basis of—how much tax savings they generate and how low the company's effective tax rate is. In one recent survey, two-thirds of corporate tax executives said that minimizing the effective tax rate is extremely or very important.[21]

The problem is that the tax department starts weighing in on business decisions. Companies may alter the way they do business not because it makes them more innovative or more efficient, but because it saves tax. Often these tax-driven decisions would make no business sense at all but for the tax savings. (To be fair, in some cases the change in behavior is exactly what Congress intends.) An inefficient company with a great tax department can be more profitable than an otherwise more efficient one that doesn't pay enough attention to tax strategies. The tax-savvy business thus finds it easier to attract capital and may even drive its more efficient, but less tax-obsessed, competitor out of business. And, of course, the fact that some of the smartest people in the company are developing innovative tax strategies rather than innovative products is a pure waste of economic resources.

Income earned by corporations is double-taxed, and tax avoidance opportunities abound. Make up your mind—is corporate income taxed too much or too little?

Whether the tax liability triggered by corporate income is remitted by the legal entity called the corporation or some other entity generally does not matter except if it facilitates the collection and monitoring of taxes. After all, we're not much concerned that most of the tax liability triggered by labor income is actually remitted by employers (via payroll taxes and withholding) rather than the workers. It's easier for the IRS to keep track of a much smaller number of firms, many with sophisticated accounting systems, than the hundred-million-plus employees. In the same way, it is easier for the IRS to collect much of the tax due on corporate income from corporations. But there is one notable difference between employers' withholding and remitting tax for their employees and corporations withholding and remitting tax for their shareholders. With minimal information from their employees, employers can tailor the withholding amount to the approximate tax liability of the employee. But even then, the withholding is almost never exact. Thus, when the employees figure their own tax liability, they credit the employer withholding against that liability, and are responsible for any additional tax due. As it happens, most households' tax liability is less than what their employer(s) withheld, so that they qualify for a refund. Either way—tax due or tax refund—the total tax owed doesn't depend on employer withholding.

Let's now carry the withholding analogy back to the corporation income tax. With a large number of anonymous shareholders, often running into the millions, it is not realistic for public corporations to calculate their tax liability based on the appropriate tax liability of all of their shareholders. But one can imagine treating the corporate tax as a credit against the tax liability of the shareholders, and indeed some countries have operated systems with this basic structure. The United States has never done this, with the result that the entity-level tax liability on the taxable income of C corporations is effectively the same for all shareholders, now about 21 percent, whether the shareholder would be in a 37 percent or 0 percent individual income tax bracket. The slightly graduated tax on dividends and capital gains personalizes the tax burden somewhat, but it only adds to, and never subtracts from, the corporate-level tax, so that the total tax is not closely related to shareholders' tax status.

What about corporate tax avoidance and evasion? One answer is to enforce the tax law better, which we discuss in chapter 9. Second, clean up the tax base to minimize opportunities for unintended tax sheltering. Finally, it makes sense to limit the preferred lower rate on dividends (and maybe capital gains) only to shareholders of companies that have remitted some minimal level of corporate tax. This was part of the original Bush administration proposal that led to the dividend tax reduction in 2003, but did not make it into the enacted legislation. Linking the tax on dividends to the corporate tax would recognize that the identity of the remitter is not critical and a sensible tax structure would recognize the two levels of tax and try to coordinate them.

What is depreciation?

At first blush, measuring business income is pretty straightforward—it's simply receipts net of the costs of doing business. Wages and salaries of employees and independent contractors are a cost of doing business, so these should be subtracted from receipts. (Even saying this glosses over some tricky accounting issues—should the wages be deducted when paid or when the products the workers make are sold, and what if the employees are compensated with stock options that cannot be cashed in for years?) Same with paper clips. In practice, though, some steps in this process can become quite complicated. Consider installment sales. For the measurement of taxable income, income generally is presumed to occur when the cash is received; for purposes of financial statements, it is recognized up front when the sale is made.

For long-lived capital goods such as an assembly line or a factory building, the central issue is *when* a deduction can be taken for the cost. If a building (or a machine) is productive over many years, measuring income accurately in each year requires allocating some fraction of the cost of the factory to each year it is in use. Deducting the entire cost of a new assembly line in the year it is purchased and installed would greatly understate the net income in that year, and slightly overstate net income in the subsequent years when the assembly line is contributing to the bottom line but triggers no deductible expense. For many decades, the tax code dealt with this issue by grouping capital goods into broad categories based on their average productive lifetime, and then allowing businesses to deduct the purchase cost over these lifetimes according to a fixed schedule. Some deviation from these schedules was allowed, but the objective was to match the time pattern of the deductions, known as depreciation allowances, with the actual depreciation of the value of the capital good due both to wear and tear and to technological obsolescence.

This way of thinking about depreciation allowances changed in 1981. The Reagan administration was looking for a way to induce more business investment by tweaking the tax code. Cutting the corporate tax rate was deemed to be politically unattractive and, besides, would provide no incentive for noncorporate businesses. As an alternative, the administration hit on the idea of allowing businesses to deduct the cost of capital goods more quickly. This reduced tax liability and thus increased cash flow in the short term, although, later in the life of the capital goods, taxes increase and cash flow falls. But remember, time is money. Getting deductions earlier, and therefore after-tax income earlier, is almost always valuable to a business.

After the Tax Reform Act of 1986 eliminated the investment tax credit, tinkering with the tax depreciation schedules became the preferred tax policy for kick-starting the economy by stimulating business investment. Compared with the alternative—a corporate tax cut—accelerated depreciation has two advantages. One that we've already mentioned is that it applies to all businesses (although more valuable to capital-intensive ones), and not just to those that are subject to the corporate income tax. Second, the tax break from accelerated depreciation rules only applies to new investment, which maximizes the "bang per buck," where the bang is the kick to investment and the buck is the tax revenue forgone. Cutting the tax rate produces a lower bang per buck because it applies to all income, including income produced by past investments. Indeed, at any point in time, current corporate profits are almost entirely the result of past investments, so that an across-the-board tax rate cut increases after-tax profits without stimulating much additional investment. Thus, a rate cut largely rewards past investments and does not effectively target new investments. This is an important issue to keep in mind when evaluating the effect of the TCJA on investment.

What are expensing and bonus depreciation?

When expenditures on capital goods can be entirely deducted when purchased, it's called "expensing." Bonus depreciation is the name given since 2002 to the policy of accelerating depreciation by allowing firms to deduct immediately— expense—some fraction of the cost of most capital goods while depreciating the remaining fraction over time. The fraction expensed has varied since then between 30, 50, and 100 percent. Of course, 100 percent bonus depreciation simply allows a business to deduct an asset's entire purchase and installation costs right away even though the income it generates usually flows over many years. The Tax Cuts and Jobs Act allows 100 percent bonus depreciation for assets other than buildings through the year 2022, after which the percentage allowed for immediate deduction is scheduled to decline by 20 percent per year until it is fully eliminated in 2027.

Why not let businesses write off their investments right away? It would make the process of determining taxable income easier, as businesses would no longer have to keep track of depreciation schedules for long-lived capital goods. The problem is that it would mean abandoning the attempt to tax business income, or at least part of it. As discussed above, only a small fraction of the cost of a factory that will last twenty years is really a cost of earning income *this year*.

It turns out that if the tax system allows an immediate deduction for the cost of long-lived capital goods in the year of purchase (expensing), a capital investment that returned just exactly the normal rate of return in the economy would effectively be subject to no tax at all. This is because the value of the immediate tax deduction exactly equals the present discounted value of the taxes paid on future returns on that investment (assuming tax rates do not change), so the net present value is zero—the deduction precisely offsets the tax due. The government becomes essentially an equal, albeit silent, partner in the business enterprise. The government "invests" a fraction of all costs, in the form of a tax deduction, and receives in return as tax the same fraction of future receipts. The government earns the same rate of return on its up-front investment (the value of expensing) as the company does.

For investments that end up offering higher than normal returns, that is, those with a positive net present value, the corporate tax would still collect some revenue.

Should businesses' interest expenses be deductible?

At first blush, yes. After all, an income tax should tax the *net* profits of a business—receipts minus the expenses incurred to earn that income—and interest payments are the cost of obtaining debt financing. But that might be wrong for two reasons. First, as already mentioned, the cost of obtaining equity capital—by, for instance, issuing new shares—is not deductible, so interest deductibility generates an inefficient bias toward debt financing, leaving the corporate sector more leveraged and, therefore, more vulnerable to bankruptcy in economic downturns. Eliminating interest deductibility would eliminate this debt bias.

The second reason is that interest deductibility plus expensing of capital expenditures implies that not only is the income from debt-financed investments not taxed, it is *subsidized*. Recall that expensing means that the tax rate on income from that investment is zero. If the business can deduct interest on top of that, the present value of taxes turns negative. As a result, some investments that would not be profitable in the absence of any taxation become profitable with tax.[22] This is a recipe for tax shelters and helps explain why the Tax Cuts and Jobs Act limited the net interest expense deduction (interest paid minus interest received) for most businesses to 30 percent of income.

Why do many corporate executives prefer tax rate cuts over expensing?

Both tax rate cuts and accelerating depreciation increase the present value of an investment's profits and therefore make it more attractive. Many corporations, however, strongly prefer lower tax rates to accelerated depreciation. As Tom Neubig, who for many years was an economist for the accounting firm Ernst & Young, has pointed out, a lower corporate rate would lower the effective tax rate corporations report on their financial statements, and therefore would increase the book net income that they present in their financial statements, making the company look more profitable to potential investors.[23] In contrast, under current accounting rules, accelerated depreciation only changes the timing of deductions and does not reduce the effective tax rate shown on the financial statement or increase book income. This is a problem with the accounting rules, because accelerated depreciation does reduce the tax burden on corporations. This problem arises because the GAAP accounting rules do not allow corporations to discount future tax payments to take into account the time value of money, presumably because corporations might be tempted to manipulate discount rate assumptions to inflate their profits. If corporations were required to realistically discount future cash flows, the benefit of expensing would show up as higher profits because each dollar of higher future tax liability would count less than a dollar of immediate tax saving. But, regardless of why these numbers are problematic, much evidence suggests that reported book income matters to financial analysts and investors, and so corporate CFOs pay close attention to it. New York University law professor Lily Batchelder even argues that the accounting rule bias against expensing could mean that it is less of a boost to investment than economic theory would suggest.[24]

Are there implicit spending programs run through the corporate income tax?

Indeed there are, and they come in several varieties. One type is the so-called rifle-shot provision, where special tax treatment is granted for a set of circumstances that apply only to one or a few companies. Because putting the company's actual name into the tax code would invite unwanted scrutiny, the circumstances are described very precisely but circumspectly. The classic example of a rifle-shot provision applied to an individual, rather than a company: a 1954 statute about the taxation of lump-sum distributions to employees was designed so only Louis B. Mayer, the retiring head of the Metro-Goldwyn-Mayer movie studio, qualified. In their wonderful book on the legislative origins of the Tax Reform Act of 1986 entitled *Showdown at Gucci Gulch*, Jeffrey Birnbaum and Alan Murray recount several examples. One benefited "an automobile manufacturer that was incorporated in Delaware on October 13, 1916" (viz., General Motors) or "a binding contract entered into on October 20, 1984, for the purchase of six semi-submersible drilling units" (viz., an Alabama firm called Sonat).[25]

Others are special tax provisions aimed at particular sectors, more or less explicitly. For example, former Senator William Roth of Delaware wanted to help chicken farmers required by EPA rules to dispose of animal waste in an environmentally friendly way. Section 45 provides a tax credit for converting the euphemistically labeled "poultry litter" (as well as other animal waste) into electricity. It sounds good, but it's basically a subsidy for what farmers were already doing. Note that tiny Delaware is home to more than 200 million chickens.[26]

For oil and gas drillers, the using up, or depletion, of the natural resource is a key cost of doing business. Depletion allowance is the term used for the tax deduction allowed to account for the reduction of reserves as a product is produced and sold; this is analogous to the depreciation allowance for other capital investments. Producers can choose either of two depletion allowance regimes: cost depletion and percentage depletion. Many experts believe this deduction scheme is way too generous if the goal is to measure income accurately rather than subsidize oil and gas production.[27]

Other provisions of the tax code provide subsidies to certain industries even though these industries are never mentioned. For example, accelerated depreciation favors those sectors that tend to utilize the kind of capital that qualifies for the most accelerated write-offs.

Are multinational corporations taxed differently than domestic companies?

Most big corporations operate not only in the United States but also in many foreign countries. For example, Nike has over 600 factories worldwide, manufacturing products in 42 countries, and McDonald's has restaurants in 101 countries.[28] Operating in many countries allows them to seek low-cost places to produce their products and profitable places to sell them.

The global nature of corporations raises a number of complex and contentious tax issues. Both the home country (where the company has its legal residence) and the host country (where the operations are) may claim the right to tax the income of the company. If both countries were to tax the income at their full rates, then the total tax rate could become so punitive that few cross-border commercial operations would ever happen, and that is not a good outcome for people in either country. Governments recognize the possibility of this kind of double taxation and design their tax codes to avoid punishing corporations that operate across national borders. But there is more than one way to accomplish this.

Should we try to tax corporations on their worldwide income?

Until the Tax Cuts and Jobs Act, the United States was the last major country that applied a so-called worldwide system to multinational corporations. Here's how it worked. The United States claimed the right to tax the worldwide income of its resident corporations (and individuals), but, to avoid double taxation, a U.S. corporation was entitled to a credit against its income tax liability for the income taxes its foreign subsidiary remitted to the foreign government. To see how this worked, first consider what happens if a U.S. corporation had a wholly owned subsidiary in a country, call it Fredonia, which had the same corporate tax rate as the United States—35 percent as of

2017. The subsidiary makes one dollar of profit, and owes 35 cents to Fredonia. The dollar was also part of the U.S. parent company's taxable income, so the dollar of profit earned in Fredonia triggered 35 cents of U.S. tax. But, because the United States allowed a foreign tax credit of 35 cents, there was no net U.S. tax owed (and no double taxation).

The story got more complicated, and more interesting, for a U.S.-based company operating in a country with a low effective tax rate. As an example, we'll consider that the "host" country for the investment is China, which had a corporate tax rate of 25 percent. The U.S. rate exceeded the Chinese tax rate, and thus the foreign tax credit, by 10 percentage points. However, this extra, or residual, tax owed to the U.S. was not due until the profits were returned, or repatriated, back to the U.S. parent company as dividends. So the residual tax could be deferred for a long time.

Moreover, by careful (and generally legal) tax planning, the U.S. parent corporation could effectively get access to the foreign subsidiary company's profits without ever being subject to the 10 percent residual tax. One other consideration was that the foreign tax credit applied on a worldwide basis (with the exception of income from a list of countries identified as tax havens), so taxes paid in high-tax foreign countries could offset part or all of the tax owed with respect to income from low-tax countries. However, most foreign nations had tax rates below the U.S. rate, so U.S. companies often would owe corporate income tax on income that they repatriated.

What is a territorial system?

In answering the previous question, we said that the United Sates was the last major country to run a worldwide system. With the TCJA, as of 2018 we have moved to a version of the alternative system that most countries use, a territorial system. A territorial system avoids double international taxation because the home country of the multinational corporation mostly cedes its rights to tax foreign income and taxes only the income earned within its borders. That said, most territorial tax systems apply minimum taxes to prevent income from fleeing to tax havens. (See page 93, "What is a global minimum tax and why does it matter in a territorial system?")

Will shifting from a worldwide to a territorial system bring American jobs home?

Probably not. Putting aside that the TCJA lowered the corporate tax rate from 35 percent to 21 percent, moving to a territorial system reduces the U.S. tax on the income from foreign operations to zero. On its own, this makes foreign operations more, not less, attractive relative to U.S.-based operations.

A leading argument for moving to a territorial system is that it would improve the "business competitiveness" of U.S.-headquartered multinational corporations operating in low-tax foreign countries. For example, if a U.S. and German company are both considering setting up a subsidiary in Ireland, both companies would owe the (low) Irish income tax, but under a worldwide system, only the U.S. company would owe, upon repatriation, a residual tax to its home country. The German company, in contrast, would be subject to Germany's territorial tax system, and thus would not owe any taxes to the German government irrespective of what it chooses to do with profits from its Irish subsidiary—invest them back in its Irish operations or repatriate them to Germany.

Some research has suggested that cross-border synergies might redound to make investment of U.S. multinational companies more profitable in the United States when foreign operations expand, perhaps leading them to expand their operations here.[29] But it's not obvious that prosperity in the United States is better served when U.S.-based multinational companies invest in the United States relative to investment done here by foreign-based multinationals. U.S. workers employed by Toyota, Royal Dutch

Shell, or Nestlé USA have learned that a job is a job. Indeed, for a U.S. multinational company a territorial tax system improves the relative attractiveness of investing in (low-tax) foreign countries compared with investment in the United States, and so it might discourage domestic investment and hiring.

Another problem with a territorial system is that, as long as the United States has a higher statutory corporate rate than many other countries (including tax havens), moving to a territorial system would greatly increase the incentive for shifting taxable income overseas, as we discuss later. Under the former worldwide system, shifting taxable income from the United States to a low-tax country merely postponed the residual U.S. tax liability until repatriation (which could, admittedly, be a very long time); in contrast, under a territorial system, it would be lost forever.

As discussed below, the TCJA includes several provisions intended to prevent the erosion of the U.S. tax base due to taxable income shifting. As we write, corporations and tax scholars are trying to assess how effective they will be and whether they might have unintended effects.

What is transfer pricing? Why is it important to multinational corporations (and taxpayers)?

Across countries, both corporate tax rates and tax base definitions vary, creating tax-planning opportunities for multinational corporations, and headaches for revenue authorities of countries with relatively high tax rates. When tax rates differ, the multinational corporation has an incentive to shift its taxable income from a country with a high tax rate to a country with a low tax rate. For example, say a U.S. car company has a manufacturing subsidiary in Ireland. The United States has a corporate tax rate of 21 percent, while the tax rate in Ireland is 12.5 percent. If the company can somehow reduce its U.S. taxable income by a dollar and increase its Irish taxable income by a dollar, its worldwide tax liability falls by

OFFSHORE OUTSOURCING

The practice of hiring an external organization to perform business functions in a planet other than the one where the products or services are developed or manufactured.

Copyright ©2010 by Barbara M. Brandt

Source: www.CartoonStock.com.

8.5 cents (21 cents minus 12.5 cents) per dollar shifted. This is very easy money.

Transfer pricing is one way to shift income from a high-tax country to a low-tax country. When the U.S. parent company sells something to its Irish subsidiary, it "charges" an artificially low price; when an Irish subsidiary sells something to its U.S. parent, it charges an artificially high price. This increases taxable income in Ireland and increases deductions—and therefore lowers taxable income—in the United States. Because the transfer prices are between two parts of the same multinational company, they have no effect on its overall pre-tax profits, but they do shift taxable income from the high-tax country to the low-tax country, and thus reduce the company's worldwide tax burden and thereby increase its worldwide after-tax profits. The high-tax country's government, though, is not pleased with this drain on its revenue and requires that the transfer prices of products be close to the prices that would be charged among parties in "arm's-length" commercial transactions. But this is very difficult to enforce, especially when intangible goods, such as the license to make use of technology developed by the parent company, change hands. This is because such intangibles are rarely exchanged between two unrelated parties, so valuing the asset is very difficult.

Clever use of inter-company loans is another way to shift income to low-tax countries. If the company in a high-tax country lends to a related company in a low-tax country, the former company can write off the interest payments against a high tax rate, while the latter company owes tax on the interest receipts at a lower tax rate. Voila, total taxes of the multinational company go down!

What are tax havens?

Although we used low-tax Ireland as an example, there are lots of countries that effectively levy a zero tax rate, so the tax saving of moving a dollar of taxable income from the United States is 21 cents on the dollar. These countries are known as tax havens. Think of the Cayman Islands or the Isle of Jersey. Tax havens are jurisdictions—often small island nations—that levy no or only nominal taxes and offer themselves as a vehicle for nonresident companies to escape taxation in their country of residence. To facilitate tax evasion, tax havens often do not readily share information about the activities of foreign tax-payers in their countries. A U.S. company might funnel enor-mous amounts of taxable income into such countries even though it has very little real economic activity there. For ex-ample, in 2010 the profits of U.S.-controlled foreign corpor-ations equaled 1,804 percent of the GDP of the British Virgin Islands, 2,066 percent in the Cayman Islands, and 1,614 percent in Bermuda. This compares to 0.4 percent of GDP in Germany and Japan, 0.3 percent in Italy, and 2.1 percent in Britain, even though U.S. corporations conduct much, much more real eco-nomic activity in those European countries than in their trop-ical post office box operations.[30]

There is considerable concern that tax havens are "para-sitic" on the tax revenues of the non-haven countries, inducing them to expend real resources in defending their revenue base and in the process reducing the welfare of their residents. One report in 1998 by a respected multilateral organization, the Organisation for Economic Co-operation and Development (OECD), concluded that "governments cannot stand back while their tax bases are eroded through the actions of coun-tries which offer taxpayers ways to exploit tax havens [and preferential regimes] to reduce the tax that would otherwise be payable to them."

In sharp contrast to this long-standing concern about their deleterious effects, some economists have argued that tax ha-vens are a device to save high-tax countries from their own bad policies. In a global economy, goes their argument, coun-tries should avoid taxing highly mobile capital (business or

" RON CHOATE, OFFSHORE TAX HAVEN CONSULTANT, SPEAKING..."

Source: www.CartoonStock.com.

investments that could easily move to another country) because it just drives capital away and is ineffective at raising revenue from capital owners who have many alternative investment opportunities. Looking the other way as corporations make use of tax havens, the argument continues, allows countries to move toward the less-distorting tax regime they should, but for some reason cannot, explicitly enact. On the other hand, though, tax havens induce wasteful expenditure of resources, both by firms in their participation in havens and by governments in their attempts to enforce their tax codes. And they siphon off tax revenues from the non-haven countries. In addition, tax havens worsen tax competition problems by causing countries to further reduce their tax rates below levels that are efficient from a global viewpoint. The same economic logic that underlies the call for lower statutory rates to address taxable income shifting suggests that there should be substantial attention paid—unilaterally and multilaterally—to defending a country's revenue base.

What is a global minimum tax and why does it matter in a territorial system?

Cutting the corporate rate from 35 percent to 21 percent as the TCJA did reduces the reward to shifting taxable income out of the United States, but it does not eliminate it, especially with regard to income shifting to tax havens. However, moving from a worldwide to a territorial system increases the return. Under the old worldwide system, if a dollar of taxable income was shifted to a subsidiary in a low-tax country, tax liability fell in the current year, but in principle the U.S tax rate was due if and when the money was repatriated to the U.S. parent company. But in a pure territorial system, that backstop is gone, period—a dollar shifted away is lost to the high-tax country forever.

The framers of the TCJA understood this problem, and along with the move toward a territorial system enacted a trio of new provisions with more or less memorable acronyms: GILTI (global intangible low taxed income), BEAT (base erosion anti-abuse tax), and FDII (foreign-derived intangible income). BEAT can be thought of as a limited-scope alternative minimum tax, applied by adding back to the parent's taxable income certain deductible payments made to related foreign companies and subjecting that expanded base to a lower tax rate to come up with a minimum tax liability. These new provisions are widely agreed to be labyrinthine. How successful they will be at stanching income shifting remains to be seen, as multinational corporations have the incentive to skirt the intent of the law to minimize their tax liability. What is certain is that the United States has not moved to a pure territorial system, but rather to a territorial system modified to constrain outward income shifting.

What is formulary apportionment? Would that be a better option
than trying to enforce transfer pricing rules?

U.S. states, which levy a variety of corporate income tax rates,
face a similar problem with taxable income shifting.[31] They
are allowed to tax only income earned in their state, while
most big companies operate in many states. Take Walmart as
an example. Imagine how difficult it would be, and ripe for
tax-minimizing schemes, if to determine taxable profits each
state tried to check on the prices Walmart charged (itself) as it
shipped goods across state boundaries. But, then, how do the
43 states that have a state corporate income tax determine how
much income was earned in their state if they don't calculate
and keep track of interstate prices?

Here's how. They all use a formula that estimates the fraction of a company's total U.S. income that is taxable within the
state. For about 20 states, that fraction is determined by the
ratio of in-state sales to U.S. sales. Other states take account
of the ratio of in-state employment to total U.S. employment
and the ratio of in-state assets to total U.S. assets. A handful
of states rely on an equal weighting of the three ratios. Using
a "formulary apportionment" scheme for determining how
much of a multistate corporation's total income is taxable by
one state eliminates the need for companies to calculate, and
the tax authority to monitor, interstate prices. But it does not
eliminate the payoff to tax avoidance schemes to reduce state
income tax liability. Such schemes, which often take advantage
of states' different formulas, proliferate.

Some experts have argued that the U.S. government should
adopt for worldwide taxation of U.S. corporations a formulary apportionment system like that used by the states. But
implementing this system for countries, rather than states
within the United States, runs into some difficult problems.
In the case of formula apportionment by U.S. states, there
is an unambiguous place from which to start the formula
calculation—total U.S. income. Compare that to how a formula

apportionment system would work for the United States in determining the U.S. share of income of a multinational company. It would be possible to calculate the ratio of U.S. sales, employment, or assets to worldwide sales, employment, or assets. But then what? There is no global tax authority that is defining, monitoring, and auditing such a concept. Moreover, countries have very different methods of calculating taxable income, so calculating worldwide income is challenging. And unilaterally adopting formulary apportionment would abrogate tax treaties we have established with many nations. For these reasons, it is unlikely that a worldwide formulary apportionment system will be implemented any time soon.

How does the U.S. corporate tax rate compare to the rate of other countries?

Before the TCJA, the United States had the highest statutory corporate tax rate among developed countries, as corporate tax rates have been falling throughout the world for 30 years while the U.S. rate stayed about the same. After the TCJA, which cut our federal statutory corporate tax rate to 21 percent, we are at about the average for advanced economies.

As we have already discussed, the statutory rate is only one component of the tax disincentive to business investment and may be outweighed by the definition of the business tax base, especially the tax depreciation schedules. Calculating the net tax disincentive, called by economists the marginal effective tax rate on investment, is much more difficult than calculating the statutory rate and is especially difficult to do in a way that is comparable across countries. One careful, but certainly not definitive, study concluded that in 2008 the marginal effective tax rate on investment due to the corporate tax for the United States was just 16.2 percent, which tied for 46th out of the 80 countries in the survey and 18th out of the 31 countries then in the OECD.[32] So, even when our statutory rate was at or near the highest, our effective rate was in the middle. After the TCJA, undoubtedly our rank in the marginal effective tax rate has gotten better (or worse, depending on your perspective).

Source: www.CartoonStock.com.

Did our relatively high corporate tax rate hurt our companies' competitiveness and the country's competitiveness?

We've slipped in one of the most prominent policy buzzwords—competitiveness. The terms "compete" and "competition" have a special resonance and a specific meaning to economists. But competitiveness does not have a clear meaning, and the term has been the source of much miscommunication. Because competition is an essential element of most athletic endeavors, sports analogies often crop up. But what is the right analogy? A running race, where each nation is an entry? A race where the prizes depend on the order of finish or one where the prizes depend only on how fast one runs? If the runner is a country, and the runner's time is income per capita, then surely the latter analogy is more apt. The benefits of prosperity are not diminished by another nation's greater prosperity. This is nothing more than what Adam Smith said over 200 years ago—global commerce allows every country to enhance its prosperity by concentrating on doing what it does best and taking full advantage of what other countries do best.

In the past, competitiveness has been associated with either the size of a nation's export sector as a share of GNP or its trade surplus. This is dangerous because maximizing either of these quantities is not a defensible policy goal. One can easily conceive of a declining economy with a thriving export sector—if, for example, the export sector is propelled by a favorable exchange rate caused by the drying up of attractive domestic investment opportunities. Conversely, the discovery of natural resources, while a boon to prosperity, often causes a decline in the manufacturing trade balance. A deteriorating trade balance may be a symptom of increasing imports, which may simply reflect a burgeoning economy with lots of demand for goods and services. Neither a trade surplus nor deficit is a reliable indicator of economic health.[33]

In some debates, competitiveness of a country is defined as the success of its resident multinational companies compared with foreign competitors, sometimes measured by their share of worldwide sales or profits. But high multinational corporation profits could be achieved simply by a transfer from taxpayers to domestic corporations, a policy that most would agree is not appropriate and would not improve the fundamental soundness of the economy. With government subsidies, domestic firms could gain market share even in cases where the revenue gained is less than the additional cost of production, which is also not in the national interest.

Properly interpreted, competitiveness is not equivalent to prosperity. Its value as a policy buzzword is to remind us that the conditions under which we strive for prosperity have changed as the integration of national economies into the world economy has progressed. Just as the training regimen for a race at high altitude is different, it may be that how to achieve prosperity is different in a globally integrated economy. In a global economy the objective of policy is to maintain (and preferably grow) the real incomes of our citizens in the face of global markets and the policies of other countries, which vary in trade policy from a free-trade orientation in some countries to aggressive promotion of exports in others. Tax policies range from domestically oriented and open to international cooperation to aggressive courting of foreign investment to the beggar-thy-neighbor behavior of tax havens.[34]

The bottom line is that there is no compelling evidence that high statutory corporate tax rates per se inhibit economic growth or suppress a nation's prosperity. The two best defenses for reducing our rate were to diminish outward income shifting that drain away tax revenues, and to bring down the disincentive to business investment.

4

TAXING SPENDING

What is a consumption tax?

A consumption tax is a tax triggered by spending. In the United States, the most common form of consumption tax is the retail sales tax administered by most states and many local governments. There are also specific consumption taxes called excise taxes that apply to items such as gasoline, alcohol, and cigarettes. In the rest of the world, the value-added tax (VAT) is by far the most common form of consumption tax, levied by over 160 countries (but not the United States). A VAT is just a sales tax that is collected from businesses at all stages of production and distribution, not just the retail stage.

Why tax consumption rather than income?

People argue for a consumption tax on the grounds of fairness and efficiency; although, as we shall see, perceptions of fairness vary dramatically. The English philosopher Thomas Hobbes (1588–1679) made the fairness argument thus: "It is fairer to tax people on what they extract from the economy, as roughly measured by their consumption, than to tax them on what they produce for the economy, as roughly measured by their income."[1] Many economists think a consumption tax is more efficient than an income tax because an income tax discourages saving, while a consumption tax does not. (See box 4.1.)

BOX 4.1 Why an Income Tax "Double-Taxes" Saving and a Sales Tax Does Not

Imagine a world without an income tax. (Yes, it is fun, but this is just make-believe.) If you earned a dollar, you could choose to spend it now or save it for a year, in which case you'd have a dollar plus interest to spend. Suppose that you can earn 4 percent interest. Your choice is between spending $1.00 now and spending $1.04 one year hence. At the prevailing interest rate, you will decide to save (or borrow) until a dollar more of current consumption is worth the same amount to you as $1.04 of consumption a year from now. The interest rate is "a return to waiting."

Now suppose you have an income tax at a flat rate of 50 percent. (This makes the math easy.) If you earn a dollar, you get to keep $0.50 after tax. You could spend it now or let it earn interest for a year. However, you wouldn't get to spend $0.50 plus interest in a year because you also pay tax on the interest. So, even though you'll get two cents in interest (at a 4 percent rate), you only keep one cent after tax. Your after-tax return to waiting is cut in half, to 2 percent, by the income tax. The income tax cuts your current consumption possibilities by half, but it cuts your future consumption possibilities by even more. Instead of having $1.04 to spend next year, you have $0.51. The original—say labor—income is taxed; subsequently any return on the portion of that income that is saved is taxed as well. This is the sense in which the income tax is said to "double-tax" saving. More precisely, deferred, or future, consumption is taxed more heavily than current consumption.

And the longer you defer consumption, the bigger the effective tax rate on future consumption. For example, if you wanted to save long enough for your money to double—about 18 years at a 4 percent annual interest rate—your dollar would grow to $2 without tax. Every dollar saved provides one extra dollar—$2 in total—to spend 18 years in the future. With the income tax, you would earn 2 percent after tax, so your $0.50 would grow only to $0.72. Future consumption would be reduced by 74 percent (from $2 before tax to $0.72 after the income tax).

Now suppose we had a sales tax at a rate of 100 percent. (Note that a 100 percent sales tax rate is equivalent to a 50 percent income tax rate in terms of its effect on current consumption possibilities.) You could take the $1 you earned and buy something for $0.50, plus tax. (There'd be $0.50 in tax just as in the income tax example above.) Or you could put the dollar in the bank (there's no tax until you spend money) and hold it for about eighteen years until it doubles. At that point, you could afford to buy something for $1. That plus the $1 in sales tax would add up to the $2 you'd have in the bank. The tax reduces deferred consumption by exactly the same percentage as current consumption—50 percent. Thus, the sales tax does not distort the choice between current and future consumption by making the latter relatively more expensive.

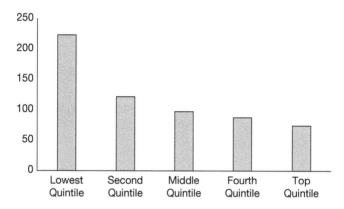

Figure 4.1 Consumption as a Percentage of After-Tax Income, by Income Group, 2013
Source: U.S. Bureau of Labor Statistics, Savings Rate by Income Group, 2013.

A consumption tax sounds great. What's the catch?

The main drawback of a consumption tax is that most versions of it seem very regressive. This is because in a given year most lower-income people spend all their income and more—people on the bottom rungs get help from friends, relatives, and government transfer programs like food stamps. Higher-income people spend a much smaller fraction of their income (see figure 4.1). Thus, a flat-rate tax on consumption amounts to a much larger share of income for poor people than for those with high incomes. For that reason, some argue that consumption taxes are fundamentally unfair.

In fact, consumption taxes are rarely flat taxes on all purchases. They often exempt necessities like food and medicine. And some have other features designed to offset the tax's regressivity, which we'll discuss later.

More important, a snapshot of one year's spending and income overstates the true regressivity of a flat-rate consumption tax. Many people with low income in a year have low income only temporarily, either because they are young or retired, or they're just having a bad year financially. These people generally choose a spending level more in line with their long-term income than their current income. If we redrew figure 4.1 to represent a lifetime of income and consumption, the height of the bars would not fall as fast. Another way to put it is, over a lifetime, all but very high-income people spend about what they earn, so that a flat-rate tax on consumption would amount to the same proportion of lifetime income for everyone but the very rich, for whom the lifetime tax burden would be a smaller share of lifetime income.

What is a retail sales tax?

It is a tax on final (i.e., to consumers rather than to other businesses) sales that is collected from retail businesses. All but five states levy retail sales taxes. The rates ranged from 2.9 percent in Colorado to 7.25 percent in California in 2017.[2] Many local governments and other jurisdictions, indeed over 11,000 of them, also collect sales taxes.[3] The combined state and local tax rate can be as high as 12 percent (in Alabama). Retail sales taxes are relatively simple, at least from the perspective of the average citizen. Retailers simply remit a fixed percentage of their taxable sales volume to the tax authority. At the cash register, the tax due is separately reported from the pre-tax price. A complication is that some consumer goods and services are exempt from the sales tax (e.g., prescription drugs are exempt in almost all states) and some are taxed at lower rates. However, modern cash registers make calculating and reporting the tax a straightforward operation for most retailers.

Retail sales taxes have some drawbacks, however. In some situations, they may be easy to evade. Some unscrupulous sellers do not remit the tax due on cash transactions. (Do you wonder why your house painter offers a lower price if you pay in cash rather than by check? It's probably *not* because he or she thinks cashing the check will be particularly burdensome.) Some buyers will cross state lines to avoid a high state sales tax—that is why

---

SIDEBAR 4.1 **State Sales Tax Havens**

"Looking for a Bargain? Delaware is the home of tax-free shopping."
    —Delaware Tourism website
"In Portland, you'll find everything you expect from big-city shopping—except the sales tax."
    —TravelPortland website

---

some Washington State residents (with a combined sales tax rate as high as 10.4 percent) like to shop in Oregon, and some Philadelphians (sales tax of 8 percent) will drive 30 miles south to Delaware. Oregon and Delaware are sales tax havens—they levy no sales tax at all.[4] And Internet vendors often do not remit tax on out-of-state sales, although, as we discuss later, that is likely to soon change.

A final drawback of a retail sales tax is that the tax can "cascade" because business purchases of materials and services from retailers might trigger sales tax and then their sales trigger the tax again. Although every sales tax has measures to exempt "business-to-business" transactions—and in principle tax only sales to consumers—they have to be fairly restrictive to limit evasion. In consequence, some intermediate inputs end up being taxed twice or more. Note that cascading does not happen under the VAT, which is also more difficult to evade entirely than the sales tax.

What is a use tax?

When you live in a state with a sales tax, what you buy is generally (i.e., other than exempt goods) taxable. But that's also true for many purchases made over the Internet or in states without a sales tax. In that case, the tax is called a use tax and must be remitted by the consumer, or at least it's supposed to be, as

---

SIDEBAR 4.2 **The First Excise Tax and the Whiskey Rebellion**

The first excise tax in the United States didn't work out well.

In 1791, to pay off debt accumulated during the Revolutionary War, the new American government imposed an excise tax on distilled spirits (i.e., whiskey). The tax varied from 6 to 18 cents per gallon, with smaller producers bearing more of the tax burden than large distillers. The small producers were mostly farmers west of the Appalachian and Allegheny Mountains who relied on whiskey sales as their primary source of income. They protested this tax by tarring tax collectors, burning houses, and other acts of violence. President Washington sent troops to quell the tax-motivated rebellion.

The excise tax on spirits was repealed in 1802.

Source: Michael Hoover, "The Whiskey Rebellion," Alcohol and Tobacco Tax and Trade Bureau, https://www.ttb.gov/public-information/whiskey-rebellion

---

long as the good is consumed in the consumer's state of residence. Many states include lines on the state income tax return where taxpayers can report out-of-state sales and add the use tax to their income tax bill. Compliance with voluntary use taxes is very low. California has estimated that $1.1 billion in use tax owed annually is never paid—a 1 percent compliance rate![5] Nationwide, uncollected sales tax is estimated at $26 billion in 2015.[6] Owners of "brick and mortar" retail stores complain that this gives online retailers an unfair (and, from a social perspective, inefficient) advantage. And they have a good point. Online retailers reply that calculating the tax due for each purchaser, which can vary by state, locality, and type of good, is unreasonably onerous; however, software could be made available that would facilitate compliance.

What is a luxury tax?

While general sales taxes are probably regressive, some specific sales taxes are intended to be highly progressive. For example, the Omnibus Budget Reconciliation Act of 1990 included a 10 percent excise tax on yachts, furs, and jewelry and high-end cars, as part of a legislative compromise that limited the increase in the top income tax rate. The theory was that the excise tax would hit mostly well-heeled consumers who could afford it. In fact, targeted industries made the case that the tax caused demand for their products—expensive boats, for example—to plummet, ultimately costing thousands of jobs. That is, at least part of the burden of the tax fell on owners of yacht retailers and their workers rather than just on the rich consumers. (See page 24, "Who really bears the burden of tax?")

Luxury taxes, familiar to Monopoly enthusiasts, have a long history. The telephone excise tax was originally a luxury tax used to help finance the Spanish-American War in 1898.[7] Back then, only the very well off had telephones in their homes. (These days, of course, having a cell phone is a necessity for most Americans.) The tax was introduced as a temporary measure, but it was continually extended and modified. In the 1960s, it was increased—on a temporary basis—to finance the Vietnam War. Some war protesters refused to pay the tax. It now applies to cell phones, as well as landlines, and there are still protesters.[8]

What is an excise tax?

An excise tax is a consumption tax on a particular item. An excise tax has a narrow base, while sales taxes tend to be broad-based. Excise taxes may also be less transparent to consumers because wholesalers remit the tax, which is ultimately incorporated into the retail price. There are currently federal excise taxes on beer and wine, alcohol, gasoline and diesel fuel, tires, airline tickets, telephone service, and cigarettes. Some excise taxes are dedicated to paying for particular activities. For example, the airline ticket tax revenue is designated for spending on airports, air traffic control, and other aviation-related infrastructure. Taxes on gasoline and diesel are earmarked for highway and transit projects.

What is a sin tax?

Sin taxes are excise taxes intended to discourage behavior deemed undesirable, at least in excess. Taxes on cigarettes, alcohol, beer, wine, and gambling are usually put in that category. The recent spate of taxes on sweetened beverages have similar motivation. Ronald Reagan liked to say, "[I]f you tax something, you'll get less of it." For a lot of taxes, that's an undesirable side effect. For example, we don't want people working less to reduce income taxes. However, sin taxes are explicitly intended to discourage the taxed activity.

What is a Pigouvian tax?

Sometimes markets don't work well in directing resources to their most efficient uses. For example, people and businesses tend to pollute too much when they treat clean air and water as a free resource. But, while it may be free to them, it exacts a toll on the society at large. The pollution that is a byproduct of economic activities is an example of what economist call an *externality*, in this case a negative externality. The polluter's activity adversely affects others who breathe the air or drink the water. Pigouvian taxes, named after the British economist A. C. Pigou, are designed to reduce externalities like pollution. The logic is similar to that behind sin taxes. The tax is intended to optimally discourage the taxed activity, but not necessarily eliminate it. Ideally, the tax rate should be set equal to the marginal social damage caused by the externality; in this way, the tax induces people and businesses to consider the extra social cost when they decide to undertake the taxed activity. The gasoline excise tax is in part a Pigouvian tax. It encourages people to drive less, which leads to less highway congestion, road wear and tear, air pollution, and emissions of greenhouse gases. Some have claimed that the cigarette excise tax is a Pigouvian tax on the rationale that it reduces second-hand smoke and public spending on health care and disability insurance for those sickened by cigarettes. (However, smoking

may save society money to the extent that higher mortality reduces spending on public retirement programs—see sidebar
4.3). Pigouvian subsidies can be justified to encourage activities with positive externalities or spillover effects. Basic research and development activities are the most prominent
example of this, and externality arguments are cited to justify
the U.S. research and experimentation tax credit.

What is a VAT?

A VAT—short for value-added tax—is a consumption tax that
is collected in stages from producers and distributors all along
the supply chain in proportion to their contribution to the final
value of a product—their value added. Because value added
sums up to the retail price of final sales to consumers, the effects of a VAT and a retail sales tax are very similar. It sounds
complicated, but there are good practical reasons for levying a
consumption tax in this way, and almost every country collects
a VAT. The United States is a very rare exception.

   There are two main ways to implement a VAT: the "subtraction method" and "credit-invoice" method. In the subtraction method, each producer calculates value added by starting
with their receipts and then subtracting the cost of inputs purchased from other firms. The quintessential example is the production process for a loaf of bread. To vastly simplify, suppose
the farmer grows wheat using only his own labor and sells it
to the miller for 10 cents. He'd owe a penny in VAT at a 10 percent rate on his sale to the miller. The miller grinds up the
flour and sells it to the baker for 40 cents. His value added is
30 cents (40 cents minus the 10 cents cost of buying the wheat
from the farmer), on which he'd owe 3 cents in tax. The baker
makes the bread and sells it to the grocery store for 80 cents,
owing 4 cents in tax on her value added. And the retailer sells
it to the consumer for a dollar, owing 2 cents in tax on the final
value added. All told, 10 cents in tax is collected—the same
amount as under a 10 percent retail sales tax—but it's collected

---

SIDEBAR 4.3 **Cigarettes Kill People. Is That a Positive Externality?**

In 1999 the Czech Republic was considering raising excise taxes on tobacco. In an effort to dissuade the government from raising this tax, Philip Morris financed a study that estimated that, while smoking costs the Czech Republic $403 million per year due to death and disability, the excise tax collected from cigarettes was $522 million—far greater than the direct costs of smoking. Moreover, the government saved $31 million on public pensions and medical care because smokers die younger and thus collect fewer benefits. Thus, smoking creates a kind of positive pecuniary externality that would diminish if excessive excise taxes caused the smoking rate to plummet.

Perhaps, not surprisingly, the public found the argument that killing people saves money kind of immoral. The story did get the Czech Republic and Philip Morris a lot of international attention.

Note: NPR's Planet Money podcast has an entertaining discussion of the Philip Morris debacle, available at http://www.npr.org/blogs/money/2010/07/16/128569258/the-friday-podcast-death-saves-you-money.

---

in stages all along the line rather than entirely from the final retailer. One advantage of this arrangement is that even if one party along the supply chain doesn't remit the tax, the government still gets tax from the other producers.

The credit-invoice VAT is the more common type. Sellers up and down the supply chain are subject to a tax on gross receipts, but they get a credit for the tax paid by suppliers so long as they receive a tax invoice verifying the tax was indeed remitted. So, in the preceding example, the baker would owe 8 cents in tax on the loaf of bread, but could credit against it the 4 cents in tax paid by the miller so long as she receives an invoice indicating that he'd remitted the tax. Her net tax bill would be 4 cents, just as under the subtraction method.

The credit-invoice VAT sounds really complicated. Why do it that way?

Countries use a credit-invoice VAT because it's easier to enforce. Taxpayers have a strong interest in doing business only with tax-compliant suppliers. To see why, think about the

"That must stand for Very Annoying Tax!"

Source: www.CartoonStock.com.

baker in the preceding example. If the miller doesn't provide an invoice, she owes the whole 8 cents in tax herself. So she's going to insist that the miller give her an invoice (or demand a price discount to reflect the extra tax that she'll owe). Thus, the miller has a strong incentive to be tax-compliant in order to attract business from other tax-compliant firms.

And the invoice method isn't as complicated as it sounds. A lot of the invoice tracking and reporting can be and is done by computers.

Are small businesses subject to the VAT?

Not usually. Most VATs exempt small businesses (such as street vendors). An advantage of the VAT over the retail sales tax is that exempting small retailers doesn't cost much revenue. Tax is still collected along the other parts of the supply chain. In some countries, small producers may opt out of the VAT, but if they sell a lot of goods to other tax-compliant businesses, they often voluntarily choose to register and remit the VAT because their business customers want a tax-paid invoice.

Why doesn't the United States have a VAT?

Despite its prevalence in the rest of the world, the United States has never come close to enacting a VAT. Al Ullman, chairman of the powerful House Ways and Means Committee, proposed a VAT in 1979 and was promptly voted out of office in the next election. While other factors clearly played a role (he disliked meeting with constituents and was widely seen as arrogant and aloof), Ullman's advocacy of the VAT while sitting in a position where he might have made it happen was perceived as an important element in his undoing.

One reason that we don't have a VAT is that—news flash—Americans really dislike taxes (e.g., "Tea Party"). Some worry that a VAT would be *too* efficient, in the sense that it could easily raise hundreds of billions of dollars per year in additional revenues, which would fuel expansion in government. They point to evidence from Europe that increases in VAT revenues are followed by increases in government spending as a share of the economy. This doesn't prove that the VAT revenues *caused* the increase in spending, but VAT critics are convinced that the VAT would fuel an explosion in government spending. Grover Norquist, head of Americans for Tax Reform, has said that "VAT is French for big government."

SIDEBAR 4.4 Larry Summers on VAT Politics

"Liberals think it's regressive and conservatives think it's a money machine. If they reverse their positions, the VAT may happen."
   —Larry Summers, former secretary of the Treasury (1988)

Source: http://www.nytimes.com/1988/12/19/business/tax-watch-the-likely-forms-of-new-taxes.html.

A distinct set of critics object to a VAT because it is regressive—just as with a retail sales tax, its burden would comprise a larger share of income for poor families than rich ones. And some worry that a VAT would interfere with states' ability to administer their own sales taxes—the largest source of revenue for state and local governments.

But there are signs that this may be changing. In the 2016 Republican presidential primary campaign, two of the candidates—Ted Cruz and Rand Paul—endorsed a subtraction-method VAT as a replacement for other taxes, although they insisted their proposals were still income taxes. In a fascinating exchange during a presidential debate, Marco Rubio insisted that Cruz's plan was a VAT, which Mr. Cruz thought was a scurrilous accusation. The irony is that Rubio's own plan was a kind of X tax, which is a more progressive VAT (that we discuss later).

How much money would a VAT raise?

It depends on how broad the base is. A very broad-based VAT, like the one in New Zealand, could annually collect about $36 billion per percentage point.[9] So a 10 percent VAT could collect $360 billion per year. If there are exemptions for food, medicine, housing, and other necessities, as is common almost everywhere else in the world, the tax would raise much less. A typical European-type VAT would raise about $22 billion per percentage point.

There would, though, be considerable costs to administering and enforcing a VAT that don't depend on the tax rate chosen, which is why a VAT would probably not be worth doing unless the rate were at least 5 percent or so (because the administrative and compliance costs would be a large fraction of revenues raised if the tax rate is small).[10]

A very broad-based VAT would almost surely require some type of offsetting subsidies to mitigate its effect on lower-income families, through the higher prices of goods and services.[11] One option would be to offer a flat refundable income tax credit designed to offset the amount of VAT paid by the average family at the poverty level. A very broad-based VAT with such a tax credit would raise about as much revenue (net of the subsidy) as the typical narrow-base European model.

What is the typical VAT rate in other countries?

They range from 5 percent for Canada[12] and Japan to 25 percent or more in the Nordic countries and Hungary (figure 4.2). The average rate is 19 percent.[13]

How would a federal VAT interact with state and local sales taxes?

States worry that a VAT could undermine states' and local governments' primary source of revenue—the sales tax—for several reasons. First, a VAT at rates common in the rest of the world would make the combined federal, state, and local retail sales tax rate quite high. (State and local retail sales taxes averaged 7.4 percent in 2018.)[14] At such high rates, tax evasion could be a serious problem. Second, the base and computation method for the VAT could vary significantly from those used to calculate sales taxes. This could seriously complicate compliance for businesses and undermine support for state and local sales taxes.

There are, however, some potentially offsetting factors. If there were a federal VAT, the state and federal government could share information for purposes of monitoring and enforcing compliance—as they do currently for the income tax. States could also choose to enact their own VATs using the same tax base as the federal tax. This would simplify compliance for businesses.

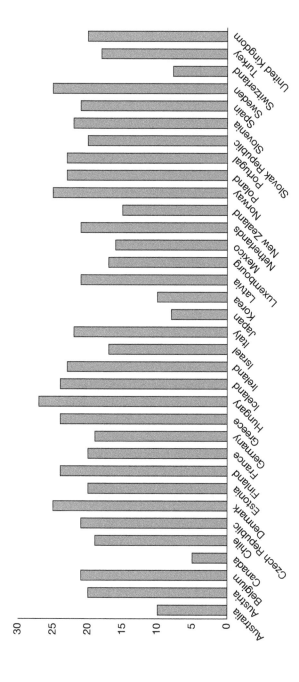

Figure 4.2 VAT Rate for OECD Countries, 2018

Source: https://www.oecd.org/ctp/consumption/Table-2.A2.1-VAT-GST-Rates-2018.xlsx.

Does a VAT promote exports?

Probably not, although this is widely asserted. Some people think that a VAT is an export subsidy because it typically applies to imports, but not exports. (VAT already remitted—as verified by invoice—is rebated to the exporter at the border.) But this treatment is exactly the same as would apply under a national retail sales tax, where the tax would apply to goods sold here, regardless of where they were produced, and would not apply to exports—just like state sales taxes. Exports would have U.S. VAT rebated, but foreign consumption taxes would be applied when the goods are sold there. The "border tax adjustment" simply maintains a level playing field between exports and imports.[15] That is why this tax treatment is allowed under international trade agreements that proscribe export subsidies, whether explicit or implicit in tax rules.

The destination-based cash flow tax (DBCFT) is a mouthful. What is it?

One might be tempted to assume that, because taxes have been around for millennia, there are no new taxes under the sun. (And we don't mean the same old taxes applied to newly invented products, either.) One would be wrong. The now-ubiquitous VAT has been around only since the 1950s. The dual-income tax system was adopted in Nordic countries beginning in the late 1980s. Many new taxes have been proposed, but not widely implemented. The X tax, mentioned later, is an example; when it was proposed, many academics swooned, but no country has adopted it, although the 2016 Republican presidential candidate Marco Rubio supported it (without mentioning its mysterious moniker).

Another new tax idea popped up in the House Republicans' tax plan released in June 2016. It wasn't given a name in that proposal, but academics have one—the destination-based cash flow tax, or DBCFT. Indeed, it wasn't pitched as a new tax, but rather as a series of modifications from the corporate income tax. Two key changes were to replace depreciation of capital purchases by expensing and eliminating the deductibility of interest payments (and taxation of interest receipts). This would yield what economists call a cash flow tax, in that the tax base is just real (i.e., non-financial) current revenues less expenses. This is the CF part, but the controversy the proposal attracted was mostly about the DB part—the destination basis. This means that export revenue is not included in the tax base, and expenses on imports cannot be deducted from the tax base.

At first blush, this is a radical change in how we tax corporations, and in some ways it is. In other ways it isn't. Let's start with how it isn't so radical. This is how value-added taxes, levied in over 160 countries, work. As we mentioned before, it's also how retail sales taxes work: goods and services consumed in the taxing jurisdiction are subject to tax whether produced locally or imported, and goods and services exported escape tax. But it's not how corporate taxes work, although as of 2018 most capital expenditures can be expensed for the next several years at least.

Why could imposing a border adjustable tax (BAT) hurt importers and help exporters?

The destination-based cash flow tax, like a VAT, would have been border adjustable, meaning that it would have applied to imports and exempted exports.[16] Many economists like it because it treats all goods the same no matter where they are produced. That is, it wouldn't provide a tax incentive for retailers to move their operations overseas. But retailers and others hated it because they thought their costs of imported goods would skyrocket.

Here's the math that so worries them: first, assume a corporate tax rate of 20 percent, which is what the House GOP proposed in 2017. Then think about a U.S. Mercedes dealer that pays the German manufacturer $50,000 for a car. Without the border adjustable tax (BAT), the dealer could take a 20 percent deduction from its $50,000 wholesale cost, reducing its after-tax cost to $40,000.

However, under the BAT, its after-tax cost would rise by 25 percent, from $40,000 to $50,000. That $10,000 in additional taxes could easily exceed the dealer's profit margin. While this feature has importers up in arms, it is also what some politicians find so appealing. As Howard Gleckman noted, they think it would penalize imports and boost exports and thereby create domestic jobs.[17]

This analysis assumes that the dollar cost of imports is fixed. But the value of U.S. currency relative to other currencies is not set in stone. Instead, it responds to supply and demand. And a rise in import prices and parallel decline in export prices would reduce demand for foreign currency and increase demand for dollars. Eventually the value of the dollar would rise, by 25 percent according to many economists. For example, that $50,000 Mercedes costs €57,000 at the current exchange rate of 1.14 euros per dollar. If the value of the dollar appreciated by 25 percent relative to the euro, a dollar would be equivalent to 1.425 euros. The cost of the car in dollars would fall from $50,000 to $40,000, and the car dealer would be no better or worse off than without the BAT.

However, for reasons that are not well understood, it can take a long time for exchange rates to return to their equilibrium levels after they get out of kilter. A summary of the literature concluded that markets only close 15 percent of the gap between current prices and equilibrium levels per year.[18] Economists Caroline Freund and Joe Gagnon found evidence based on the introduction of VATs, which are also border adjustable, that exchange rates adjust more quickly—with perhaps half of the exchange rate response happening in the first year.[19] But Freund also warned of "lots of complications about the exchange rate adjustment that will happen with BAT that aren't necessarily there with the VAT." Similarly, former Federal Reserve Board chair Janet Yellen cautioned at a House hearing that "[i]t's very difficult to know just what would happen" to exchange rates.[20]

A further complication is that many international contracts are denominated in dollars, not foreign currency, so even if exchange rates adjusted right away, some importers would face much higher after-tax costs until they could negotiate new contracts.

So it's no surprise that this great idea (in theory) went nowhere.

A DBCFT sounds like a VAT with a longer and unpronounceable acronym. How is it different?

It's pretty close. The only difference is the payments to workers are not deductible under a VAT but are deductible in a DBCFT. Put another way, with a 20 percent tax rate a DBCFT is a 20 percent VAT plus a 20 percent subsidy on labor payments. This has led some to ask supporters of a DBCFT, why not just levy a VAT, which would raise vastly more revenue because it taxes labor. This is a good question, and the answer lies more in the realm of politics than economics. (See our discussion earlier in this chapter, "Why doesn't the United States have a VAT?")

What is the flat tax?

Many proponents of tax proposals featuring a single rate of tax have named their plans a flat tax. To economists, *the* flat tax is a design first outlined by Alvin Rabushka and Robert Hall of Stanford University in 1980.[21] Their flat tax is a VAT split into two parts, a tax on labor income and a tax on businesses, both usually set at a rate of about 20 percent. Recall that a subtraction-method VAT allows businesses a deduction for all purchased inputs except labor. Under the flat tax, companies can deduct wages, too. (This kind of tax is sometimes called a modified cash flow tax.) Workers are subject to a tax on wages (but not capital income) at the same rate as the business tax, typically after deducting an exemption. The wage tax thus isn't really flat because there are two brackets—zero and the single tax rate—but wages above the exemption are taxed at a flat rate.

The advantage of the flat tax is that it is a consumption-based tax—a modified VAT, really—but is more progressive because of the exemption in the labor income tax base. To achieve that, the flat tax exempts all capital income from its individual tax, and allows businesses to write off their purchases of capital goods in the year purchased.

Wouldn't a flat tax be super simple and fair?

A flat tax could be considerably simpler than our current system, but taxing income at a single rate would be far less progressive than applying graduated tax rates.

Under a pure flat tax, there would be no deductions or credits, and only one exemption per household. But the current income tax would also be a lot simpler under those circumstances. It's true that calculating tax when there's only one rate is simpler than calculating tax when there are multiple rates, but most people look up their tax in a table, use software, or a hire a paid preparer, so the value of this simplification is negligible. Because capital income (interest, dividends, etc.) would be exempt from tax, that would simplify reporting and record-keeping for most taxpayers. On the business side, depreciation accounts could be dispensed with because capital purchases are expensed, and financial flows no longer have tax consequences; interest payments are not deductible, nor are interest receipts taxable. Overall, a flat tax would be substantially simpler than a similarly comprehensive income tax.

Source: Cagle Cartoons, Inc.

Another practical advantage is that, with a flat tax, taxpayers would be more likely to know their marginal tax rate than under a more progressive schedule (such as current law).

Armed with better information, in principle, they would be able to make better economic decisions.

Fairness is another matter. It would be hard to make a flat tax as progressive as our current income tax. (See page 188, "What makes a tax system fair?") For one thing, you would need not just an exemption but also refundable tax credits, because low-income people on average get refunds under our income tax. Second, a flat tax would surely reduce tax liability at the top of the income distribution, where currently much higher rates apply. To raise the same amount of revenue as our current income tax, middle-income households would inevitably owe a lot more.

There are flat taxes all over Eastern Europe. Are they the same as the flat tax advocated for the United States?

No. The flat taxes common in Eastern Europe are flat-rate income taxes, not consumption taxes. That is, the base includes capital income, not just wages and other compensation. That makes the European flat taxes more progressive than the consumption-style flat tax just discussed, but less progressive than an income tax with graduated rates.

What is the X tax?

David Bradford was a brilliant economist who taught at Princeton University and was an outspoken and articulate consumption tax advocate. He was intrigued by the flat tax but was very concerned about its regressivity, so he developed a more progressive alternative that he labeled the "X tax," reportedly to distract attention from whether it is a consumption tax or an income tax.[22] It is basically a version of the Hall-Rabushka flat tax with multiple tax rates applying to the labor income base where the top labor income tax rate equals the flat business tax rate. At least in principle, the X tax could be made as progressive as the current income tax while still offering many of the economic advantages of a consumption tax.

The Treasury Department developed a variant of the X tax for President George W. Bush's tax reform panel. The panel concluded that, with a very broad base, an X tax with a top rate of 35 percent and refundable tax credits to protect workers with low incomes would collect about as much revenue as current law (circa 2005) and have a similar distribution of tax burdens. The Treasury model also predicted that the "progressive consumption tax" (Treasury's name for the X tax) would increase economic output (GDP) by 6 percent over the long run, although, as we discuss later, such predictions are by no means airtight.[23]

What is a consumed income tax?

Under a consumed income tax, individuals would file a personal tax return, but the taxable base is income minus saving (which equals consumption).[24] Taxpayers are allowed unlimited deductions for their net contributions to savings and retirement accounts, essentially an unlimited (traditional) IRA. Loan proceeds must be added to the tax base. Like the X tax, this approach allows for much more progressivity than a VAT or flat tax, because a graduated rate schedule can be applied to this tax base. Former senators Sam Nunn (D-GA) and Pete Domenici (R-NM) proposed a version called the Universal Savings Account (or USA) Tax in 1995, but it never garnered much support because it was perceived (probably correctly) as too complex.

Are tax breaks for saving and retirement indirect steps toward a consumption tax?

Sort of. For most Americans, who have limited savings, the income tax is very much like the consumed income tax already discussed. They can save as much as they want tax-free so long as they put the money in one of a variety of tax-preferred savings accounts. There's a catch, though—the savings accounts are all earmarked for particular activities. There are several types of such retirement accounts, the most common of which are Individual Retirement Accounts (IRAs) and 401(k) plans.

There are also tax-preferred accounts to pay for education and health expenses. Typically, contributions are deductible and withdrawals are taxable, although some more recent accounts like Roth IRAs and "529" (college savings) plans do not allow a deduction up front but don't tax withdrawals. In both kinds of accounts, earnings accrue tax-free. However, there are penalties if the money is withdrawn for non-designated purposes. This is a key difference with the tax treatment under a consumed income tax, which would allow tax-free savings for any purpose.

"I used to get toys as birthday gifts but now that I'm in pre-school, all I get is money for my college fund."

Source: www.CartoonStock.com.

Because a significant fraction of saving is tax-free under our "income tax," many analysts believe that our tax system is more properly viewed as a hybrid between an income tax and a consumption tax.

Do these tax breaks actually encourage saving?

This question is the subject of much debate among economists. Most, but not all, empirical research suggests that saving is not very sensitive to its rate of return. This might sound surprising because you'd expect people to be more likely to save when the after-tax rate of return is higher than when it is lower. There's a bigger reward to waiting to consume one's wealth in the former case. However, there's another offsetting factor at work. When the rate of return increases, you have to sacrifice less current consumption to achieve any particular level of future consumption. Most people don't save because they like saving per se but because they want a higher level of future consumption. This motive can actually cause people to save *less* when the rate of return increases. Effectively, the higher rate of return makes it possible to consume more both now and later.

Empirical evidence suggests that these two effects roughly balance out. When the rate of return increases, some people save more and some save less. Overall, there doesn't seem to be much effect; more precisely, research has not yet compellingly demonstrated such an effect.

Based on that evidence, you might expect tax incentives for saving to be pretty ineffective, as all they do is raise the after-tax rate of return. Actually, it's even worse than that for high-income people who account for most of the saving. They often save much more than the amount they can put in limited tax-free accounts. When they're deciding whether to save more or less, that is all done in taxable forms, unaffected by the tax subsidy. All the subsidies do for them is lower their tax liability without affecting the return to additional saving.

Because the tax break increases their after-tax income, they're likely to consume more now (and later), which means that aggregate saving goes down.

However, tax-free retirement accounts or education accounts might encourage people to save through other mechanisms. For one thing, by tying up people's money for many years, these accounts can help them to follow through on their savings plans. Also, to the extent that the accounts run through employers, they make it easier to set aside saving in small manageable pieces. Payroll withholding turns out to be a more effective way to get some people to save than relying on them to set aside money on their own.

So these accounts can be somewhat effective in increasing saving for some people. However, there has been a massive expansion in retirement savings incentives while the personal saving rate has plummeted. Before the Great Recession, it stood near zero, although it has crept up since then. So these incentives don't appear to have been hugely effective (or they've been more than offset by other factors).

If the economy runs on consumption, why would we want to encourage saving?

A New Year's Eve, 1965, *Time* magazine article quoted iconic free-market economist Milton Friedman as saying, "We are all Keynesians now."[25] Friedman later explained that the quote was taken out of context. He meant that even though the language of John Maynard Keynes—famous for recommending fiscal policy as a tool to manage the economy—had pervaded popular consciousness, most people had no idea what this meant.

We have thought of Keynesian misunderstandings many times in discussing tax policy with reporters and others. For example, critics sometimes complain that a flat tax or consumption tax would hurt the economy because "The economy runs on consumption." President George W. Bush urged the nation to visit Disney World as our first response to terrorism. Clearly, the public, our political leaders, and at least some members of the press have decided that spending is a civic virtue.

That is a dangerously misguided view of macroeconomics. Sure, a sudden drop in spending could bring on a recession, and more spending (and investment) is a tried-and-true Keynesian prescription for a downturn. But when the economy is performing well, inadequate consumption is not a problem we have to worry about. Instead, too little saving is the real threat.

Experts debate how to measure personal saving, but by any reckoning it has been trending south for a long time. By some measures, the saving rate approached zero in the last decade. It increased somewhat during, and since, the Great Recession, but is still low by historical standards. Lower interest rates and the rapid rise in stock market prices in the 1990s followed by soaring house prices until 2007 likely contributed to the decline in saving. But part of the problem may be that we have gone from believing that thrift is a virtue—a lesson learned the hard way during the Depression—to thinking that it is a vice.

Spending beyond our means—both privately and publicly (through deficits)—is a big problem. To start, when we spend more than we produce, the difference has to be made up by imports. There's a direct connection between our spendthrift ways and our massive trade deficits and the shrinking dollar.

Second, at the household level, people need to save to buffer themselves against financial shocks—an unexpected layoff or medical expense, for instance—and to finance retirement. The baby boomers should have been saving like crazy during their peak earning years instead of spending like there's no tomorrow.

Third, baby boomers' retirement and the continuing rise in medical costs will impose unprecedented demands on the government. Our best option would be to put entitlement programs—Social Security, Medicare, and Medicaid—on a secure financial footing. But there's no sign of that happening any time soon. Next best would be to leave our children and grandchildren enough financial resources to cover the hefty taxes needed to fund the promises we've made to ourselves.

Bottom line: Saving is still a virtue.

What's the difference between Roth and traditional IRAs?

Roth IRAs are named for former Senate Finance Committee chairman William Roth (R-DE). Contributions to traditional IRAs are deductible and earnings accrue tax-free, but withdrawals are fully taxable. Roth IRAs reverse the tax breaks: contributions are not tax-deductible and withdrawals are not taxable, while earnings accrue tax-free. (Both kinds of accounts assess penalties for withdrawals before the age of 59½.) Under certain circumstances, the tax breaks under the two kinds of accounts end up being equivalent. To see this, suppose you're in the 25 percent tax bracket and contribute $1,500 to a Roth IRA. Alternatively, you could contribute $2,000 to a traditional IRA. Because of the deductibility of the latter, the after-tax cost of the contribution is the same in both cases. In retirement, you can withdraw the $1,500 plus interest in retirement from the Roth IRA and it's all tax-free. For the traditional account, you'll have to pay tax, but if the tax rate stays at 25 percent, you'll still get to net three-quarters of the $2,000 plus interest for retirement consumption. That is, you end up (after tax) with $1,500 plus interest—the same as with the Roth. Note that this conclusion holds whatever the rate of return.

Obviously, this example makes several assumptions. The key ones are that you contribute the same amount after tax under each plan, and that the tax rate stays the same. In fact, if the limits on contributions to Roth and traditional IRAs are the same, you can squirrel away more tax-free income in the Roth. And if you expect tax rates to go up in the future, then a Roth becomes a much better deal, because the higher tax rates you'd face when withdrawing your funds from a traditional IRA don't apply. Also, you have to start withdrawing funds from a traditional IRA at a certain age, but you can hold onto a

Roth until you die, which is especially valuable for people who don't really need the money during retirement. And there are estate tax advantages of the Roth.

Finally, Roth IRAs can turn out to be a bad deal for the federal budget because, if they really became popular, they could significantly reduce revenues in the future. Recall that withdrawals from traditional IRAs are taxable, whereas Roth IRAs are tax-free forever. Given that our long-run budget situation is very bleak because of an aging population (and expensive Social Security benefits) and rising health care costs (which impact Medicare and Medicaid), reducing future tax revenues seems like a dubious policy (box 4.2).

BOX 4.2 **Stupid Tax Tricks: Roth IRA Conversions**

As part of a bill raising the limits on retirement plan contributions, Congress allowed high-income taxpayers, starting in 2010, the option to convert their traditional IRAs into Roth IRAs in exchange for remitting tax on the balance at the time of conversion. (People with moderate incomes were always allowed to do this.) To sweeten the deal further, tax due on conversions done in 2010 could be postponed and remitted in two equal installments in 2011 and 2012. Even though most taxpayers would only take advantage of this option if they expected to save taxes over the long run, the official estimators scored this as a short-term revenue raiser because they expected many taxpayers to take advantage of this option and remit extra tax in 2010, 2011, and 2012.

Here's why Roth rollovers were so good for taxpayers and so bad for the Treasury. By pre-paying tax on accumulated IRAs, rich folks could effectively increase their tax-free savings by close to half. And the rollover option is worth most to people who don't actually need retirement accounts to finance their old age.

The policy didn't serve any goal other than to further enrich the already wealthy. It didn't encourage saving (or work, for that matter). And although it brought revenue into the Treasury coffers for a few years, it meant that billions of dollars of future tax revenues would never be collected because the accounts, once converted, were forever exempt from income tax.

In fact, the rollover gambit is really borrowing on very unfavorable terms to the government. When this boondoggle was enacted in 2010, the implicit interest rate on that borrowing was about 14 percent compared with an interest rate on long-term government bonds of about 4 percent.

If the Congressional Budget Office and Joint Committee on Taxation had scored the rollover provision as borrowing rather than revenue, Congress probably would not have enacted it. The revenues produced from the conversions would have been disregarded, and the implied interest arising from the substantial and growing revenue losses would have been scored as a multi-billion-dollar cost over the budget period.

Note: Converting a traditional IRA into a Roth increases the amount of tax-free savings because in a traditional IRA, a portion of the account will go to pay off tax on the eventual withdrawals. On a Roth IRA, the entire account is tax-free. At a 35 percent tax rate, that means more than 50 percent more tax-free retirement income (1 / 0.65 = 1.54, so the Roth produces 54 percent more tax-free savings). The 14 percent implicit interest rate on government borrowing via Roth IRA conversions is derived from the revenue estimates in Leonard E. Burman, "Roth Conversions as Revenue Raisers: Smoke and Mirrors," *Tax Notes*, May 22, 2006, 953–956. At an interest rate of 14 percent, the stream of small tax revenue gains in the short term and large revenue losses in the long run just balance out in present value. (Put differently, 14 percent is the internal rate of return.)

Do consumption taxes disproportionately burden the old?

While spending is a very large share of income—often more than 100 percent—for the elderly, they are somewhat insulated from consumption taxes because most elderly people get most of their income from Social Security, which is indexed for inflation. If consumption taxes translate into higher prices, Social Security benefits automatically increase. (This protects current retirees, but not future retirees because future benefits depend on wage histories, and real wages would fall under a consumption tax.)

Moreover, for older people with substantial wealth, the *transition* from an income tax to a consumption tax may be quite burdensome. Consider a couple on the eve of retirement. The couple has been subject to income tax on their earnings, and expects to live off their savings during retirement without facing much more tax. If, though, we were to switch to a consumption tax, say a retail sales tax, there is a tax hit as they draw down their savings to live the good life they've planned during their working years.[26]

That said, a lot of high-income elderly people continue saving a fair amount well into their retirement, and they would continue to benefit from the fact that saving is exempt from consumption tax. A broader point is that the impact of taxes should properly be evaluated from a lifetime perspective. Over the life cycle, savers benefit more from a consumption tax than an income tax, even if they end up paying high taxes as a share of income in retirement.

5

OTHER KINDS OF TAXES

The estate tax is a tax on the wealth held by people when they die. (The "estate" is the legal entity that holds assets between the time of death and payment of any tax and distribution to heirs of the remaining assets.) The federal tax applies only to people with considerable assets—at least $11.2 million for singles and twice that amount for couples as of 2018. Because of this large exemption, the tax applies to less than 0.1 percent of decedents. There is also a parallel gift tax, which is "unified" with the estate tax to prevent avoidance of the estate tax by giving away one's money while still alive. This means that gifts made before death are also subject to the estate tax to the extent they exceed the exempt threshold. However, annual gifts below $15,000 per recipient are exempt from estate and gift tax.[1]

The estate tax has generated some intense political controversy. Opponents call it the "death tax" and paint a macabre picture of the grim reaper (played by the IRS) snatching from their grieving families the hard-earned wealth of the most productive members of society. They see the tax as a complex, unfair, and inefficient levy that violates every norm of good tax policy.

Supporters see it as a pillar of a progressive tax system, because it applies only to the very richest Americans, discourages large concentrations of wealth (which some people believe are undesirable), and has the added virtues of plugging income tax loopholes and encouraging charitable contributions.

In attempting to reconcile these divergent views, politicians have debated three estate tax options: live with it, reform it, or throw it out. Remarkably, in 2001 they chose all three! The 2001 tax bill (the first of the Bush tax cuts) changed the estate tax rules, phased in lower tax rates and a higher exempt threshold, and ultimately repealed the tax—but for only one year, 2010. In 2011, along with the rest of the Bush tax cuts, the estate tax returned from the dead like Freddy Krueger with the old rates, exemptions, and rules back in force.

People respond to incentives, and the incentives created by a one-year estate tax holiday provoked gallows humor about keeping Grandma alive until 2010 and "throwing Mama from the train" at the end of the year.

"With all the uncertainty surrounding the repeal of the federal estate tax, I will need your advice -- should I be planning to die this year or shouldn't I?"

Source: © Arnie Glick.

Billionaires like New York Yankees owner George Steinbrenner, who died in 2010, were admired for their tax savvy. As far as we know, there's no evidence of heirs deliberately hastening the demise of their loved ones (although it seems to have happened in earlier estate-tax change episodes in the United States and some other countries!), but there certainly was a powerful financial incentive to do so for some rich families.[2] The Joint Committee on Taxation estimated that the one-year hiatus from the estate tax cost the U.S. Treasury $14 billion in 2010 compared with the revenue that would have been raised if the 2009 rate and exemption had been extended. Had Congress done nothing, the estate tax would have returned for all estates larger than $1 million at rates up to 55 percent.

Ultimately, Congress and the president agreed to a temporary extension of the Bush tax cuts. The estate tax was reincarnated with a $5 million exemption and a 35 percent rate, but only for two years. Starting in 2013, the estate tax rate was reinstated permanently with a 40 percent tax rate, and the exemption level was indexed for inflation. The Tax Cuts and Jobs Act doubled the exemption level to $11.2 million ($22.4 million for couples), with indexing, but only through 2025.

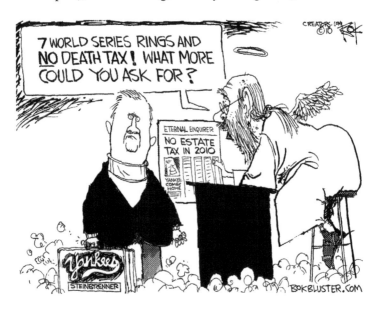

Source: By permission of Chip Bok and Creators Syndicate, Inc.

How is estate tax liability calculated?

At present, it's basically a flat tax on taxable estates larger than the exemption level. To calculate the taxable estate, various deductions are subtracted from the gross value of assets held at death. The largest is an unlimited marital deduction—any transfers to a spouse are tax-free. Gifts to charity are deductible, as are state and local transfer taxes (inheritance and estate taxes). There are some tax breaks for farmers and small business owners; most notably, the taxable estate may often include less than the full value of a farm or closely held business. Farmers may value land based on the value of what it produces rather than the market value. This can substantially reduce the estate tax value of land held close to a city (which might be worth much more as a housing development or an office park than as a farm). People who own a large share of a family business may claim "valuation discounts" on the logic that the business would be worth much less if broken into pieces than as a whole. The argument is that a partial share of a business is worth less because of a lack of marketability and the drawbacks of minority ownership, such as less say in making business decisions. All told, researchers have estimated that these discounts may reduce the total taxable value of farms and businesses by up to 59 percent.[3]

The estate tax can be extremely complex, mostly because it attempts to address many sorts of complicated trusts and other legal arrangements. Most of these reduce the ultimate amount of tax liability. Some are designed to protect the interests of spouses or other heirs while minimizing tax liability. Some also allow deductions for gifts of income-generating assets to charities before death with the understanding that the donor will receive the income generated by the donated asset and full control passes to the charity only after the donor dies.

Critics of the estate tax bemoan the complexity of the tax, but every one of the complex provisions has a powerful constituency of estate lawyers and wealthy people who benefit financially from it. Proposals to simplify the estate tax have a poor track record in Congress.

Stu's Views   © Stu All Rights Reserved www.STUS.com

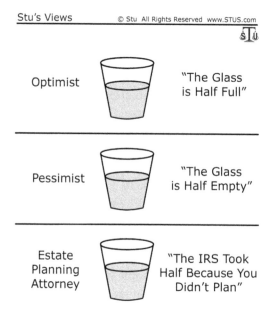

Source: stus.com.

Why tax estates when the assets that went into them were already subject to plenty of tax?

Critics of the estate tax argue that it amounts to double, or even triple, taxation. Consider the following example: Someone builds a business from scratch and pays tax on the income it produces every year and saves enough of the income (after tax on the return to saving) so as to accumulate substantial wealth. Doesn't an estate tax on that wealth amount to double (or triple) taxation? That sounds unfair and also inefficient (because it penalizes hard work and thrift).

Supporters of the estate tax respond that a lot of income is never taxed, that it is an important backstop preserving the integrity of a loophole-ridden income tax, and that it makes important contributions to the progressivity of the federal tax system. The most obvious example of income that may never be taxed is capital gains, which can escape individual income tax entirely if an asset is held until death. (See page 46, "What is the 'Angel of Death' loophole?") Recognizing that fact, the "Angel of Death" loophole was partially rescinded (on very large capital gains) for the one year when estates were tax-free in 2010. More generally, there are thought to be numerous ways that wealthy individuals can accumulate income and wealth and owe little or no income tax. (Even income that is eventually taxed as capital gains is only subject to tax at most a 20 percent statutory rate, while the top ordinary income tax rate is 37 percent.)

For sure, the estate tax is the most progressive tax in the federal tax system. The Tax Policy Center estimates that, in 2018, 88 percent of the tax will be collected from the estates of households in the top 5 percent of the income distribution, and 71 percent from the richest 1 percent. By comparison, in 2018, only 63 percent of personal income tax revenues are expected to be collected from the top 5 percent and 43 percent from the top 1 percent.[4]

What are the estate tax's effects on work and saving?

Some are concerned that the estate tax discourages work, saving, and entrepreneurship—all activities that contribute to a prosperous society. For those people rich enough that extra income would be mostly passed on to their heirs, an estate tax reduces the return—leaving a bigger bequest—to earning and saving income. Some economists have tried to measure how big this discouragement effect is, and our reading of the empirical evidence suggests that the overall effects are fairly modest.

The full picture must, though, also consider how an estate tax affects the heirs. The picture is somewhat mixed. On the one hand, there's evidence that inheritances encourage entrepreneurship, so bigger after-tax bequests might boost this kind of economic activity (although the main operative factor might be that children of very successful entrepreneurs—who owe estate tax—are more prone to entrepreneurship themselves, and would be regardless of the size of bequest).[5]

On the other hand, heirs expecting an inheritance have less incentive to work and save. As Andrew Carnegie noted in 1891, "The parent who leaves his son enormous wealth generally deadens the talents and energies of the son and tempts him to lead a less useful and less worthy life than he otherwise would." (The argument would certainly apply to daughters as well.) Indeed, empirical evidence suggests that heirs work and save less if they expect to receive a large bequest. To the extent that the estate tax diminishes inheritances (both because the tax reduces the after-tax estate and also because it encourages gifts to charity to avoid the tax), it would be expected to raise the energy and productivity of potential heirs.

How does the estate tax affect small businesses and family farms?

How the estate tax impacts small businesses and family farms has been an especially contentious issue. Critics complain that it forces heirs to break up family businesses in order to be able to afford the tax. In fact, very few small businesses and farms appear to be affected by the tax, mainly because the threshold is so high. It's debatable whether a business worth over $11 million, the current exemption level, should be considered small. The vast majority have much smaller net worth. Moreover, the Tax Policy Center estimates that just 140 out of the 1,890 taxable estates filed for 2018 hold primarily farm or business assets. The valuation provisions already mentioned often reduce tax liability, and special provisions are available to help heirs pay the tax without dissolving the business, including interest-free and reduced interest loans to defer the tax. Finally, any competent accountant would advise the owner of a family business to purchase life insurance to cover the estate tax liability; this doesn't eliminate the tax burden—the policy premiums comprise the tax burden—but this simple bit of planning keeps the estate tax from being a devastating cost to the next generation of owners.

Should the United States adopt a wealth tax?

The United States does not have a net wealth tax. At least not yet. Senator Elizabeth Warren, who aspires to be the Democrat's 2020 presidential candidate, has made a wealth tax a centerpiece of her primary campaign. She has proposed an annual tax of 2 percent levied on household net worth above $50 million, with a 3 percent rate applying to net worth above $1 billion.

Other countries have tried a net wealth tax. About half of developed countries had one in 1990, but only three still levied the tax by 2018. These taxes had many exemptions and deductions, high levels of avoidance and evasion, and high costs of administration and compliance. Policymakers worried about wealthy individuals moving capital overseas to skirt the tax. (Senator Warren's proposal has a very broad base and provisions aimed at deterring capital flight.)

A wealth tax would not be completely unprecedented for the United States. After all, local governments' primary revenue source is a kind of annual wealth tax, the property tax, whose base is "immovable" property, and which usually does not have a high exemption or a graduated rate schedule. The United States relies more on property taxes than most other countries.

Advocates of a wealth tax that applies only to the very wealthy argue that it would reduce wealth inequality and the political and market power that comes with extreme concentrations of wealth. The tax can also plug holes in the coverage of capital income taxation, such as the low effective tax rate on capital income in the form of never-realized capital gains.

The statutory rates of tax, 2 percent and 3 percent in Senator Warren's proposal, may look benign, especially in comparison to estate tax rates that reach 40 percent. But don't be fooled—the estate tax is a one-time tax, while a net wealth tax is levied every year. Imagine a household with $100 million of wealth above the $50 million threshold (so $150 million in total). A wealth tax of 2 percent above the exemption exacts 2 percent of taxable wealth each year, so, ignoring further accumulation, the

$100 million falls to $98 million the next year, then $96.04 million the year, $94.12 the year after that, et cetera. This adds up to a lot more than 2 percent. Even under the more reasonable assumption that the wealth accrues income, a 2 percent annual wealth tax can constitute a large share of income. For example, 30-year Treasury inflation-protected securities currently yield 1 percent above inflation. A 2 percent wealth tax would turn that 1 percent pre-tax real gain into a 1 percent after-tax loss (before accounting for income taxes). It's true that high-wealth people often make investments that pay higher rates of return, but those investments are also riskier. In some years, they lose money, but they'd be subject to the wealth tax every year.

For some readers, this arithmetic may fail to elicit much sympathy for the very wealthy, especially as the revenue it brings in could be used to fund programs that help those in need. Even so, the redistribution that a wealth tax would achieve comes at some cost. It would certainly reduce the return to saving and therefore potentially reduce national saving and capital accumulation, which could ultimately reduce business investment and thus wages, offsetting some of the desired redistribution. (That is, part of the burden of the tax could fall on workers.) Its efficacy also depends on how susceptible it would be to avoidance and evasion. The incentive to move assets abroad to escape the tax net would be enormous, and would strain the recent initiatives to exchange tax information across countries, such as the U.S. Foreign Account Tax Compliance Act rules we discuss in chapter 9. (To supplement these measures, the Warren proposal includes a 40 percent exit tax on the net worth above $50 million of U.S. citizens who renounce their citizenship.) It would also create incentives to invest in assets that are less easily monitored by the tax authorities, such as diamonds, rare antiquities, and digital currencies. And, just as under the estate tax, wealthy people might be able to avoid the tax by moving assets into trusts or accelerating contributions to charity that they might otherwise have planned to make at death.

What is the difference between an estate tax and an inheritance tax?

Many people think these are the same, but they're different. An estate tax is assessed on the estate, rather than heirs, and applies to the entire value of the estate. An inheritance tax applies to heirs, and the tax liability could depend on how much each heir inherits, the heir's other income, as well as the relationship of the heir to the decedent. Many states and some foreign governments impose inheritance taxes, and the tax rate is almost always lower the closer is the blood relationship of the heir to the decedent. Inheritance taxes can be stand-alone taxes or integrated with the income tax. One particularly simple option would be to have heirs include in taxable income any gifts and bequests they receive above a threshold amount—say $1 million per heir.

There are several arguments in favor of this approach versus an estate tax. One is that the graduated income tax gives donors an incentive to break up large estates and therefore to some extent discourages large concentrations of wealth. A second argument is that, while donors might be very wealthy, their children and grandchildren might have more modest incomes. A progressive inheritance tax can account for that by taxing the bequest based on the circumstances of the heir.

Finally, some advocates argue that replacing the estate tax with an inheritance tax would offer political advantages by shifting the focus of the debate away from the tax treatment of the people who accumulated the wealth toward those who will receive a bequest (Paris Hilton rather than Conrad Hilton). And it would be harder to call an inheritance tax a "death tax," as it would apply to the living heir.

It would, though, be more complicated to administer an inheritance tax, because it requires that each heir calculates his or her tax liability separately. One administrative virtue of an estate tax is that it is levied at the same time that probate rules require that the estate be valued.

What is a financial transaction tax?

A financial transaction tax is a tax on the gross value of certain financial transactions such as bank withdrawals or stock sales. It is fairly common in less developed countries because it can collect a lot of money with an apparently low rate levied on a small number of well-heeled financial institutions.

Several years ago, a financial transaction tax was proposed in the United States as a way to recoup some of the costs of the financial crisis that led to the Great Recession. A few prominent economists—most notably, the late James Tobin, a Nobel laureate from Yale University—have argued for it as a way to discourage "noise trading." The idea is that investors often buy or sell based on rumors and misinformation—what economists call noise. Noise can prevent asset prices from accurately reflecting their fundamental or long-term value, so, at least in theory, discouraging noise trading might make markets work better.

There are, though, some serious problems with financial transaction taxes. One is that they are as likely to discourage trading based on real information as on noise. Thus, they can exacerbate inefficiencies by preventing markets from responding to news. Second, the taxes can cascade. For example, banks make numerous bond transactions to balance their portfolios, meet reserve requirements, and satisfy customers' demands for funds. This can result in a relatively large burden as a share of financial institutions' income.

Finally, if the tax applies to bank deposits and withdrawals, people may avoid dealing with financial institutions subject to the tax and instead conduct transactions using cash or barter. There is an incentive to come up with an alternative means of exchange, such as IOUs, that can become a de facto sort of currency. There is an incentive to try to move transactions offshore so that they are done using financial institutions not subject to the tax. Because financial intermediation is generally quite efficient, allowing safe financial transactions to occur at low cost, this kind of disintermediation is inefficient. Disintermediation also makes tax enforcement more difficult, as the electronic trail dissolves, and it is also sometimes unsafe (see box 5.1).

BOX 5.1 **Stupid Tax Tricks: The Bank Debit Tax in Colombia**

Colombia has a bank debit tax, which applies to all financial transactions. In particular, it applies to check transactions. The tax rate is low, only 0.4 percent of the check amount, but that can still be a significant share of profit margins when they are small (as in retail or financial services). People have reacted to the tax in a number of ways. Instead of cashing checks at a bank and triggering the tax, check recipients endorse the check over to their suppliers or other creditors, and the supplier endorses the check to another business or person, and so on, until the back of the check is covered with lots of tiny signatures. If 20 signatures could be squeezed onto the back of the check, the tax as a share of the transaction volume was cut by 95 percent. That is, if a 100-peso note changed hands 20 times, it is financing 2,000 pesos in transactions. The ultimate tax of 0.4 peso is 0.4 percent of the note value, but only 0.02 percent of the total transaction amount.

The Colombian authorities ultimately banned multiple endorsements and thus squashed this form of tax avoidance. However, a more straightforward way to avoid the tax exists, which is to conduct transactions in cash. At the time both of us were studying the Colombian tax system, it was one of the most dangerous countries in the Western Hemisphere, and the financial transactions tax was encouraging people to carry around brief cases full of currency to avoid the tax. This gave new meaning to the economic concept of "deadweight loss."

Note: See María Angelica Arbeláez, Leonard E. Burman, and Sandra Zuluaga, "The Bank Debit Tax in Colombia," in *Fiscal Reform in Colombia*, ed. Richard M. Bird, James M. Poterba, and Joel Slemrod (Cambridge, Mass.: MIT Press, 2005), 225–246. Thornton Matheson assesses financial transaction taxes in "Taxing Financial Transactions: Issues and Evidence," International Monetary Fund Working Paper, 2011. See also Deloitte, "International Tax: Colombia Highlights 2019," https://www2.deloitte.com/content/dam/Deloitte/global/Documents/Tax/dttl-tax-colombiahighlights-2019.pdf?nc=1.

What is the property tax?

The property tax is an annual wealth tax that applies to particular kinds of property, usually homes, commercial property,
and sometimes automobiles. Typically, state or local governments assess these taxes. Overall, real estate property taxes are
the largest source of tax revenue for local governments and are
often earmarked to finance schools.

Some economists question whether property taxes should
even be considered taxes rather than a fee for services provided
by local governments. For example, if a town invests in excellent public schools, that will make the town more attractive to
current and potential residents, who would be willing to pay
more to live there. If the property tax revenues are well spent,
the increase in property values should at least offset the higher
tax burden. And, alternatively, if a community underinvests
in key public services, citizens will vote with their feet by
leaving and property values will fall, negating the tax savings
from having an underfinanced public sector. Because people
have different willingness to pay for public services, the mix
of property taxes and services will vary among communities.
Households that place a relatively high value on, say, excellent
public schools will be attracted to communities with high taxes
and very good schools, while others will tend to gravitate to
low-tax, low-service communities. The higher property taxes
are thus the price for better schools.

This view of responsive local governments providing services that citizens are willing to pay for is not universally accepted. Public choice theorists have put forward an alternative
hypothesis, called ominously the Leviathan hypothesis. The
idea is that citizens will never have as much incentive to monitor and control their governments as bureaucrats have in
perpetuating and expanding public spending. In this sense,
the public sector is like an ever-growing leviathan, or mon-
ster. Over time, its activities can substantially diverge from the

needs and desires of citizens. There is some empirical evidence in support of this theory.

Interest in taming leviathan has been one motivation behind property tax and spending caps that have spread around the country.

What is a lump-sum tax?

On one dimension a lump-sum tax is an economist's dream tax system. Everyone is assessed a tax bill that does not depend on how much they earn, spend, or own. For example, the tax might be $10,000 per adult per year. In 2017 this would have raised about $2.5 trillion, enough to replace the revenue collected from both the individual and corporation income taxes, plus some payroll tax revenue. Such a tax is sometimes called a "poll tax" because it used to be common for local governments to require a flat payment before someone could vote. Of course, this tax could be avoided by not voting, so it could still distort behavior (and, indeed, in many places it was intended to discourage low-income people—and especially people of color—from exercising their franchise, which is why the Supreme Court ultimately struck the poll tax down). In principle a lump-sum tax could also vary from individual to individual, so long as it doesn't depend on anything that people can voluntarily change.

Such a tax is in theory quite efficient. It collects revenue without changing any prices. As a result, it doesn't favor any activity over others and therefore does not, in economists' jargon, distort behavior. There's no disincentive to working, saving, or consuming. Of course, in the real world, some people simply wouldn't be able to afford to pay the tax and it is hard to convince voters that it is fair that Mark Zuckerberg owes no more tax than a single mother just getting by on a minimum-wage job. In the United Kingdom, Margaret Thatcher, who was a big fan of economics, once got a small lump-sum tax enacted.[6] It was enormously unpopular and is thought to have been a significant factor in the Tories' defeat in the next parliamentary election.

Do economists have other goofy ideas about ideal tax systems?

Why, yes, we do. One idea is a tax based on innate ability. In principle, if you could measure income-earning ability, the government could assign tax bills based on that, regardless of what people actually earned. In theory, this could be a very progressive tax, as high-ability people could be assigned much higher tax bills than those of modest abilities. And so long as the tax can be collected, it doesn't distort workers' decisions about, for example, how much and how hard to work, as one's actual income—and anything else other than ability—does not affect tax liability.

In practice, this is a nonstarter for several reasons. One is that ability is impossible to measure accurately, in part because if people suspected that a test would be used to determine tax burden, they'd have a strong incentive to produce a low score. (Ideally, the test would be administered after earning ability is to some extent observable, but before a child could fathom why her parents were telling her, "Annie, on *this* test you should always give the WRONG answer.") Second, are you really going to assess a tax burden of $100,000 per year on high-ability Annie because she *could be* a Wall Street hotshot even though she has chosen to be a journalist earning $25,000 per year? Even if ability could be measured, collecting the tax might appear unseemly.

Gregg Mankiw and Matthew Weinzierl put forward as a parody another theoretically brilliant (goofy) idea: a tax on height. Research shows that height is correlated with lifetime income. Because tall people earn more than shorter people on average, a tax based on height would be progressive and efficient—as people are extremely unlikely to try to alter their height in response to tax rules. Even a small tax on height could allow cutting back on progressive, but distorting, income taxes.[7]

Certified offbeat economist Joel Slemrod (winner of the Ig Nobel Prize for Economics) and coauthor Kyle Logue have gone further to suggest that, in the future, when each person's genome can be charted and its average effects on lifetime income prospects understood, a genome levy could tax people who have the "most likely to invent the next Facebook" genes and subsidize those prone to debilitating diseases, thus achieving some progressivity with no disincentive to work, save, or invent.[8]

Do these ideas explain why people don't like economists?

No comment.

"There's a thin line between thinking outside the box
and a caffeine-induced wacko idea."

Source: © Steve Smeltzer.

PART II

THE COSTS AND BENEFITS OF TAXATION

6

TAXES AND THE ECONOMY

How do taxes affect the economy?

In many, many ways. They reduce the reward to working, saving, and investing and so diminish the incentives to undertake these activities, which can lower GDP and hamper growth. When they discriminate among different activities, they affect how the economy's resources are allocated and may direct them to relatively wasteful uses. In some cases, taxes can mitigate negative consequences like excessive pollution. People and businesses spend real resources complying with the tax system and trying to avoid or evade taxes. Those resources could otherwise be spent on activities that would make us happier, so that also represents a cost to society. Although economists are divided on the efficacy of Keynesian fiscal policy, many, including us, think that enlightened tax policy can help an economy recover from a severe economic downturn and poorly chosen tax policies can exacerbate a recession. (There's a near consensus among economists that monetary policy is the better tool to manage economic fluctuations during normal times.) At all times, taxes affect the distribution of well-being.

Of course, the uses to which tax revenues are put may boost the economy by supporting such things as a legal system, national defense, productive infrastructure, education, and health care. And, putting the abstraction of an "economy" aside, tax revenue funds the Social Security and Medicare systems and provides income support for tens of millions of low-income households.

Why do economists think that raising funds costs much more than the tax sticker price?

Because the act of raising taxes hampers the economy. Consider a bridge that costs $100 million to build. Raising $100 million extra in taxes will exacerbate all the adverse incentive effects caused by taxes: the disincentive to work, the disincentive to save, the incentive to engage in unproductive tax sheltering, and so on. Raising $100 million more in a $20 trillion-plus economy means that the extra disincentive caused will be a tiny fraction of the existing distortions, but it will not necessarily be tiny relative to the $100 million price tag for the bridge. Because of this, the true social cost of building the bridge is the dollar cost plus the extra cost of all the disincentives caused by the higher tax. For technical reasons, it is hard to accurately measure the economic cost of taxation, and estimates vary widely, but the midpoint estimate among economists would probably be about 30 cents on the dollar, in which case the bridge should provide at least $130 million worth of benefits to make it worthwhile. While economists are far from consensus on just how much distortion taxes cause, there is near-unanimous agreement that the total economic cost exceeds the sticker price.

Do some taxes help the economy?

Earlier in chapter 4 we discussed Pigouvian taxes, which are designed to induce people and businesses to consider the cost their activities impose on other people. (See page 106, "What is a Pigouvian tax?") These sorts of taxes, of which carbon taxes are an example, help the economy in the sense that they improve the allocation of resources. Indeed, they could be

Taxes and the Economy   151

justified even if the government needed to raise no revenue at all.

What is the Laffer Curve?

It's something that economist Arthur Laffer drew on a napkin showing the relationship between tax revenues and tax rates. Laffer asserted that tax revenues would be zero both at a zero tax rate (not surprisingly), and also at a 100 percent tax rate because people would choose not to earn and/or report any income to the tax authorities if it would all be taxed away. We can imagine scenarios where the tax authorities might still be able to collect tax revenue, as there would likely be rampant tax evasion at a 100 percent tax rate and the authorities could probably catch some cheaters, but we will avoid delving into the implications of this dystopia.

Laffer conjectured that if revenue is zero at both a 0 percent and a 100 percent tax rate and positive in between, a graph of tax revenues on the y-axis and the tax rate on the x-axis might have an inverted-U shape. This has come to be known as the Laffer Curve. The basic insight is that at sufficiently high tax rates, at the right end of the inverted-U shape, revenues would fall substantially. Thus, there must be a revenue-maximizing tax rate (where the inverted-U shape reaches its highest point) beyond which further rate increases would be counterproductive.

Even accepting the hypothesis that revenues are zero at the end points, the rate at which revenues are maximized—the peak of the Laffer Curve—could in principle be anywhere between 0 and 100 percent. A survey by economists Peter Diamond and Emmanuel Saez estimated that the revenue-maximizing federal income tax rate was "conservatively" 48 percent assuming the existing tax base and could be as high as 76 percent if the tax base were much broader (because there would be fewer avenues for tax avoidance). Evidence from other studies also suggests that current tax rates are safely below the revenue-unproductive level.

Which is a better economic stimulus, cutting taxes or spending more?

Bringing up the word "stimulus" reminds us that tax policy can play another role—altering the length and severity of a cyclical downturn. The use of tax cuts and increased government spending to ward off or dampen recessions is sometimes called Keynesian policy, after the British economist John Maynard Keynes, who in the 1930s championed the notion that active fiscal policy can minimize the effect of recessions. Although the belief in the potential efficacy of fiscal policy was widespread among economists in the 1950s, 1960s, and 1970s, by the end of the 1970s many economists had soured on the notion of active countercyclical fiscal policy, in part because of the late-1970s phenomenon of stagflation—high unemployment combined with high inflation—which was not easily explained within the framework of Keynesian economics. These days it remains a controversial and divisive topic among economists.

What is certain is that, since 2001 and especially after the financial crisis and Great Recession, activist fiscal policy made a comeback in the United States. Major tax cuts were part of the stimulus bills passed in 2008 and 2009, and even in 2012 the debate about whether to extend cuts in payroll taxes revolved around Keynesian issues such as whether, and to what extent, it would boost aggregate spending. All of these stimulus programs contained both tax cuts and additional government spending. Although tax cuts provide an instant, visible boost to people's disposable income (and firms' cash flow), most economists believe that the "bang per buck" of direct government purchases exceeds that of tax cuts, because tax cuts are effective in stimulating economic activity only to the extent the extra disposable income is spent. Especially in light of recent evidence, discussed subsequently, that people often save a significant portion of any tax cut (either directly or by using the money to pay down credit card and other debt), direct government spending seems like the more effective stimulus.

The problem with direct spending as stimulus is that it's much better if the direct spending creates something of value, and it is not easy to have a large list of worthwhile projects that are ready to go as soon as Congress gives the word—the projects should be "shovel ready," as well as of intrinsic value. If there is a long lag before the projects can get underway, the stimulus might arrive too late, when the economy is back on track, when the hurdle for such projects is higher because the projects will use less idle resources and are more likely to draw resources away from valuable competing uses.

What kinds of taxes provide the most stimulus?

Tax policy can provide a short-term boost to the economy in at least two different ways. One way is to increase taxpayers' income, in an attempt to get them to spend more. Because most consumers generally base their spending not only on their current income but also on their expected future income, how effective this will end up being depends on how temporary or permanent the tax cuts are perceived to be. Tax cuts that are perceived to be long-lasting will increase consumption more (as long as the taxpayers don't think too far ahead, to when the deficits caused by tax cuts will lead to higher taxes and lower after-tax income). How much spending rises with higher income depends on that term famous from Economics 101, the marginal propensity to consume (MPC)—how much extra spending an additional dollar of income induces. This will in general vary by taxpayer characteristics. For those who live paycheck to paycheck, spending everything they get, the MPC could be close to one—even for a very short-lived tax cut. It might also be high for people who try to maintain a target level of saving per pay period. Until recently the conventional wisdom was that, on average, low-income people will have a higher MPC than high-income folks, because they are more likely to have unmet immediate spending needs. If this is true, tax cuts aimed at lower-income households would have a bigger bang per buck, producing more stimulus through higher spending per dollar of tax cut. But evidence based on taxpayer surveys has called this received wisdom into question. When asked how the stimulus checks sent out in 2009 affected behavior, the percentage of people who said it would mostly increase their spending was no higher for low-income people than high-income people; it was low—under 20 percent—for both groups.[1] There are reasons to question how much people's actions track such self-reports, but the responses suggest that even well-targeted temporary tax cuts may be less effective than previously thought.

Another kind of stimulus works by inducing consumers and businesses to change the timing of their spending and investment, respectively—to move it forward to when times are bad. Recent examples in the United States abound. Beginning in 2017, businesses were allowed to immediately write off for tax purposes (rather than deduct over the course of many years) their expenses for investments made before a certain date. From 2008 to 2010, households were offered a tax credit for buying a house, and in 2009 for trading in their old clunker for a new car, for a limited time only. In some cases this type of policy might induce more total investment, but its primary effect is often to accelerate planned future economic activity to the low-tax period, without much increasing total spending. This doesn't sound very helpful, but it can make sense to shift economic activity into a period when unemployment is high and capital is cheap. It does, though, require a high degree of foresight by policymakers. Otherwise, the expiration of the tax break and the resulting drop-off in spending can hurt a still-weak economy.

In December 2008, the United Kingdom cut its value-added tax rate from 17.5 percent to 15 percent until the end of 2009 with the hope of stimulating consumption due to the temporarily low tax rate. It seems that Americans are not the only people who love a sale. In contrast to a disposable-income-increasing stimulus, a retiming stimulus works best when it is perceived to be temporary, for only that provides an impetus to consume or invest now, before the tax "sale" ends.

What are built-in stabilizers?

Taxes tend to fall and spending increases automatically when the economy falters, even without explicitly enacted stimulus programs. When the economy slows, incomes decline, which automatically reduces income tax liability. Drops in earnings often result in larger Earned Income Tax Credits (although some may have earnings so low that their EITC is reduced or eliminated). Certain non-tax spending programs, such as unemployment compensation and food stamps, also increase during a recession. All of these "built-in stabilizers" tend to dampen the decline in after-tax income and soften the resultant decline in consumer spending.

How do taxes affect prosperity and growth?

We've been talking about the role, and effectiveness, of tax policy in combating a cyclical downturn. This is an important question when the economy falls into, or is danger of falling into, a recession. But how the tax system affects the economy is *always* a crucial question, because it always matters and can always be changed.

Shortly, we will offer our wisdom—or at least our best guesses—about how tax systems affect the level of GDP per capita, overall and by income group, as well as future growth in these measures of how prosperous we are. Before we get to that, we must admit the painful truth—we don't know for sure. It's not just that we are unenlightened, but that the economics profession usually does not provide definitive

BOX 6.1 The Liberal-Conservative Divide on the Cost of Government

Nick is a conservative economist and Adam is a liberal

"People like free services and monthly checks in the mail, but people don't realize the true cost—not just in terms of higher taxes, but in lower productivity. And slower growth will hurt our kids a lot more than deficits."

"There's no compelling evidence that taxes at the level we pay—just about the lowest in the industrialized world—have much effect on work, savings or investment," Adam said. "Besides, why assume away the positive role that government can play in fostering economic growth? Think of all the government dollars shelled out to protect property rights, provide infrastructure and support education."

I found my chance to intercede. "Why is it that so many liberals believe the effect of taxes on incentives is small, while their conservative counterparts believe that taxes create huge distortions? Since this is an empirical question, you'd expect the conclusions to be independent of one's politics."

"Not necessarily," Nick responded. "Some conservatives are skeptical about government because we view the costs of paying for it as very high."

"Do any Republicans believe that taxes don't affect behavior much?" I asked. "Do any Democrats believe that taxes are costly?"

Source: Leonard E. Burman and Joel Slemrod, "My Weekend with Nick and Adam: Tax Policy and Other Willful Misperceptions," *Milken Institute Review* (September 2003): 50–58. Reprinted by permission.

answers, even if some economists offer answers in an entirely self-confident way.

One reason for this somewhat embarrassing state of affairs is that getting a definitive answer is inherently difficult. Say we would like to know how the 2017 tax law has affected the economy. We have, or soon will have, great statistics on what happened after the new tax law took effect. We also have great statistics on what was going on with the economy before the tax law took effect. What we don't know is how the economy would have performed if the Tax Cuts and Jobs Act *had not* become law—what economists call the counterfactual. And we can never know for sure. Economists have all sorts of ingenious methods to make educated guesses about the counterfactual. We have statistical methods for estimating the counterfactual, and thereby estimating the effect of the policies actually implemented. But these methods can never be perfect. Consider that, just a few weeks after the TCJA came into force, President Trump announced tariffs on solar panels and washing machines, and a looming trade war sank the stock market and caused many businesses to reassess their prospects. It would be a mistake to ascribe the effects of the trade war to the new tax bill, but there is no way to exactly purge the economic data of the effects of the tariffs so as to isolate the consequences of the changes in the tax system.

Recently, many economists have tried to learn from randomized field experiments, where alternative versions of a policy are applied to different people or businesses, and the differential impact is studied. For example, some but not all taxpayers suspected of noncompliance are sent a letter informing them about the penalties for tax evasion; if on average their subsequent behavior changes significantly compared with people who did not get the letter (the "control group"), we may confidently conclude that the difference in behavior was caused by receipt of the letter. This method works well for learning about the impact of small, localized policies, but it is useless for big, macroeconomic policies like tax policy changes. What government would allow, for the sake of learning how policies work, a big tax cut in some regions and a small tax cut elsewhere? The people who get the small tax cuts would be (understandably) outraged, and it would be difficult to control for any spillover effects of the policies across regions. And while random selection is ideal for scientific experiments, turning the tax code into a lottery is probably unconstitutional. For all of the ingenuity and statistical sophistication of researchers, these methods remain inexact and, as a result, substantial uncertainty persists about the answers to these central questions that should inform policy.

However, the evidence is good enough for us to say with a lot of confidence what kinds of claims are *not* true.[2] It is not true that cutting taxes by itself will guarantee a spurt of growth. We know this by observing that some countries with substantially higher tax takes are doing quite well, thank you. We know that higher tax rates on the rich do not guarantee economic disaster, because in the 1950s and 1960s, when the U.S. top individual tax rates exceeded 90 percent, the U.S. economy performed very well, indeed—better than in decades since, on the whole, in the rate of growth of GDP and productivity. We know that lowering tax rates from current levels will not boost the economy so much that revenues will go up rather than down. We know this by observing that recent tax cuts in the United States and in other countries were inevitably followed by bigger deficits.

But we also know that taxes can blunt the incentives that people and businesses have to do the things they must do to prosper: work hard, educate themselves, invest in physical capital, and so on. These disincentives must be taken seriously in the formulation of tax policy.

How do taxes affect working and saving?

Two decades ago the conventional wisdom was that the labor supply of prime-age males hardly budges when tax rates changed; these men, often family breadwinners, have to work regardless of what their labor brings in. Some recent research has found a greater responsiveness, suggesting that a tax rate cut from 30 percent to 25 percent might raise labor supply as much as 2 percent, still fairly small but enough to imply nontrivial economic costs from sharp increases in taxation. Most economists believe that the labor supply decisions of women are much more sensitive than men are to the after-tax wage, especially with regard to the decision of whether to be in the labor force at all.[3] This is especially troubling given our household-based income tax system, where a spouse considering working faces a marginal tax rate determined by the earnings of his or her spouse, so income tax rates of as much as 37 percent plus payroll taxes may be imposed on even small amounts of income.

We know much less about the responsiveness of saving to the real after-tax rate of return, in part because it is much more difficult to measure saving than hours worked. Over time there seems to be no clear correlation between this rate of return and aggregate personal savings rates. This doesn't necessarily mean there is no relationship, as it could be that so many other factors affect savings that it is not possible to identify the effect of taxation alone. Thus, a key economic argument against taxing the return to saving, as a pure income tax does but a consumption tax does not, rests on a theoretical, not empirical, argument that any such effect is especially harmful to the long-run growth prospects of the economy.

How do taxes affect entrepreneurship?

Some research has suggested that one aspect of progressive tax systems in general, and capital gains taxes in particular, inhibits risky entrepreneurial activity. It is that they levy a higher tax on successful ventures than they rebate on unsuccessful ones. This is an unavoidable outcome of a graduated rate schedule, under which higher returns push one into higher tax brackets, while losses push one into lower tax brackets or negate current tax liability altogether. Thus, the government is an unequal and unhelpful business partner; it takes a hefty share of profits, but shares little or none of losses. For businesses that are liquidated or sold at a loss, the law limits the amount of capital losses that may be deducted from other positive income. Offsetting this are the preferential tax rates levied on capital gains; indeed, the asymmetric treatment of gains and losses is one argument made for the preferentially lower tax rates. (See page 44, "What are the arguments for and against lower capital gains tax rates?")

Entrepreneurs often toil for years earning low wages, and therefore incurring low tax liability, while they build their business. If all works out, they will earn back their labor contribution with a fair return (more if the business is especially successful). That return will often be taxed as a capital gain at low rates if they end up selling the business. This is even better than the tax treatment of traditional IRAs or 401(k) plans. In that case, they may deduct the up-front investment—just as they do for sweat equity—but the ultimate return is fully taxed as ordinary income rather than capital gain. Moreover, for very talented (high-earning) people, the contribution of labor may far exceed the limits on contributions to retirement accounts.

How do taxes affect research and innovation?

Like many countries, the U.S. government subsidizes basic research and development (R&D), both via direct funding (mostly dedicated to defense and health) and, since 1981, through tax credits related to R&D activity. The subsidy is motivated by the belief that basic R&D has important spillover effects that benefit not just the businesses that do it, but other businesses as well—it generates positive externalities (as opposed to the negative externalities that polluting activity generates), which suggests that a Pigouvian subsidy is appropriate. The tax law provides a credit of 20 percent of a taxpayer's qualified research expenditures that exceed an amount based on past activity. Although the basic form of the credit hasn't changed much since it was first enacted, the credit was a temporary measure that expired and had been extended multiple times, making it difficult for businesses to make long-term commitments based on its continued existence. In the tax act of 2015, though, it was made permanent, which means it need not be explicitly extended each year but does not ensure it will never change, as no legislation can bind future Congresses.

Most studies conclude that the credit stimulates more R&D. One credible study estimated that a 10 percent fall in the after-tax cost of R&D induces just over a 1 percent rise in the level of R&D in the short run, but almost a 10 percent rise in the long run.[4] This and many (but not all) other studies suggest that the credit is effective in the sense that each dollar of forgone tax revenue causes businesses to invest an additional dollar in R&D.

What is "trickle-down" economics?

This term is generally applied in a pejorative way to policies that heavily feature tax cuts for rich folks, but which are defended on the grounds that they will eventually benefit everyone through job creation and investment. The term has been attributed to the humorist Will Rogers, who said during the Great Depression that "money was all appropriated for the top in hopes that it would trickle down to the needy." In modern terminology, tax cuts for the 1 percent help the 99 percent. The idea behind trickle-down economics is not illogical. For example, if tax cuts for high-income people induce them to hire more people in a business they own, some of the benefit could go to the working population broadly. The problem is that it doesn't usually work that way.

One careful recent study makes the point that income growth for the 99 percent was highest in the United States from 1933 to 1973, when top income tax rates were high, and has slowed down since the 1970s, when top tax rates came down.[5] A statistical analysis of the data shows that, other things equal, lower marginal tax rates for the 1 percent are associated with lower, not higher, real income for the 99 percent.

Why do smart, serious people disagree about optimal tax policy?

For at least two reasons. The first is that even smart, serious people can disagree about how the economy works. For example, whether higher tax rates dampen the incentive to work a lot or a little is a critical input into optimal tax policy, but even after decades of research, economists still disagree. Second, what is appropriate tax policy also depends on noneconomic values, most importantly what priority to put on reducing economic inequality. For any given set of beliefs about how the economy works, people with more egalitarian values will favor more progressive tax systems. Economic arguments cannot resolve differences in values. For that we need ethicists, philosophers, theologians, and deep introspection, but not economists.

For outsiders trying to make sense of disagreements among economists about policy prescriptions, this creates a dilemma. If economist X says she favors shifting the tax burden toward high-income people, is that because her professional expertise has convinced her that the economic costs—in terms of disincentives to work, invest, and so on—are low, or because her own values are more egalitarian, or some of both? Economists should have some claim to expertise about the former, but we have no special claim to be heard about values. A citizen who wished to be enlightened by experts must try to sort out the path that leads an economist to the policy prescriptions, or else ignore them entirely and try to make sense of the evidence about how the economy works.

Actually, it's even worse than that. If economics were a purely scientific venture, then we would expect that economists' judgments about such things as the magnitude of tax disincentive effects would bear no relationship to their values. After all, do we expect that physicists' views about the nature of black holes are correlated with their political party affiliation? Of course not. We expect that it depends on how they assess theory and evidence about the universe. But this doesn't work in economics. Most economists with conservative values believe that the economic costs of taxation are high, which leads to conservative policy prescriptions (low taxes and small government). Liberals tend to believe that taxation entails much smaller costs—a view consistent with liberal policies. A careful study of the policy preferences and values of economists in the top 40 academic departments found not only considerable disagreement among economists about policy proposals in their areas of specialization (probably no surprise), but also that policy positions are usually more closely related to differences in values than to differences in estimates of relevant economic parameters.[6] The same study found a statistically significant correlation between values and reported economic parameters. Now, in principle that could be because economists' scientific conclusions about how the economy works influence their attitudes toward such matters as income distribution. But a more unsettling possibility is that their estimates of economic parameters may be influenced by their values. To be clear, we are not arguing that most economists fudge the numbers to conform to their values, but there may be subtle biases at work that can move us to more readily accept evidence that comports with our worldview (box 6.1). This issue was fully on display in the debate leading up to the Tax Cuts and Jobs Act of 2017, which we discuss shortly.

It may be that the same phenomenon arises in other politically charged scientific disciplines where values or personal dispositions end up influencing research design or interpretation of research, so that experts' apparently scientific claims are correlated with their nonscientific worldview.

Where does that leave the citizen looking for professional expertise from economists? Forewarned. In an ideal world, economists would describe what they think they know about how the economy works, and, if asked about what policy they favor, they would be clear about how their answer depended both on what they think they know and on what values they hold. The reality is that this rarely happens.

Why not run deficits forever?

The United States can run a structural deficit (meaning noninterest spending is greater than revenues) forever so long as the debt doesn't rise faster than GDP. If debt rises slower than GDP, the debt/GDP ratio will fall over time.

Whether we *should* run deficits is a much more complicated question. We should borrow to finance investments that will pay off over time. That includes obvious things like many roads and dams, and also spending on wars and homeland security if those investments make us safer over the long run.

But we should save (that is, run surpluses) if, as is true now, we have large underfunded future obligations. The enormous projected shortfalls in Social Security, Medicare, and Medicaid may outweigh the returns on public investments, so the optimal policy might be to run surpluses right now.

A further complication is that the optimal policy depends on future economic growth. Running deficits is a way to smooth our aggregate consumption over time if we know that the economy will be growing. Basically, we're sharing in our grandchildren's good fortune. If future and current generations care equally about each other, this sort of makes sense. There is, though, tremendous uncertainty about future economic growth. Historically, the economy has grown at an average rate of around 2 or 3 percent per year. If that continues, then our grandchildren will be much richer than we are. However, there are many risks. For example, what will climate change do to the economy? Will resource constraints (e.g., finite clean water and cropland) become binding, slowing growth? Will a new era of innovation stimulate productivity gains?

On balance, it's not at all clear what the optimal deficit policy is, but there's a pretty good chance that it's *not* to run structural deficits forever.[7]

One final caveat. There's a very strong argument for running a temporary structural deficit when the economy is operating far below capacity, which was true at the time the first edition of this book was written (in 2012), but it is not true in 2019.

Are the benefits of tax cuts diminished, or eliminated, if they
increase deficits?

Diminished, for sure. Higher deficits push up interest rates
and crowd out private investment. The extent they do so depends on how much the higher interest rates induce greater
private saving and inflows of foreign capital. Reviewing the
empirical evidence, the Congressional Budget Office's central
estimate is that each dollar of increase in the budget deficit reduces domestic investment by 33 cents, which depresses economic growth.[8] Increased foreign investment may help out, but
a good portion of the induced future income would be owed
to foreigners who lend funds to finance the excess of induced
investment over induced domestic saving. The significance of
this factor is reflected in the Congressional Budget Office pro-
jection that real GDP (income generated in the United States)
could be 0.7 percent higher over 2018–2028 due to the TCJA,
but real GNP (income of Americans) could rise by only 0.4 percent. That is, the CBO predicts that nearly half of the increased
income generated within the United States would accrue to
foreigners.[9]

Some prominent economists would go farther, and argue
that deficit-financed tax cuts *reduce* national income in the long
run, although if coupled with appropriate reforms, the overall
mixture could expand the size of the economy.[10]

However, some analysts believe that there is a surplus of
capital in world markets. If so, the expected increase in the
deficit may not have much effect on interest rates (and the
economy). Interest rates have been very low for a while, with
no clear sign that growing public debt in the United States and
other countries is pushing them up. If world interest rates do
not respond to additional U.S. public debt, then government
borrowing does not crowd out private investment, and deficit-
financed tax cuts may not be especially problematic. We are
skeptical, however, that cheap capital will persist. Moreover,
even if world interest rates remain low, lenders may begin to

doubt the American government's ability to make all of its debt payments, which would increase the interest rate on U.S. debt and could rapidly spiral into a fiscal crisis with potentially disastrous consequences.[11]

If people care about their children, won't they just save more to make up for any deficits? That is, do deficits matter at all?

Former vice president Dick Cheney once famously said, "Ronald Reagan proved that deficits don't matter." His comment attracted scorn and derision, but some very smart and thoughtful economists have made a similar argument—without the reference to President Reagan.

The basic idea is this: If people care about their children and grandchildren, then they will, as private citizens, take steps that offset government's actions that have long-term negative consequences. If people behave this way, then when the government borrows, citizens know that will just translate into higher future taxes on their children and grandchildren, so they will save more and bequeath more to offset these consequences and smooth out consumption across generations. If taxpayers are infinitely farsighted and perfectly rational, private saving will completely offset any public borrowing.

David Ricardo, the brilliant political economist of the early nineteenth century, was the first to articulate this possibility, which is often called "Ricardian equivalence" in his honor. Long considered an interesting but implausible scenario—Ricardo himself viewed his model as simply a thought experiment—it was resurrected by Harvard economist Robert Barro in the 1980s.[12]

Although there is certainly something to the idea that individual saving and borrowing could be affected by deficit policies, we think full Ricardian equivalence does not hold in practice, for many reasons. To start, people obviously do not live forever (Ricardo's scenario). Barro replies that all that matters is that people care about their kids, who in turn care about their kids and, by a kind of transitivity property (economists call it an "overlapping generations model"), that means that they effectively care about all their future descendants. Critics have pointed out that, in the limit, this implies the implausible notion that everyone cares about everyone else's descendants because given enough time, everyone becomes related. Other problems include that the argument assumes that everyone borrows when the government is running a surplus, which isn't plausible given that most people face borrowing constraints. More fundamentally, people don't know how future tax burdens and spending cuts will be distributed, so it is unclear how much (if at all) to save to offset the consequences of future policies on one's descendants.

And—this is a hard thing for economists to say—there's a lot of evidence that people aren't ultra-rational (and sometimes aren't even slightly rational). If they were, you'd expect to see substantial boosts in private saving when deficits soar. But if there is a relationship, it's a very subtle one. The government has been running large and growing deficits for the past two decades, and until the Great Recession, saving rates were very close to zero.

Will the Tax Cuts and Jobs Act boost the economy and make most Americans better off?

We've now come to the 64-million-dollar question. The tax law was sold as boosting the growth rate of the economy, raising both the pre-tax and after-tax incomes of most everyone, and providing more jobs. Will it work? We've already admitted that even applying sound economic reasoning can't provide a definitive answer to this kind of question. But we owe you our best educated guesses.

First we should note what others have said. The official arbiter of the revenue cost of tax changes, the Joint Committee on Taxation (JCT), estimated that because of the Tax Cuts and

Jobs Act the level of GDP would be 0.8 percent higher on average over the 10-year budget window due to increases in labor supply and investment. Other prominent groups came out with growth estimates on either side of those offered by the JCT. For example, the Penn Wharton model estimated that GDP by 2027 would be between 0.6 percent and 1.1 percent larger than otherwise. A letter to the Treasury secretary, Steven Mnuchin, signed by nine prominent economists suggested a larger response, a gain in the long-run level of GDP of just over 3 percent, or 0.3 percent per year for a decade.[13]

Not all of this is pure gain. Some arises because people work more hours, and part of it arises because people forgo some consumption. As mentioned above, some of the GDP increase—perhaps as much as half—will be owed to foreigners who buy the government's debt raised to cover the deficits that TCJA necessitates. Finally, as we discuss in chapter 8, exactly whose income is likely to change matters. The fact is that it is impossible to tell who benefits from deficit-financed tax cuts because we do not know how those deficits will ultimately be repaid. Future taxes might increase on high-income earners, making the TCJA a boon to low-income households. Or safety net programs that primarily benefit low- and middle-income households may be cut, costing those households far more in benefits than they gained from the tax cuts.[14] If deficits are allowed to grow unchecked, the ultimate debt crisis might make everyone worse off.

Thus, we believe that the stimulus to growth provided by TCJA will be modest, far short of many supporters' claims, and could even turn out to be a net negative in the long run.

"SINCE IT'S FALLING ON ME TO HELP PAY OFF THE BUDGET DEFICITS WHEN I GROW UP, I THINK YOU NEED TO INCREASE MY ALLOWANCE, DAD!"

7

THE HIDDEN WELFARE STATE

Are a trillion dollars in middle-class entitlement programs really hidden in the tax code?

Yes, give or take ... The actual amount is in dispute for reasons we'll get to, but many spending programs, big and small, are run through the income tax.[1]

When policymakers want to support or penalize a certain activity or group of people or businesses, they have a choice about whether to do it through traditional spending agencies—like the Department of Housing and Urban Development—or through the tax code. One would like to think that the choice of delivery vehicle depends only on how the program can most effectively be administered, but there are good reasons to think that our political system is biased in favor of the tax delivery mechanism.

Economists and lawyers call spending programs run through the tax code "tax expenditures." No doubt this sounds like an oxymoron—"jumbo shrimp" comes to mind—but bear with us. Congress's nonpartisan Joint Committee on Taxation counted 202 different tax expenditures in 2007, a more than 50 percent increase from 1987. Despite the passage of the Tax Cuts and Jobs Act, there are still more than 200 tax expenditures in the code. There are tax expenditures in every budget category. For example, military officers and soldiers get benefits like free housing on base or an allowance to help pay for off-base housing. These benefits are tax-free, saving recipients $5.5 billion of tax liability in 2018. The tax savings on the housing allowances are equivalent to a boost in pay—albeit one that depends on the soldier's tax bracket—but, unlike a direct increase in salary, they don't show up as Department of Defense spending. Instead, the extra after-tax compensation is counted as a reduction in taxes.

To take a better-known example, taxpayers who itemize deductions can deduct charitable contributions, providing a tax saving proportional to the taxpayer's rate bracket. But, rather than allow a deduction for charitable donations, the government could directly subsidize qualified charities by sending them a check related to the amount of private donations they receive; this is how it's done in the United Kingdom. Under either method, charity is subsidized, but in the first case it appears to be a cut in taxes, while in the second case it appears to be an increase in spending.

The biggest tax expenditures are the tax exclusion for employer-sponsored health insurance, lowered rates on capital gains and dividends, and the tax break for 401(k) retirement plans (table 7.1). (If pensions and 401(k) plans were grouped together as retirement breaks, they'd be the second largest tax break.) An obvious aspect of the big tax expenditures is that they affect a broad swath of the population (unlike the military housing allowance exclusion) and are enormously popular. Even though some of them have dubious merit as public policy, changing them would be politically difficult.

What exactly is a tax expenditure?

The broad definition of tax expenditures—spending programs run through the tax code—is not in dispute, but there is far from consensus about what exactly belongs in that category. The Office of Management and Budget uses the definition proposed by Treasury assistant secretary Stanley Surrey, who invented the concept in 1967, and his coauthor, Paul R. McDaniel:

Table 7.1 Largest Estimated Tax Expenditures in Fiscal Year 2018, in Billions of Dollars

	Provision	Amount
1	Exclusion for employer-sponsored health insurance	249.3
2	Lower rate on capital gains and dividends	128.7
3	401(k) plans	125.5
4	Child Tax Credit	104.2
5	Pensions	87.9
6	Tax deferral for multinational corporations	73.9
7	EITC	71.6
8	Depreciation of equipment in excess of the alternative depreciation system	62.6
9	Subsidies for insurance passed through the health benefit exchanges	48.5
10	Charity deduction (other than education, health)	42.8

Note: The health insurance estimate includes $92 billion in payroll tax expenditure (because employer contributions to health insurance are exempt from both income and payroll taxes). We approximate the payroll tax portion by applying a ratio of payroll tax expenditure to income tax expenditure for health insurance for 2018 estimates (found in the FY 2019 budget) to newer JCT estimates. The Child Tax Credit, EITC, and health care exchange subsidy include the refundable parts—$44.1, $63.3, and $43 billion, respectively—which are considered outlays (spending) rather than tax cuts under the budget rules. The depreciation measure includes bonus depreciation.

Source: Joint Committee on Taxation, Estimates of Federal Tax Expenditures for Fiscal Years 2017–2021 (JCX-34-18), May 25, 2018; U.S. Budget, Analytical Perspectives, FY 2019; authors' calculations.

The tax expenditure concept posits that an income tax is composed of two distinct elements. The first element consists of structural provisions necessary to implement a normal income tax, such as the definition of net income, the specification of accounting rules, the determination of the entities subject to tax, the determination of the rate schedule and exemption levels, and the application of the tax to international transactions. The second element consists of the special preferences found in every income tax. These provisions, often called tax incentives or tax subsidies, are departures from the normal tax structure and are designed to favor a particular industry, activity, or class of persons. They take many forms, such as permanent exclusions from income, deductions, deferrals of tax liabilities, credits against tax, or special rates. Whatever their form, these departures from the normative tax structure represent government spending for favored activities or groups, effected through the tax system rather than through direct grants, loans, or other forms of government assistance.[2]

The controversies all revolve around what constitutes the "normal" or "normative" tax structure. The most important one is whether tax expenditures should be defined with respect to an income tax or a consumption tax. If the normal tax were taken to be a consumption tax, which does not tax the return to saving, then the tax breaks related to pensions, 401(k) plans, capital gains, and the exclusion of net imputed rental income on homes would not be on the list. Nonetheless, many items would be included regardless of the definition of "normal tax." Economists Donald Marron and Eric Toder have estimated that 70 percent of tax expenditures (by dollar amount) would be classified as such under either benchmark.[3]

Measuring the value of tax expenditures is also challenging. By convention, the estimates simply reflect how much the relevant tax breaks reduce taxpayers' liability in a year, without accounting for how taxpayer behavior, and therefore tax liability, would change if the tax breaks were repealed. Longtime Ways and Means Committee tax counsel John Buckley has argued that repealing or scaling back tax expenditures could raise far less revenue than the conventional method suggests because taxpayers would change their behavior to avoid paying more tax.[4] For example, if the mortgage interest deduction were repealed, some taxpayers would sell taxable assets and use the proceeds to pay down their mortgage. Tax revenue would then decline by the amount that otherwise would have been due on the diverted assets' income.

Why do we call tax expenditures entitlement programs?
They're tax cuts.

Many tax expenditures are similar to mandatory spending programs (commonly called entitlements) because they provide subsidies to everyone who is eligible and they are not subject to annual appropriation. Like entitlements, they continue forever unless Congress makes an explicit decision to modify or repeal them. This isn't true of every tax break. For example, most of the tax cuts enacted in 2001 and 2003 were originally scheduled to expire at the end of 2010 but were extended through 2012, at which time most were made "permanent." Many of the provisions in the TCJA are set to expire at the end of 2025 (although many in Congress would like to make those provisions permanent, too). The low-income housing tax credit is actually allocated by state housing agencies and subject to a state-by-state cap. These tax expenditures are not appropriated, but they are not open-ended entitlement programs either.

Like entitlement programs, tax expenditures are large, growing, and hard to control.

Who benefits from tax expenditures?

Most taxpayers qualify for at least some tax expenditures. Whether taxpayers benefit or not compared to a world with no tax expenditures at all is a much more difficult question to answer, as tax rates could be lower—or explicit expenditure programs increased—if there were not so many exclusions, deductions, and credits, but exactly how tax rates would be cut is impossible to know.

Eric Toder, Daniel Berger, and Yifan Zhang estimated the distribution of tax expenditures by income groups in 2015 (see table 7.2).[5] Tax expenditures are a significant share of income for households at all income levels. Strikingly, they are largest for high-income people—worth about 13.4 percent of income

Table 7.2 Benefit as a Percentage of Pre-tax Income for Various Categories of Income Tax Expenditures, 2015

Cash income percentile	Exclusions	Capital gains and dividends	Itemized deductions	Above-the-line deductions	Non-refundable credits	Refundable credits	Other	All provisions
Lowest quintile	0.6%	0.2%	0.0%	0.0%	0.1%	5.4%	0.0%	6.7%
2nd quintile	2.7%	0.4%	0.1%	0.1%	0.2%	4.0%	0.0%	7.5%
3rd quintile	3.5%	0.6%	0.4%	0.1%	0.1%	1.5%	0.0%	6.3%
4th quintile	3.3%	0.9%	0.7%	0.1%	0.1%	0.6%	0.0%	6.3%
80–90th percentiles	4.0%	1.3%	1.2%	0.1%	0.1%	0.3%	0.1%	7.2%
90–95th percentiles	4.4%	1.4%	1.5%	0.1%	0.1%	0.0%	0.1%	7.6%
95–99th percentiles	4.3%	1.9%	1.7%	0.1%	0.0%	0.0%	0.1%	7.9%
Top 1 percent	2.7%	7.3%	2.1%	0.1%	0.1%	0.0%	0.3%	13.4%
Total	3.4%	2.1%	1.1%	0.1%	0.1%	0.9%	0.1%	8.1%

Note: Separate categories do not add up to total because of interactions among provisions.

Source: Eric Toder, Daniel Berger, and Yifan Zhang, "Distributional Effects of Individual Income Tax Expenditures: An Update," September 26, 2016, Tax Policy Center, table 3.

for the richest 1 percent, about 7 percent of income for the richest 10 percent, compared with 6.7 percent for the poorest 20 percent, and 8.1 percent overall.

Higher-income people benefit most from exclusions and deductions, whereas low- and middle-income people benefit more from tax credits. This isn't surprising, because in a graduated income tax, deductions and exclusions from taxable income are most valuable per dollar to taxpayers in high tax brackets. Credits typically are at the same rate for everyone, and some phase out at higher income levels. Low-income households benefit most from the refundable EITC and Child Tax Credit, which are akin to vouchers in the sense that families can benefit even if they do not have income tax liability.

Why has the use of tax expenditures been growing in recent years?

Income tax expenditures have been proliferating since the mid-1990s. According to data from the Joint Committee on Taxation, the number of individual income tax expenditures increased by 50 percent between 1996 and 2018—from 130 in 1996 to over 200 in 2018.[6]

It is not entirely clear why, but we suspect that politics is a big part of it. Taxpayers dislike paying taxes, but they like getting help from the government. In an antitax environment, a politician who proposes a new spending program is open to attack for being a "tax and spend" liberal. In contrast, if a nearly equivalent program can be run through the tax code as a tax expenditure, it can be defended as a tax cut rather than a new spending program. Its cost does not appear in calculations of the cost of government (although it obviously does affect the deficit or tax rates that households face). In that way, it may appear more benign and more affordable than direct spending programs.

How should policymakers decide whether to run a subsidy through the tax system?

Some tax purists believe that subsidies should be delivered through program agencies rather than the IRS because, they argue, the tax system's only role is to collect revenue. But there are cases where the tax system is the more efficient delivery mechanism. This is especially true if eligibility can easily be determined using information already on tax returns or that tax authorities can easily obtain, for example via information reporting of third parties such as employers. There are also issues about the timing of tax subsidies. Usually, tax subsidies are claimed when filing a tax return, potentially long after the qualifying activity occurs. This can make the subsidy less effective if taxpayers are short on cash. On the other hand, establishing eligibility for cash transfer programs can be difficult and time-consuming, and there may also be a welfare stigma associated with applying for a benefit. Tax subsidies have the advantage of being relatively easy to claim and anonymous, so there is little or no welfare stigma.

Many potential subsidy programs have been derailed because there is no plausible way for the IRS to enforce them without an audit. Ideally, an independent third party would report eligibility to the IRS. Often, however, there is no such entity. That is presumably why the Tax Cuts and Jobs Act eliminated a provision allowing employers to deduct up to $20 per month in reimbursements to employees for "qualified bicycle commuting" expenses if "the bicycle is regularly used for . . . a substantial portion of travel between" home and work. We like bicycling (one of us is a bicycle nut), but this policy was completely unenforceable. How could an employer verify that employees qualify? By counting how many times a month they show up in spandex? Who was supposed to scrutinize employees' bike shop receipts to be sure that the expenses are for the employee's bike and not her kid's?

How should tax expenditures be designed?

Many choices arise in the design of subsidies. First, there's the question of whether the subsidy should be delivered by way of a tax credit, an exclusion, or a deduction from taxable income. Exclusions are often used for fringe benefits. For example, if your employer offers health insurance at work as part of your compensation, the value of that insurance is not included in your taxable income; alternatively, the government might tax all employee compensation—cash and fringe benefits—and then provide subsidy payments to those who receive fringe benefits. The big advantage of the exclusion is that it's very simple from the point of view of the recipient. But here's the rub: the rate of subsidy is larger for taxpayers in high brackets than those in low tax brackets. A deduction is similar except that the taxpayer subtracts it from income on the tax return rather than simply excluding it from income in the first place. Why designers of a tax system would want to offer a higher rate of subsidy for charitable donations to higher-income people is beyond us.

Exclusions and deductions make more sense when the objective is not to subsidize an activity but rather to better measure a taxpayer's standard of living. Excluding certain costs from income may result in a better measure of the taxpayer's true economic status. This argument justifies the deduction for extraordinary medical expenses, which reduce a family's wellbeing below what their pre-deduction income suggests.

A tax credit is more like a voucher. It reduces tax liability by the same amount for all households with sufficient tax liability to use the credit. However, a tax credit may be of little value to households that don't have much tax liability. For that reason, a few tax subsidies are offered as refundable tax credits and available even if the taxpayer has no tax liability, so that net tax liability becomes negative—the household gets money from the government in excess of pre-credit tax liability. In addition, policymakers have to choose whether to

off the mark.com   by Mark Parisi

MS. KELLY, TAKING SOMEONE OUT ON A PITY DATE DOESN'T QUALIFY AS A CHARITABLE CONTRIBUTION...

D. HARMON CPA

©2007 MARK PARISI DIST. BY UFS INC.

Source: Cartoon © Mark Parisi. Permission granted for use, www.offthemark.com.

provide a fixed dollar amount or a percentage of qualifying expenditures, whether there is a limit on the total credit, and whether the credit phases in or phases out with income. The advantages of phasing out a credit (or deduction) are that the revenue cost of the subsidy is lower and that the benefit is targeted to those with lower incomes. The disadvantages are that the phaseout complicates tax compliance and can create undesirable incentive effects. Phasing out a credit as income rises is tantamount to a marginal tax on income. (See page 53, "What are hidden tax brackets?") Thus, policymakers have to trade off the incentive effects caused by the phaseout and the efficiency costs of raising more tax revenue to make up for a more widely available credit.

Does the mortgage interest deduction encourage homeownership?

Probably not much, and it might even discourage some home purchases. This may seem surprising. People who itemize their deductions may reduce taxable income by all or part of their mortgage interest. At a 25 percent tax rate, a $2,000 per month interest tab only costs $1,500 after subtracting the $500 reduction in tax liability, which lowers the cost of homeownership. However, few households now benefit from the deduction, because as of 2018 only about 11 percent have itemized deductions in excess of the standard deduction. (see p.32, "What is the standard deduction?"). So 91 percent of households—all non-itemizers plus a small number of itemizers who do not claim the deduction—get no benefit from the mortgage interest deduction. Even some who itemize don't save much on their taxes because their deductions are barely above the itemization threshold. For example, suppose a married couple in 2018 had $10,000 in mortgage interest plus $15,000 in other itemized deductions. The $25,000 in total itemized deductions is just $1,000 above the $24,000 standard deduction, so itemizing doesn't lower their taxes much. Without mortgage interest, the couple would not itemize and would claim the standard deduction instead. Their taxable income would rise by $1,000, not $10,000. Assuming a 25 percent tax rate, they'd save $250 in total taxes, or 2.5 percent of their mortgage interest.

The subsidy is only valuable to higher-income people who are most likely to own a home, and the largest subsidies go to households with large homes and big mortgages. Most low-income households get no benefit. Indeed, some might be worse off if the subsidy for high-income households raises housing demand and thus pushes prices up, making housing *less* affordable for those who do not itemize.

More households benefited from the mortgage interest and (property tax) deductions before passage of TCJA, but there's not much evidence that the subsidies boosted homeowner-ship. Homeownership in the United States has tracked owner-ship in Canada over time, despite the fact that Canadians have never been able to deduct interest.

There are other policy options that might boost homeown-ership. For example, Bill Gale has suggested that the mortgage interest deduction be replaced with a refundable tax credit to support first-time homebuyers.[7]

Why does tax-free health insurance push up health care costs?

Your employer's contribution toward your family's health in-surance never shows up in your paycheck and is completely disregarded for purposes of calculating income and payroll taxes. Employer-provided health insurance is a very valuable fringe benefit. The average employer who offered insurance spent about $5,000 per single worker in 2017, but it isn't con-sidered taxable compensation.[8] Individuals who get health in-surance at work saved a total of almost $250 billion in income and payroll taxes (including the employer's share) in fiscal year 2018. (See table 7.1.) It is the single largest individual in-come tax expenditure.

It's a popular and costly subsidy, but most economists think it is also complicit in America's high health care costs. The issue is that the tax expenditure makes health insurance cheaper, the very quality that makes it popular. If your com-bined income and payroll tax rate (including any state income taxes) is 40 percent, a dollar of health insurance only costs you 60 cents in after-tax wages (assuming the employer passes on the cost to workers). With the 40 percent off discount, you're willing to "buy" much more expensive health insurance than you would if you had to pay the full price. That means em-ployees tend to resist health insurance offerings that provide access to fewer doctors, restrict coverage of costly procedures or drugs, or include other effective but annoying cost-control features—even if it means that wages are lower than they would be otherwise. Fewer cost controls is one reason that the United States spends a lot more per person for health care than other rich countries.

Policymakers recognize this problem, but the politics of fixing it are challenging. When John McCain ran for president in 2008, he proposed to replace the unlimited exclusion for employer-sponsored health insurance with fully refundable flat dollar tax credits for qualifying coverage, whether acquired at work or purchased in the individual nongroup market. This would have been a very progressive change—the credit would have been worth much more than the income and payroll tax exclusions for low- and middle-income workers because they face relatively low income tax rates. McCain's opponent, Barack Obama, attacked him, saying, "He wants to tax your health insurance," and it is likely that the attack hurt McCain at the polls. Having waged this somewhat disingenuous attack, Obama could not have adopted the eminently sensible policy or anything like it as part of health reform.

Instead, health reform included an excise tax on employers who offered especially generous health insurance plans, sometimes called the Cadillac Plan Tax, as a backdoor limit on the value of the tax exclusion. But the Cadillac Plan Tax has been so unpopular that legislators have postponed its effective date several times, and it may never be allowed to take effect.

Was the Affordable Care Act (Obamacare) actually a giant tax law?

Many major elements of the ACA were implemented through the tax code. And a key element—the "individual mandate"—survived a constitutional challenge when the Supreme Court narrowly decided that the requirement to get coverage was permissible because it was enforced by means of a tax. Writing for the majority in the five-to-four decision, Chief Justice John Roberts wrote:

The individual mandate cannot be upheld as an exercise of Congress's power under the Commerce Clause. That Clause authorizes Congress to regulate interstate commerce, not to order individuals to engage in it. In this case, however, it is reasonable to construe what Congress has done as increasing taxes on those who have a certain amount of income, but choose to go without health insurance. Such legislation is within Congress's power to tax.[9]

Ironically, the bill's drafters did not want to call the mandate penalty a tax. Its technical name is the Individual Shared Responsibility Payment. But that is water under the bridge, because TCJA eliminated it as part of an effort to undermine the ACA.

Source: Cartoon © Mark Parisi. Permission granted for use, www.offthemark.com.

There were many other tax provisions in the ACA. The biggest is the premium tax credit, a fully refundable credit designed to help low- and middle-income people pay the premiums of insurance offered in the health insurance exchanges. Including the refundable portion (which is technically considered a cash outlay rather than a tax cut in the government's accounts), the premium credit is the ninth largest tax expenditure, totaling almost $50 billion in 2018. (See table 7.1.) The ACA also included a number of new taxes, including surtaxes on the labor and capital income of those with high incomes, the aforementioned Cadillac tax, taxes on health insurance providers, pharmaceutical manufacturers and importers, and medical device manufacturers and importers, plus some oddball provisions like a new excise tax on tanning salons. Besides their objection to the government's intrusion into health insurance markets, part of the motivation for Republican efforts to repeal the ACA was a desire to eliminate a lot of taxes.[10]

SIDEBAR 7.1 **A Tax Credit for People Who Don't Get Tax Credits?**

One April Fool's Day many years ago, a Treasury economist who shall remain nameless (it wasn't either of us) proposed a tax credit for people who don't get other tax credits. His memo was in standard format for new proposals. He noted that, under current law, a minority of taxpayers do not qualify for any tax credits. The reason for change was that the credit-deprived folks thought this was unfair, with some justification. His proposal was to create a new tax credit that would only be available for taxpayers who are not eligible for any other tax credits.

Although this proposal never made it into legislation, or even a public legislative proposal, it illustrated one of the key drawbacks of the proliferation of tax expenditures. Surveys show that most taxpayers think they are not getting their fair share of tax benefits.

Are all tax expenditures run through the income tax?

No. Several large fringe benefits are exempt from payroll tax, as well as income tax. The Treasury estimated that the exclusion of the value of employer-sponsored health insurance from the payroll tax base cost the Treasury $134 billion in 2018, as compared to a cost of $228 billion for the income tax expenditure. The payroll tax savings are partially offset by reduced future Social Security benefits, so it is not entirely clear how to measure this kind of tax expenditure, but it is surely significant.[11]

The late Treasury economist Bruce Davie pointed out that there are also excise tax expenditures.[12] For example, different kinds of beer are subject to different levels of excise taxes, conveying an effective subsidy for microbrews. Davie questioned the wisdom of this tax expenditure on both equity grounds—microbrews are generally favored by those with higher incomes—and efficiency grounds. The Treasury published a list of tax expenditures under the estate and gift taxes until 2002.

And, arguably, the many preferences given to particular goods and services under state and local sales taxes constitute tax expenditures.

Is the whole concept of tax expenditures based on the fallacious assumption that government owns all your money?

One recurring critique of the tax expenditure concept is that it rests on the assumption that all income belongs to the government unless government deigns to refund it in the form of tax breaks. Interestingly, neither this argument nor the concept of tax expenditure is a new one. Canadian economist Neil Brooks reports that in 1863, William Gladstone, then a Tory member of the British Parliament, railed against the exemption from income tax of charitable contributions. He complained that the charitable deduction would make no sense as a direct expenditure, conflicting as it would with efforts to bring "the whole expenditure of the State . . . within the control, and under the eye, of the House of Commons. If this money is to be laid out upon what are called charities, why is that portion of the State expenditure to be altogether withdrawn from view . . . and to be so contrived that we shall know nothing of it, and have no control over it?" The rebuttal from Sir Strafford Northcote would be familiar to modern critics of tax expenditures: "The right hon. Gentleman, if he took £5 out of the pocket of a man with £100, put the case as if he gave the man £95."[13]

BOX 7.1 **Len Burman Takes on Jon Stewart, Host of** *The Daily Show*, **on Tax Expenditures**

Dear Jon,

"The Daily Show" is my favorite TV show. I think you're the smartest policy analyst on television. (Okay, as you prove time after time, that's a really low bar, but, seriously, you're brilliant.)

Last month, however, your satire missed the mark. You had a lot of fun with President Obama's pledge to make "spending reductions in the tax code":

What??? The tax code isn't where we spend. It's where we collect. . . . You managed to talk about a tax hike as a spending reduction. Can we afford that and the royalty checks you'll have to send to George Orwell?

Jon, meet me at camera 3.

I know you say it's fake news, but when you riff on policy, people take you seriously. And, with respect, in this case, you don't know what the hell you're talking about.

For 40 years, tax geeks like me have been trying to explain that there's a boatload of spending programs masquerading as tax cuts, and they're multiplying. Their number increased by almost 60 percent between 1987 and 2007.

The fact that pols can claim credit for "tax cuts" (good) rather than "spending" (bad) has made them irresistible to legislators of both parties. Never mind that the IRS doesn't have the budget or expertise to effectively administer a couple hundred spending programs (sorry, tax cuts) or that many of them make no sense. The tax code's cluttered with this junk.

Finally we get the president of the United States to acknowledge this and you drill him a new one.

You don't believe there's spending in the tax code??? Here's a real life example: the chicken-s**t tax credit. Really, section 45 of the Internal Revenue Code. You can look it up. The late Senator Roth of Delaware (home of lots of chickens and "poultry manure," as it's euphemistically called) put this little goody into our tax laws. Here's the backstory: the EPA said that enormous chicken farms could no longer put their poultry waste in pools or bury it because it poisoned the ground water. One of the best options to meet the new requirement was to dry the vile effluent and burn it to make electricity, but that was still costly. Roth didn't want chicken farmer profits to plummet or chicken and egg prices to rise just because farmers couldn't use the earth as a giant toilet, so he pushed through the chicken s**t tax credit to create a profitable market for that (as well as all sorts of other crap).

There are lots of chicken s**t tax subsidies. The mortgage interest deduction is basically a housing voucher for rich people. Those who really need help get bupkes. The tax-free health insurance you get at work is heavily subsidized by the tax code, but those with low incomes rarely get health coverage, and, if they do, the subsidy is worth little or nothing. The ethanol tax credit is a farm price support program that is literally starving people.

It's spending, Jon. Often really dumb spending. And when we're talking about cutting food stamps, nutrition programs for mothers and infants, and environmental protections to save money, those spending programs in the tax code should be on the table too.

Tax subsidies add up to more than $1 trillion per year. That's not chump change, but, until recently, it's been off limits in any bipartisan budget negotiations in Congress because Republicans have been unwilling to consider anything that might be labeled a tax increase.

But there's a glimmer of hope. The president, his bipartisan debt commission, the bipartisan Domenici-Rivlin task force that I served on, and even Paul Ryan want to slash tax subsidies. Arch-conservative Oklahoma Senator Tom Coburn, leader of the bipartisan "gang of six," has said that he'd support tax increases so long as they didn't include rate increases. That is, he wants to rein in subsidy programs run by the IRS.

This is important. Coburn was willing to take on Grover Norquist, who has very effectively prevented any sensible compromise on the budget by insisting that cutting tax subsidies would violate the taxpayer protection pledge that he strong-armed most Republicans to sign. Now Grover can use your laugh line to reinforce Republican intransigence and doom any chance of bipartisan cooperation.

In all seriousness, Jon, this is not helpful.

With respect,

Len Burman

Source: Originally published on Forbes.com.

The fact is that tax expenditures have the same effect on incomes and allocation of resources as direct spending programs. Tax expenditures and direct expenditures are functionally equivalent—whatever they are called—and should be subject to scrutiny both by those who care about efficient delivery of public services (and small government) and by those who care about the integrity of the tax system.[14]

8

THE BURDEN OF TAXATION

What makes a tax system fair?

The issue of tax fairness is highly contentious, and, unfortunately, economics provides little precise guidance. For example, some people think that a flat tax on wages is fair because it taxes everyone at the same rate; to those who believe in tax progressivity, that epitomizes unfairness.

Defining fairness is tricky. One notion of fairness—so-called horizontal equity—is the idea that, other things equal, the tax burden should not vary much among people at about the same standard of living; in other words, the tax system should not discriminate on the basis of irrelevant characteristics or tastes. That means, for example, that the tax system shouldn't discriminate between equally well off owners and renters, people with health insurance and people without, or those who choose to drive an electric car and those who drive an old clunker. Of course, the tax system does discriminate in each of those cases, always with the rationale that a higher goal is being advanced: building community (mortgage interest deduction), encouraging health insurance coverage (health insurance exclusion), and improving the environment and reducing reliance on foreign oil (electric vehicle tax credit). Thus, even when we have an apparently reasonable standard of fairness such as horizontal equity, other goals may trump it.

The consequence is that neighbors with identical standards of living might bear very different tax burdens.

A more controversial notion is that of vertical equity—how the tax burden should vary across households of different levels of well-being. Most, but not all, people accept the idea that higher-income people should owe a larger share of their income in tax than those less able to pay—but how much more? The vertical equity concept underlies our progressive federal income tax, but many of the loopholes and preferences in the tax system undermine progressivity. Also, an income tax violates horizontal equity in the sense that it taxes people who choose to save more than otherwise similar people who prefer to spend all of their income and those who choose to work more than otherwise similar people who prefer to lie on a beach. (See page 99, "Why tax consumption rather than income?")

What is the benefit principle?

The benefit principle is another notion related to fairness—the idea that the tax burden should be related to how much one benefits from what government provides; that is, taxes are a quid pro quo. This principle suggests that if you can identify the people who benefit from a particular government service, they should pay for it. So, for example, people pay a fee for visiting many national parks, and local governments often charge a fee for water use and trash collection.

This principle is straightforward and unobjectionable in the cases mentioned, but identifying the beneficiaries of *all* government services is impossible. Adam Smith argued that the value of services such as national defense, police, and courts increases with income, and suggested that a proportional income tax would be the appropriate levy. Bill Gates Sr. (father of Microsoft's Bill Gates) has argued that very wealthy people owe an enormous debt to their country because the educated populace, investment in research, robust legal institutions, and so on create an environment especially conducive to wealth creation. On those grounds, he defends both a progressive income tax and an estate tax as a kind of user charge.

Note, though, that the benefit principle more broadly applied would also conflict with other social objectives. For example, taxing recipients for the food stamps they receive would completely undermine the program.

Do special fairness concerns come into play when tax laws change?

Yes. People often make decisions with long-lasting implications assuming a particular set of tax rules. If the rules change, some people can be hurt more than others. For example, if the mortgage interest deduction were eliminated, existing homeowners would likely be hurt in two ways. First, their after-tax mortgage costs would increase. Second, the value of their homes might fall. A transition rule, sometimes called a grandfather clause, could be put in place to protect homeowners from the first, but not the second, factor.

How is the tax burden distributed?

Using data from individual income tax returns, it is possible to estimate how tax burdens are distributed by income levels (figure 8.1)—sometimes called distribution tables. Here the word "estimate" is crucial. Typically, the calculations are based on a single year of data, so they represent a snapshot of households' economic status. The calculations account for non-filers—including many elderly households and low-income households without children. As discussed in chapter 2, to make such a calculation, one must make assumptions about what group of people end up bearing the burden of the tax, as distinct from who writes the checks to the government. In the Tax Policy Center's tabulations, the individual income tax is assumed to be borne by the taxpayers, payroll taxes are borne

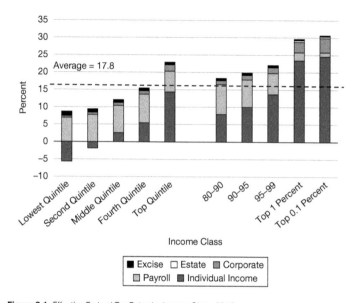

Figure 8.1 Effective Federal Tax Rates by Income Class, 2018

Source: Tax Policy Center, table T18-0083, https://www.taxpolicycenter.org/model-estimates/baseline-average-effective-tax-rates-august-2018/t18-0083-average-effective-federal.

entirely by workers (including the part technically levied "on" employers), the Social Security and Medicare benefits tied to taxes collected are ignored, the estate tax is borne by decedents, and the corporate tax—whose ultimate burden is very controversial—is assumed to be borne in part by corporate shareholders, in part by capital owners, and in part by workers. These are all reasonable assumptions based on evidence and economic reasoning, but they are not incontrovertible.

Under those assumptions, the federal tax system is fairly progressive overall. In 2018, taxes comprised about 3 percent of income for the poorest 20 percent of households, but 23 percent of income for the richest quintile.[1] At the very top of the income distribution—the richest 1 in 1,000—federal taxes comprise about 30 percent of income. At very low income levels, the individual income tax burden is negative—meaning that refundable tax credits more than offset households' income tax liability. The payroll tax, however, is larger than the tax credits, so the combined income and payroll burden is positive. A small portion of the corporate tax is assigned to this group—mostly reflecting older families with a small amount of income from pensions and 401(k) plans but otherwise modest incomes.

At higher income levels, income taxes—both individual and corporate—become a larger share of income, while the payroll tax dwindles in importance, due to the cap on taxable payroll, for those with high incomes. The estate tax is a factor only for those with very high incomes, but even for them it's a small percentage of income (mostly because few of them die each year and are subject to the tax).

State and local taxes tend to be regressive, so that the total tax burden of all government is less progressive than figure 8.1 suggests. States heavily rely on regressive sales and property taxes and even their income taxes tend to be much flatter than the federal income tax. The Institute on Taxation and Economic Policy (ITEP) estimates the distribution of state and local taxes (figure 8.2). By their estimates, the federal, state, and local taxes together comprise a growing share of income, but only

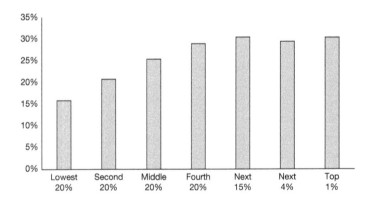

Figure 8.2 Total Federal, State, and Local Effective Tax Rates in 2018

Source: "Who Pays Taxes in America in 2018?," Institute on Taxation and Economic Policy (ITEP) Tax Model, April 2018, http://www.ctj.org/pdf/taxday2018.pdf.

up to about the 95th percentile. Some of the very wealthy actually experience a decline in tax burdens as a share of income.

Why can analysts draw different conclusions about whether a particular tax change is progressive?

The U.S. Treasury measures the progressivity of a tax change in terms of how much it changes people's after-tax incomes at different income levels.[2] The idea is that after-tax income is an indirect measure of well-being because people have more money to spend if they have more income left after taxes (and vice versa). Thus, a tax change that raises after-tax income by proportionately more for high-income people than for low-income ones is regressive. That was indeed what the Tax Policy Center found when it estimated the effects of the TCJA; the TPC estimated that in 2019, the tax cuts would equal 2 percent of after-tax income for the highest-income 20 percent of households compared with only 0.3 percent for those in the bottom quintile.[3]

Chris Edwards of the Cato Institute looked at the same bill and drew the opposite conclusion. He pointed out that the high-income quintile would receive 62 percent of the tax cuts, but that was less than their share of overall taxes—67 percent.[4] As a result, their share of tax liability would increase if the Senate legislation were enacted. He concluded that means the bill was overall progressive.

Chris's math is right, but his conclusion is debatable. To see why, imagine a very small island economy with two people on it. (Economists like island economies because the math is so much easier than in an economy with millions of people and foreign trade.) Joe works hard every day harvesting coconuts by hand and finds about 10 a week. Sally has a ladder and other tools and manages to harvest 90 a week. Before tax, Joe has 10 percent of the coconuts and Sally has 90 percent. The "government" on this island is a hungry monkey who needs coconuts to be held at bay (which pretty much conforms to the view of government by people in Chris's camp). Joe pays a tax of 1 coconut a week and Sally pays 20. After tax, Joe has 11.4 percent (9/79) of the coconuts and Sally's share is 88.6 percent (70/79). That is, the progressive coconut tax reduced the disparity in after-tax income. Now suppose that "tax reform" eliminates Joe's tax altogether while it cuts Sally's from 20 to 1. The distribution of after-tax income is now very close to the pre-tax distribution. Joe has 10.1 percent of after-tax coconuts (10/99) while Sally has 89.9 percent (89/99). That is, the new tax system hardly makes a dent in pre-tax inequality. The tax cut is worth 11 percent of after-tax income for Joe and 27 percent for Sally, reflecting this. However, Sally's share of tax is now 100 percent and Joe's is zero. Chris would say that shows the tax change is progressive.

Note also that this plan leaves Joe and Sally with a debt to the monkey, because he won't accept the 95.2 percent (20/21) cut in coconuts without the promise of future coconuts (with interest). The ultimate burden of the deficit-financed tax cut will depend on who is going to have to pay him back. In this sense, it is impossible to know who wins and who loses from a deficit-financed tax cut, but we think the percentage change in after-tax income provides the better short-run estimate.[5]

What is the burden of deficits?

Typically distribution tables ignore the burden represented by deficits. For this reason, according to distribution tables such as figures 8.1 and 8.2, the tax cuts in the TCJA made almost everyone seem better off. They provided a free lunch. If tax cuts paid for themselves because of more robust economic growth, then this assumption might be warranted. But, as we noted earlier, that is simply not true; thus, current deficits imply higher taxes in the future, a lower level of government services, or some combination of the two. (See page 163, "Why not run deficits forever?")

Because it is impossible to know ex ante how the resulting deficits will be addressed, it is also impossible to determine the winners and losers when a tax cut is financed with borrowed money. For example, table 8.1 shows the distribution of tax changes by income percentile arising from the Senate version of the TCJA tax cuts under different assumptions about who will eventually bear the burden that deficits create. The first column assumes that nobody pays—the standard assumption. This creates a tax nirvana in which every income class gets at least a small tax cut—averaging $40 for households in the bottom quintile and $5,420 for people in the top quintile. The average family could expect a tax cut worth $1,210 in 2019.

If we consider that the tax cuts must ultimately be offset by spending cuts or tax increases (or some of both), the story changes dramatically. The last three columns show the distribution of tax changes under different assumptions. In the first, the tax will be offset by equal lump-sum tax increases

Table 8.1 Average Estimated Federal Tax Change in 2019 Due to the Tax Cuts and Jobs Act as Passed by the Senate, under Different Financing Assumptions, in Dollars

Cash income percentile	Financing Method			
	None	lump-sum	proportional	
			To income	To tax
Lowest Quintile	−40	1,170	160	−20
Second Quintile	−300	900	170	180
Middle Quintile	−840	370	40	−410
Fourth Quintile	−1,560	−350	−50	−500
Top Quintile	−5,420	−4,210	−880	1,230
All	−1,210	0	0	0

Note: The table is based on the Tax Policy Center's analysis of the Senate-passed tax bill. TPC estimated that the conference agreement for the TCJA would provide larger cuts for each income quintile under the "no financing" assumption in column 1.

Source: William Gale, Surachai Khitatrakun, and Aaron Krupkin, "Winners and Losers after Paying for the Tax Cuts and Jobs Act," Tax Policy Center (December 8, 2017), tables 9–12; and TPC Staff, "Distributional Analysis of the Conference Agreement for the Tax Cuts and Jobs Act," Tax Policy Center (December 18, 2017).

of $1,210. This makes the plan revenue neutral, but now the bottom three quintiles come out much worse off, the fourth quintile is somewhat better off, and only the top 20 percent is significantly better off. While it is unrealistic to expect a future Congress to enact a large lump-sum tax to pay back the loans taken out to finance the tax cuts, it is certainly plausible that broad-based spending cuts might result. In that case, lower-income families could be much worse off than if the tax cuts had never been enacted; tax cuts that favor the rich are offset later by cuts in expenditures that benefit the poor.

The last two financing options are more progressive. One option would be a surcharge set as a flat percentage of income (column 3). In that case, the bottom three quintiles are still made worse off than without the tax cuts, but the burden on low-income families is more modest. However, it is also possible that the high-income people who seem to be the big winners from the policy will ultimately end up worse off. If the tax cuts are ultimately financed with a tax increase proportional to tax liability, the top quintile's apparent $5,420 windfall turns into a tax increase of over $1,200. The message of this exercise is that deficit financing does not reduce the burden of government spending—on the contrary—but it certainly blurs which people will bear the burden.

It should also be noted that the efficiency effects of tax cuts also depend on how they are ultimately financed. But it is impossible to discern for sure either the effects on the economy or on the distribution of well-being without knowing how the tax cuts will be financed.

Is progressive taxation class warfare?

No. All societies must determine how to assign the burden of funding government, and how much to weigh fairness in this determination. In the United States, most people agree that the tax burden should depend on how well off one is. Exactly how the tax burden should vary between the poor, the middle class, and the rich will always be contentious, but the resolution of this issue—which depends on economic matters, as well as values—should be confronted rather than dismissed by sloganeering.

9

RUNNING A TAX SYSTEM

ADMINISTRATION AND ENFORCEMENT

How much does it cost to run the U.S. tax system?

The easy part of answering this question is to add up the budgets of the various tax administration agencies across the country. At the federal level, that would be the Internal Revenue Service, or IRS. In fiscal year 2017 IRS expenditures amounted to $11.5 billion, which comes to just 0.34 percent of all the taxes it oversees.[1] The 0.34 is a stunning decline of over one-third since 2010, when the percentage stood at 0.53. Over this seven-year period, collections rose by 46 percent while the nominal IRS budget fell by 7 percent.

Collecting revenue at a cost of just 34 cents per hundred dollars sounds pretty good, and indeed the IRS often trumpets this percentage as a sign of its great efficiency. Among developed countries, this is one of the lowest cost-to-revenue ratios.[2] But this percentage by itself doesn't tell us much about the efficacy of our tax collection process or tax administration. For one thing, countries vary widely in the scope of responsibilities placed on the tax authority. More importantly, a low ratio could simply mean that the task of collecting taxes is carried out poorly on some important dimensions, such as deterring evasion, so that revenue is collected in a capricious, inequitable, and inefficient manner. Thus, the drop from 0.53 to 0.34 could reflect improved efficiency or could be a sign that the IRS cannot enforce the tax system as effectively as it once could.[3]

The biggest reason why the 0.34 percent is an inadequate and incomplete measure of the cost of collecting taxes is that the IRS budget is only the tip of the iceberg. The bulk of the iceberg is the value of the time and the out-of-pocket expenses incurred both by taxpayers and by third parties such as employers who withhold and remit tax on behalf of their employees and provide information reports to the IRS. These costs, known as compliance costs, greatly exceed administrative costs, and therefore comprise most of the cost of collection. Our best estimate for the U.S. income tax compliance cost, done for fiscal year 2004, comes to 14.5 percent of individual and corporation income tax receipts—more than 40 times as large as the administrative costs! Extrapolating the 14.5 percent figure to fiscal year 2017 receipts yields a compliance cost of about $273 billion.[4] And it's possible that the precipitous drop in IRS funding has affected compliance costs. For example, with fewer resources the IRS is able to answer a smaller fraction of taxpayers' telephone calls, which might prompt them to seek out other, more costly sources of advice. Not to mention the fact that the taxpayers who do get through spend more time on hold waiting for their call to be answered.

More than half of compliance cost is the value of the time individuals spend on their tax affairs—an estimated 3.5 billion hours—including record-keeping, researching the law, and completing the returns. Assuming a 2,000-hour work-year, these hours translate into the equivalent of 1.75 million "hidden" IRS employees—you and us—who are essential to operating the self-assessment income tax system.

How does tax remittance and collection work?

Everyone would like the tax system to collect revenue with a minimum of hassle and invasion of privacy. But everyone also knows that some people will seek any advantage and escape their tax liability when they can get away with it, leaving everyone else—the dutiful and those without the opportunity to evade successfully—facing a higher tax burden. Thus, no government can simply announce a tax system and then rely on taxpayers' sense of duty to remit what is owed. Some dutiful people will at first undoubtedly pay what they owe, but many others will not. Over time, the ranks of the dutiful will shrink, as they see how they are being taken advantage of by the others and realize there are no adverse consequences from noncompliance. Thus, paying taxes must be made a legal responsibility of citizens, with enforcement and penalties for noncompliance. Effective tax administration, and substantial taxpayer involvement, is needed to operate the tax collection system and to ensure that it runs efficiently and equitably.

For tax liabilities to be legitimate—neither arbitrary nor capricious—they must be based on observable and verifiable information. For a tax system to be cost-efficient, the information must be obtainable at a relatively low cost. For a tax like a retail sales tax, the key information is the volume and nature of transactions between businesses and consumers. For a personal tax like the individual income tax, information about individuals—their total income, sources of income, marital status, and perhaps also information about their charitable donations, medical expenses, and so on—must also be provided to the tax authority and monitored.

There are three key components of tax administration and enforcement: audits, information reporting and matching, and withholding. Although the dreaded tax audit gets the most attention, and therefore we'll talk about it first, the other two are no less important.

Who gets audited and why? What's the DIF?

The IRS publishes the percentage of income tax returns that are audited in broad classes of taxpayers. Overall, in fiscal year 2017, 0.6 percent of individual income tax returns, 1 percent of corporation income tax returns, and 8.2 percent of estate tax returns were audited.[5] The audit rate is highest for those who report high income: 4.4 percent if your total reported positive income exceeds $1 million, 0.8 percent if your income is between $200,000 and $1 million, and 0.2 percent for returns with income less than $200,000. Among corporations, the bigger ones are more likely to be audited: about 0.7 percent of corporations with total assets of less than $10 million, 6.4 percent for corporations with assets between $10 million and $1 billion, and 58.4 percent for the largest category—the 616 corporations with assets over $20 billion. Indeed, a majority of the very biggest corporations are subject to a continual IRS audit, with the audit team given a more or less permanent office at corporate headquarters.

While the likelihood of audit generally increases with income, returns that claimed the refundable Earned Income Tax Credit were more likely to be audited than any income category except millionaires. In 2017, 1.4 percent of such returns, which are filed by low-income working households, were selected for examination.

To economize on its resources, the IRS would like to target its audits to those tax returns more likely to have some funny business going on. To do so, it uses a procedure known as the DIF, standing for the Discriminant Function System, which calculates a numeric score for each individual and some corporate tax returns that reflect the potential for a tax liability increase upon audit, based on past IRS experience with similar returns.[6] Getting a high DIF score increases the likelihood that an examination of your return will result in a change to your income tax liability and is an important—but not the only—factor in determining which returns are audited. A return may also be selected for audit if information received via third-party documentation, such as a Form W-2 from your employer, does not match the information on your return. In addition, your return may be selected for audit—or you may be contacted about whether you should but didn't file a return—as a result of information the IRS acquires from a host of other sources, including newspapers, public records, and from other individuals. The IRS Whistleblower Office pays people who identify persons who fail to remit the tax that they owe. If the whistleblower provides specific and credible information that the IRS uses to collect taxes, penalties, interest, or other amounts from a noncompliant taxpayer, it may award the whistleblower up to 30 percent of the additional collections.

Source: Cartoon © Mark Parisi. Permission granted for use, www.offthemark.com.

What is information reporting?

Certain transactions that trigger tax liability must be reported to the tax authority, even though the party that reports the information does not have statutory liability for the tax. This system provides the tax authority with information that can be compared against the amount of tax liability actually reported, allowing suspect returns to be identified and followed up on. In this case, successful evasion requires coordination between the party providing the information report and the party responsible for remittance, but—and here's the key—their incentives and willingness to falsify the data are unlikely to be the same and may even work in opposite directions.

Thus, a working system of information reporting discourages noncompliance by increasing the risk of detection at relatively low cost to the tax authority. It forms a central element of all modern tax systems. In common with all other developed countries, the United States requires information reporting (and withholding—see below) by employers on wages and salaries. Information reporting, but generally not withholding, is also required of financial institutions that pay interest and corporations that pay dividends. Information reports also cover certain gambling winnings, mortgage interest, proceeds from sales of stock and homes, student loan interest, tuition payments, IRA and health savings account information, as well as partnership and S corporation income and estate or trust distributions. In fiscal year 2017, the IRS received 3.6 billion information returns, 90 percent of them electronically. Discrepancies between information returns and tax returns resulted in $6.7 billion of additional assessments.[7]

A law passed in 2008 expanded the scope of information reporting to credit cards. As of 2012, financial firms that process credit or debit card payments were required to send their clients and, more importantly, to the IRS, an annual form documenting the year's transactions. Form 1099-K must be filed when a merchant has at least 200 payment transactions a year totaling more than $20,000, and applies to all payment processors, including PayPal, and others that service very small businesses. A small business reporting less revenue than what shows up on the 1099-K forms has some explaining to do.

How far to expand information reporting involves a delicate policy trade-off. Certainly having more third-party information makes the job of the IRS easier. But it requires the reporting party to track information and to send this information both to the IRS and to the taxpayer.

How can the United States "require" foreign financial institutions to report on U.S. taxpayers?

By making them an offer they couldn't refuse—the Foreign Account Tax Compliance Act (FATCA), which was signed into law by President Obama in March 2010. The law contains detailed provisions regarding the steps to be taken by foreign banks to identify accounts owned by U.S. taxpayers, including cases where accounts are held through corporate entities, and to report to the IRS about those accounts and the income they produce, either directly or via their home government. What was the irresistible offer? Payments of U.S.-source income to any noncompliant foreign bank are subject to a 30 percent withholding tax—a killer charge for any financial institution doing significant international business. FATCA was passed to address the concern that many wealthy Americans were evading tax by keeping their money in foreign banks.

What is tax withholding?

Withholding refers to the situation where some or all of a tax liability must be remitted to the tax authority by someone other than the party that nominally "owes" the tax. Withholding allows the tax authority to collect the bulk of personal tax liability from a much smaller number of larger entities—usually businesses—who have more sophisticated record-keeping and accounting systems. It also acts as a revenue safeguard, ensuring that some tax is remitted even when the statutory bearer fails to file a return or otherwise disregards their tax obligations. And some taxpayers may value the forced saving aspect of payroll withholding because it usually guarantees that they do not have to write a check at tax time. (See page 216, "Do most people get tax refunds?")

Withholding is usually restricted to businesses and government agencies. Individuals in their capacity as employers and consumers are usually excluded—they are too numerous, with too high fixed costs, to be suitable withholding agents. A common source of tension is the conditions under which an employer is required to withhold for someone who works for the company. It must withhold with respect to payments to workers deemed to be employees but not those deemed to be independent contractors. Which category a worker falls under depends on the degree of control the company exerts over working conditions and the worker's independence. This has become a big issue for companies like Uber, which classifies its drivers as independent contractors.

To be able to withhold the appropriate amount of tax, the withholding agent must have an ongoing relationship with the statutory bearer of the tax, or, alternatively, the withholding scheme must be sufficiently simple to avoid the need for such a relationship, as is true for impersonal, usually flat-rate, taxes.

Who ultimately bears the burden of the compliance costs associated with withholding and information reporting? In the short term, it falls on the owners of the withholding businesses, although, like other business expenses, the costs can usually be deducted from taxable income (reducing tax liability), and so get partially transferred to the government. Who ultimately bears the burden of compliance costs depends on the same demand-and-supply forces that determine the incidence of taxes themselves—they may be passed on to customers, workers, or others.

A few countries provide explicit compensation to income tax withholding agents. Most (the United States included) do not, but may partially compensate withholding agents by allowing a time lag between when tax liability is triggered and when remittance is due, so interest can be earned on the tax withheld before being remitted. Some American states offer "vendor discounts" to retailers who remit retail sales tax, often justified as a recompense for the compliance costs incurred.[8]

Upon further reflection, though, employer withholding is just the most familiar example of the general irrelevance of who remits tax for the question of who bears the burden of tax. (See page 24, "Who really bears the burden of tax?" for the general rule, and page 26, "Are there cases in practice where it does matter who writes the check?")

Why do people cheat on their taxes? Why do they comply?

Tax evasion has been around as long as taxes have.[9] The history of taxation is replete with episodes of evasion, often notable for their inventiveness. During the third century, many wealthy Romans buried their jewelry or stocks of gold coin to evade the luxury tax, and homeowners in eighteenth-century England temporarily bricked up their fireplaces to escape notice of the hearth tax collector. Over the years many prominent people have been caught, or at least accused of, tax cheating. Perhaps the most famous American convicted of tax evasion was Al Capone, who was sent to Alcatraz for that crime rather than the more lurid illegal acts he is commonly associated with. More recent examples of Americans tainted with tax scandals include Nicolas Cage, Martha Stewart, and Donald Trump's lawyer, Michael Cohen.

Economists have an instinctive answer to why people cheat on their taxes—people evade when they think they can get away with it. This is consistent with what humorist Dave Barry had to say about tax compliance—"We'll try to cooperate fully with the IRS, because, as citizens, we feel a strong patriotic duty not to go to jail." People consider the chances of getting away with evasion and the likely penalty if they are caught, and decide whether to evade in just the same way they would decide whether to take any other gamble; that it is illegal is only relevant because penalties may apply. This cost-benefit story for tax evasion explains well the broad facts about

Milton Friedman and the Invention of Income Tax Withholding

Renowned economist and Nobel laureate Milton Friedman was a fierce advocate of free markets and limited government. But during his time at the Treasury Department during World War II, he was part of a small group that implemented income tax withholding, in part to combat wartime inflation. Given the circumstances, he didn't regret his role, but became an opponent of withholding later in life. He recounted the origins of withholding in a 1995 interview:

> I was an employee at the Treasury Department. We were in a wartime situation. How do you raise the enormous amount of taxes you need for wartime? We were all in favor of cutting inflation. I wasn't as sophisticated about how to do it then as I would be now, but there's no doubt that one of the ways to avoid inflation was to finance as large a fraction of current spending with tax money as possible.
>
> In World War I, a very small fraction of the total war expenditure was financed by taxes, so we had a doubling of prices during the war and after the war. At the outbreak of World War II, the Treasury was determined not to make the same mistake again.
>
> You could not do that during wartime or peacetime without withholding. And so people at the Treasury tax research department, where I was working, investigated various methods of withholding. I was one of the small technical group that worked on developing it.
>
> One of the major opponents of the idea was the IRS. Because every organization knows that the only way you can do anything is the way they've always been doing it. This was something new, and they kept telling us how impossible it was. It was a very interesting and very challenging intellectual task. I played a significant role, no question about it, in introducing withholding. I think it's a great mistake for peacetime, but in 1941–43, all of us were concentrating on the war.
>
> I have no apologies for it, but I really wish we hadn't found it necessary and I wish there were some way of abolishing withholding now.

Source: "Best of Both Worlds: An Interview with Milton Friedman," interview by Brian Doherty, *Reason* magazine, June 1995, quoted in Timothy Taylor, "How Milton Friedman Helped Invent Income Tax Withholding," Conversable Economist blog, April 12, 2014, http://conversableeconomist.blogspot.com/2014/04/how-milton-friedman-helped-invent.html.

tax evasion. The IRS calculates that the rate of noncompliance is just 1 percent for wages and salaries. This is not surprising, because information reporting and withholding by employers means that the chances of getting away with this type of evasion are very small—your employer has told the IRS what it paid you, and the IRS computers will check that you reported this income. In sharp contrast, the estimated noncompliance rate for self-employment income is an astounding 63 percent.[10] Most self-employment income is not reported on information returns and there is no tax withholding, which makes evasion much more difficult to detect.

Nonetheless, considerable experimental (and anecdotal) evidence suggests that, for many people, tax evasion involves more than amoral cost-benefit calculation. Some social scientists stress the importance of intrinsic motivation—the idea that taxpayers comply with tax liabilities because of civic virtue or a sense of duty. Given intrinsic motivation, more punitive enforcement policies could backfire by making people feel that they pay taxes because they have to, rather than because they ought to. They switch from thinking of taxpaying as a civic duty to thinking of it as a cost-benefit calculation. A field experiment conducted in Israel found evidence of intrinsic motivation in another setting. In order to encourage parents to pick their children up from day care on time, a center implemented fines for parents who were late. To their surprise, this led to an *increase* in the number of parents arriving late, probably because parents stopped feeling guilty about late pickups and started viewing added minutes as a purchase like any other.[11]

Others argue that the decision to evade tax may depend on perceptions of the fairness of the tax system or what the government uses tax revenues for. Henry David Thoreau resisted the payment of poll taxes to support the Mexican-American War in protest of what he viewed as an immoral government policy.[12] During the Vietnam War, a number of pacifist war protesters, including Joan Baez, Noam Chomsky, and Gloria Steinem, argued that it was immoral to pay income taxes that would go toward supporting an "imperialistic" American military machine, and refused to pay some or all of their income taxes. Such individual judgments can be complex; for example, expenditures on warfare might be tolerated in a patriotic period, but rejected during another period characterized by antimilitarism. This idea that people are more likely to comply with their tax obligations, even against their short-term material interest, if they believe in what government is doing is certainly plausible and intuitive, but there is little hard evidence, for the United States anyway, that this is a big part of the tax evasion story.[13]

Tax noncompliance seems related to some other observable characteristics of taxpayers. On average, married filers and taxpayers younger than 65 have significantly higher average levels of noncompliance than others. There is some evidence that men evade more than women. There also seems to be substantial heterogeneity in tax evasion. The IRS tax gap studies, discussed subsequently, concluded that, within any group defined by income, age, or other demographic category, there are some who evade, some who do not, and even a few who overstate tax liability.[14]

A recent study based on IRS audit data found that the percentage of true income not reported on tax returns rises with income, while the ratio of underreported tax liability to true tax owed is higher for low-income individuals. The latter is a result of our graduated tax structure, which implies that the same percentage reduction in reported income results in a higher percentage of underreported tax for a low-income individual relative to a higher income taxpayer.[15]

How much cheating is there?

This is not an easy question to answer—would a cheater respond honestly to a survey question about this? The IRS has produced the best estimates of the extent and nature of tax noncompliance anywhere in the world. Beginning in 1979, the IRS has periodically estimated what it calls the "tax gap," which measures how much tax should be paid, but is not paid voluntarily and on time. These studies provide separate estimates of the failure to pay the proper amount of tax due to underreporting of tax due on tax returns, non-filing, and non-payment or late payment of taxes owed. The IRS comes up with its estimates by combining information from a program of random intensive audits with information obtained from ongoing enforcement activities and special studies about sources of income—like tips and cash earnings of informal suppliers such as nannies and housepainters—that can be difficult to uncover even in an intensive audit. It does its best to adjust the information obtained from the random audits to account for what a typical auditor would miss during an examination.

The most recent tax gap estimates, published in 2016, pertain to tax years 2008 through 2010. The average overall annual gross tax gap estimate for these years was $458 billion, of which the IRS expected to eventually recover $52 billion, resulting in a "net tax gap"—that is the tax not expected to be collected—of $406 billion, or 16.3 percent of the tax that should have been paid (table 9.1).[16]

More than two-thirds of all underreporting of income happens on the individual income tax. For the individual income tax, understated income—as opposed to overstating of exemptions, deductions, adjustments, and credits—accounts for over 80 percent of individual underreporting of tax. Taxpayers who were required to file an individual tax return, but did not file on time (or ever), accounted for less than 10 percent of the gap. While the individual income tax comprises about two-thirds of the estimated underreporting, the corporation income tax accounts for about 11 percent, and the payroll tax gap makes up about one-fifth of total underreporting.

The extent of misreporting varies enormously by the type of income or deduction. Based on an earlier tax gap study, only 1 percent of wages and salaries are underreported, and

Table 9.1 Tax Gap Estimates, Tax Years 2008–2010 (money amounts are in billions of dollars)

Tax gap component	
Estimated total true tax liability	2,496
Gross tax gap	458
Overall voluntary compliance rate	81.7%
Net tax gap	406
Overall net compliance rate	83.7%
Non-filing gap	32
Underreporting gap	387
Individual income tax	264
Nonbusiness income	64
Business income	125
Adjustments, deductions, exemptions	19
Credits	40
Corporation income tax	41
Small corporations (assets < $10M)	13
Large corporations (assets > $10M)	28
Employment tax	81
Self-employment tax	65
FICA and unemployment tax	16
Estate tax	1
Underpayment gap	39

Source: https://www.irs.gov/pub/newsroom/tax%20gap%20estimates%20for%202008%20through%202010.pdf.

7 percent of taxable interest and dividends (plus some other income sources) are misreported. (These percentages exclude amounts associated with non-filing.) Of course, wages and salaries, interest, and dividends must all be reported to the IRS by those who pay them; in addition, wages and salaries are subject to employer withholding. Self-employment business income is subject to little or no information reporting, and its estimated noncompliance rate is sharply higher. As mentioned earlier, an estimated 63 percent of nonfarm proprietor income is not reported, which by itself accounts for more than one-third of the total estimated underreporting for the individual

income tax. All in all, over one-half of the tax gap is attributable to the underreporting of business income, of which nonfarm proprietor income is the largest component.[17]

Given the difficulty of accurately measuring tax evasion, it's very hard to say whether it's been going up, down, or staying roughly the same. The estimated tax gap percentage for 2008–2010 is not much different from earlier tax gap estimates. Accounting for changes in methodology and the uncertainty of the estimating procedures, one cannot infer any statistically significant trend in compliance through 2010.

How much more tax could the IRS collect with better enforcement?

Claiming to be able to raise more revenue without increasing tax rates and sparing honest (hard-working) Americans has in the past proven irresistible for many, especially Democratic, politicians. The $400 billion-plus tax gap becomes an inviting target. But, realistically, more and smarter enforcement could bring in no more than about one-fifth of that total. This would come from expanding information reporting and targeting the cash economy and from special initiatives such as the crackdown on offshore bank accounts. However, while only a small portion of the tax gap could cost-effectively be collected with more enforcement, it remains the case that spending on enforcement, at least at current levels, brings in much more revenue than it costs.

Should states be able to tax Internet and mail-order sales from other states?

The Internet and e-commerce have a direct and important impact on states' retail sales taxes. Imagine if a Michigan resident buys a bookcase over the Internet from Ikea. Like residents of all 45 states with a retail sales tax, Michigan residents owe tax at the retail sales tax rate on purchases from out of state that are used in their home state. Technically, this is called a use tax, but the base and rate are the same as the sales tax. But who must remit this tax liability? Ikea? Until very recently, the answer was probably no, because the Supreme Court had ruled that out-of-state retailers need not remit the sales tax liability to the purchaser's state of residence unless that company happens to have a physical presence, such as a store, business office, or warehouse in that state. The Court ruled in 1992 that requiring the remote seller to remit the tax would violate the Commerce Clause of the Constitution.

The problem with requiring consumers to remit the use tax is that very few did so; for example, the Michigan Treasury estimated that in 2010, it collected about 1.3 percent of the use tax due on remote sales to Michigan residents.[18] Overall, estimates put the revenue loss to all states at between $8 and $33 billion per year.[19] Many prominent "brick-and-mortar" retailers, including Walmart, argued (reasonably, in our opinion) that there's no reason to provide remote retailers with a tax-connected advantage.

The landscape of taxing online sales has recently changed a lot. First, the elephant in the online sales room, Amazon, by April 2018 had agreed with each state that levies a retail sales tax to remit the applicable sales tax to the state where the purchaser resides (for its own sales, but usually not for third-party sellers that use Amazon's platform). Then, in June 2018, the Supreme Court effectively reversed its previous decision by ruling that all but very small Internet sellers could be required to remit sales tax even in states where they have no physical presence. Thus, the tax disadvantage for brick-and-mortar sellers looks to soon shrink substantially.

Why not audit everyone?

A more interesting question is how much more tax the IRS *should* collect. The IRS does not audit everyone, for good reason—for the same reason we don't station a police officer at every street corner, or a parking enforcement officer at every meter: it would be too costly, relative to the social benefits of reduced—or even eradicated—crime. The same is true for beefing up income tax enforcement so much that no one attempts to evade. The costs to the IRS—as well as to compliant taxpayers who would face costly and highly intrusive audits every year—would far outweigh any benefits.

Source: Cagle Cartoons, Inc.

Why not ramp up the penalty for evasion?

Jacking up the penalties for tax evasion might also reduce tax evasion. Right now a "substantial understatement" penalty applies to individuals whose tax is understated by the greater of 10 percent of the correct tax or $5,000, and a "negligence or disregard of rules or regulations" penalty is assessed on individuals who "carelessly, recklessly or intentionally disregard IRS rules and regulations." Both penalties are equal to 20 percent of the net understatement of tax. The civil penalty for underpayment resulting from fraud—intentionally falsifying information on a tax return—is equal to 75 percent of the underpayment of tax. Attempting to evade or defeat tax is a felony carrying a fine up to $100,000 ($500,000 in the case of a corporation) and imprisonment for up to five years. In fiscal year 2017, the IRS assessed 39 million civil penalties amounting to $27 billion, $13 billion of which was eventually abated.[20] They initiated over 3,000 criminal investigations, which led to 2,300 convictions and incarceration of 2,043 people.[21] One new development is the use of what is known as "collateral sanctions" in tax enforcement policy. A law passed in 2015 allowed the IRS to deny new or renewed passports to people with substantial tax debts, defined as tax debt of $51,000 or more—including assessed tax, penalties, and interest. The IRS says at least 362,000 people are affected.[22]

We resist substantially increasing the penalty for tax evasion for a couple of reasons. There is a vague but widespread belief that the punishment should fit the crime, and we are also reluctant to inflict very high penalties when the IRS occasionally misidentifies perpetrators.

Are refundable tax credits especially prone to tax evasion?

Soon after the Earned Income Tax Credit was introduced, an IRS audit program found that 34 percent of claimants filed for too large a credit, and 29 percent of claimants were simply ineligible.[23] Part of the EITC error rate is honest mistakes—determining eligibility is complicated, especially for low-income households that may share housing with partners or relatives who might themselves be eligible for credits that they did not claim. But the audit statistics provoked indignation. Congress required more audits of returns with EITC claims, and several statutory and administrative changes were made.

Whether the EITC is especially prone to fraud is hard to tell. Only millionaires are audited at a higher rate than EITC recipients. When the Treasury Inspector General for Tax

Administration examined tax compliance among EITC recipients, he concluded that they were most likely to cheat in the same circumstances as higher-income taxpayers. For example, self-employed people were much more likely to misstate their incomes to appear to qualify for a higher EITC than wage and salary workers.

Do most people get tax refunds?

Of all individual income tax returns filed in fiscal year 2017, 80 percent of taxpayers received a refund, averaging about $3,200.[24] Why this is so is somewhat of a mystery. It is not hard to see why the IRS set up the standard employer withholding tables so that withholding usually exceeds tax liability and generates a refund. This provides a financial incentive for people to file a tax return in order to receive a refund, and the filing provides the IRS with information about the taxpaying population that is helpful in monitoring the tax collection process. Also, taxpayers are more likely to underreport if they owe money at tax time than if they expect a refund. And, finally, the IRS probably thinks that sending out refunds helps its public image.

But why do taxpayers go along? By filing a Form W-4, taxpayers can adjust their withholding to minimize or even eliminate their refund. This way their refund would be lower, but their tax payments early in the tax year would be lower, too. By so doing, they could stop providing the government the equivalent of an interest-free loan. These days, when interest rates are very low, the cost of having the government take a larger bite of one's paycheck only to have it refunded back at the end of the year with no interest paid is not large, but most people were getting refunds even when interest rates were sky-high in the early 1980s.

Several factors might come into play. Some people may be afraid of incurring the penalty for under-withholding. Others may simply not be aware that they can adjust how much is withheld from their paychecks. Finally, for some people overpaying their tax during the year so as to qualify for a large refund is the best, or maybe only, way to accumulate a substantial sum of money, so that the refund is a form of self-induced forced saving.[25]

How many people use tax preparers? Do they help or hinder compliance?

The IRS has estimated that there are between 900,000 and 1.2 million paid tax return preparers.[26] In tax year 2016, 53.5 percent of individual income tax returns were filed with the help of a paid tax preparer. Amazingly, 46.2 percent of individuals filing the simple Form 1040A used a paid preparer, as did 37.5 percent of those filing the even simpler 1040EZ.[27] Somewhat surprisingly, of those returns that qualify for the EITC, generally low-income individuals and families, 47 percent used a paid preparer in 2015.[28] The 53.5 percent overall rate is certainly one of the highest in the world, but is not the highest—in 2015, 72 percent of Australian income tax returns were filed with professional preparer assistance.[29] The high U.S. preparer usage rate is in part a symptom of the complexity of the income tax system, as taxpayers want to be sure they comply with the law but also want to make sure that they take advantage of all the tax breaks they legally qualify for. It certainly makes sense that not everyone becomes an expert on the tax system, and that professional expertise is available for hire. In this capacity tax preparers may improve the quality of the income tax system. Notably, the percentage using professional tax preparers has come down a bit in recent years—it was 58 percent in 2008.

Tax preparers are a heterogeneous bunch, to be sure. Most view their job as helping taxpayers comply with the law, and alerting them to credits, deductions, and other tax-saving provisions they qualify for. But a few are in cahoots with unscrupulous taxpayers, and a few others actively encourage tax cheating. Such fraud generally involves the preparation and filing of false income tax returns with inflated personal or business expenses, false deductions, unallowable credits, or excessive exemptions. Preparers may also manipulate income figures to fraudulently obtain tax credits, such as the Earned Income Tax Credit. In some situations, the taxpayer may not even know about the false expenses, deductions, exemptions, or credits shown on their tax returns.

In 2011, the IRS announced that tax preparers would have to register with the IRS and pass a competency test. However, a court ruling in 2013 found that the IRS lacked the statutory authority to regulate preparers and Congress has not yet chosen to authorize the program.

10

SIMPLICITY AND COMPLEXITY

How complicated is the U.S. income tax?

In a 2015 poll, 72 percent of Americans said they were bothered by tax complexity, with 44 percent declaring it bothered
them a lot.[1] How complex it actually is depends on who you
are or, more precisely, how complicated your financial affairs
are. If you have only wage and salary income, minimal capital
income, no dependents, and too few deductible expenses to
make itemizing worthwhile, it's a breeze. You can file Form
1040EZ, which fits on just one page and has just 14 lines. If,
however, you have not only wage and salary income, but also
rental income, capital gains, itemized deductions, foreign income, partnership income, and so on, calculating taxable income and tax liability can be bewilderingly complicated.

How is tax complexity measured, and how should it be measured?

According to the Tax Foundation, as of 2015 the number of words
in the Internal Revenue Code, not just pertaining to the income
tax, came to 2.4 million and the regulations comprised 7.7 million, amounting to just over 10 million words between the code
and the regulations explaining the code. This compares to their
estimate of the total for 1955 of 1.4 million, suggesting a seven-
fold increase in 60 years.[2] Ten million-plus words to lay out the

tax law seems pretty darn complex. But hold on. The problem with the number of words or pages as a measure of complexity is that, although more pages and more words in the tax code and tax regulations are symptomatic of more complexity, it is also true that more words may clarify otherwise uncertain areas of the tax law, and thus reduce complexity in some cases. In addition, many of these words concern issues that will never come up for the vast majority of taxpayers. So talking about millions of words gets attention but is not very informative.

A more useful summary measure of tax complexity is the total resource cost of collecting the revenue—also called the cost of collection. The cost of collection is the sum of the tax authority's budget (administrative costs) and the compliance costs incurred both by taxpayers themselves and by third parties such as employers, who withhold and remit tax on behalf of their employees and provide information reports. This measure includes both the costs that must be incurred to comply with the tax law and costs that are incurred voluntarily to facilitate avoidance (tax plan) or even evasion of tax liability. It has the advantage that aspects of the tax code that affect few people will not count for much, and aspects that affect many people will tend to count a lot.

Although the resource cost of collection is a useful measure of complexity, it does not capture all of its policy implications. To see this, consider the following "simplification" proposal: relax the record-keeping and calculation requirements of a particular tax credit, so that the average taxpayer would need to spend only half as much time to qualify for the credit. Suppose that, in response to this change, the number of people who apply for and receive the credit quadruples. If judged solely on the resource cost measure, the tax system has become more complicated—total costs have doubled, after all. The policy question, though, is whether the process simplification is worthwhile, and to assess that one must also consider the social value of the credit being made available to more households who "deserve" it (and maybe also to some who do not).

Do fewer tax brackets promote simplicity?

Not really. Although many tax reform plans tout that they will cut the number of brackets (sometimes to just one, under a flat tax), the number of brackets does not matter much for tax simplicity. The complicated part of income tax is figuring out one's taxable income. Once that's done, figuring out tax liability is easy. In the old days, you could look it up in a tax table printed in the 1040 instruction booklet; these days tax software does the calculation for most people in a nanosecond.

Why is there a trade-off between simplicity and other goals such as fairness?

For one thing, fine justice, rather than rough justice, is costly. If we think it is fair that taxable income should be measured net of medical expenses, then people have to report—and the IRS has to monitor—people's medical expenses. If we think it is a good idea that people should get to deduct their charitable contributions, then we have to measure and monitor these deductions. Otherwise we could dispense with having to track these things and have a simpler income tax, but one in which tax liability would be the same between two families, each with $70,000 of income, but where one family incurred $20,000 of medical expenses and the other incurred none.

How fast are we moving toward e-filing?

In fiscal year 2017, 70 percent of all the returns the IRS received were filed electronically, as were 87 percent of the individual income tax returns. Of the 132 million individual returns filed electronically, 53 million were filed online by taxpayers, and 79 million were practitioner filed.[3] Two and a half million taxpayers, all with adjusted gross income below $66,000, used the IRS Free File program, a free federal income tax preparation and filing service developed through a partnership between the IRS and a group of private-sector tax software companies that can be accessed through www.irs.gov. For those with income below $66,000, it provides brand-name software for free; for those with higher income it offers online versions of the IRS paper forms and performs only basic calculations. Many believe the government should expand access to this free software, but this has been fiercely resisted by the software companies, who see it as an incursion into their business.

Processing and managing a tax return filed electronically is less resource-intensive than processing one filed manually, which is why the IRS prefers e-filing. The rapid increase in electronically prepared returns suggests that most taxpayers prefer it, too, in part because refunds are received significantly faster.

If almost everyone uses tax software or paid preparers, should we stop worrying about complexity? Should we start worrying about democracy?

Once most everyone, or their tax preparer, uses software, the consequences of complexity change. If the data inputted must be subject to complex calculations, they are done automatically and correctly, so calculation complexity becomes a nonissue. (If more and more data must be inputted, that remains a concern.) Thus, the outcry of citizens might be less of a bulwark against an even more labyrinthine tax system in the future.

This would be a problem for two reasons. First, an opaque tax system, where taxpayers have little sense how their income, expenses, and other attributes affect their tax liability, limits how engaged they can be in the tax policymaking process. Tax filing would provide little basis for evaluating the fairness—or any other criterion—of the tax system, as it applies to them or to others. As Charles McLure of the Hoover Institution has said, "Taxation without comprehension is as inimical to democracy as taxation without representation."[4]

An incomprehensible tax system may also render ineffective the incentives it is meant to provide, such as encouraging charitable contributions. This might not be a bad thing if those incentives were misguided, but it would be a very cynical policymaker who voted for incentives hoping that taxpayers wouldn't notice them.

Could most taxpayers be spared any filing requirement (as in the United Kingdom)?

In several countries with an income tax, most people need not file tax returns at all. We could do it here, but it would require major tax law changes. Return-free filing relies heavily on a process called "exact withholding," in which employers, financial institutions, and others remit tax liability on taxpayers' behalf in exactly the right amount so that no end-of-year reconciliation is necessary.

The main requirement for a return-free system is a relatively flat-rate tax schedule and few deductions and credits. In the simplest case, if we had a flat 25 percent income tax with no credits or deductions, then employers could withhold and remit 25 percent of wages and banks could withhold and remit 25 percent of interest and that would equal final tax liability for a taxpayer with only those two forms of income. However, under our current income tax, the standard deduction varies with filing status and there are multiple income tax brackets. Even if your employer knew your family size and filing status, your actual tax liability depends not only on your earnings from that job, but earnings from other jobs, spouse's earnings, and income from other sources. Deductions complicate tax liability even more, as do tax credits, eligibility for which may also depend on income and filing status. For that reason, return-free filing is infeasible without significant simplification and substantial reform.

The Bipartisan Policy Center's debt reduction task force (which co-author Burman served on) proposed a tax reform plan that the Tax Policy Center estimated would eliminate the tax filing requirement for about one-half of households. The proposal would have replaced personal exemptions (now eliminated), child-related tax credits (including the EITC), and the standard deduction with two refundable tax credits—one based on the number of children in the household and another based only on earnings of each spouse. The deductions for mortgage interest and charitable contributions would have been replaced with flat 15 percent refundable tax credits, paid directly to the mortgage holder or charity. There would be only two tax brackets—15 and 27 percent—and wages, interest, and dividends would be subject to withholding at a 15 percent rate. For most households in the 15 percent bracket, withholding would exactly match income tax liability, and so on April 15 no tax would be due and no tax return would have to be filed. Households with income from self-employment, in the 27 percent tax bracket, or with complex tax situations would still have to file.

Could the IRS fill out our tax returns for us?

It is feasible, at least for relatively simple returns, but it's not easy to implement. The basic idea is that data from information returns (e.g., wages from W-2 forms, interest and dividends from 1099 forms) would automatically be entered onto a web-based return for taxpayers, and all they would have to do is check to make sure that the information is accurate and complete, and sign (electronically). If information was missing or inaccurate, the taxpayer would have to do some work, but this process could still give most taxpayers a head start on filing. Australia, Belgium, Denmark, Finland, Norway, Spain, and Sweden prepare such "pre-filled" or "pre-populated" returns for their citizens.

But it's not something the IRS could implement tomorrow. For one thing, the IRS does not get some information returns until after the filing season is over. Employers and financial institutions would have to file sooner and the IRS would have to overhaul its information systems to match the data with taxpayer IDs early in the tax season. The IRS would also have to invest in people to track down anomalies and answer questions from taxpayers. Economists Joseph Cordes and Arlene Holen concluded that it would likely cost the IRS, employers, and financial institutions more than it would save taxpayers.[5] Apparently, policymakers in the aforementioned countries have concluded otherwise.

For many years, California offered the option of a pre-filled return, called ReadyReturn, for singles and heads of households with straightforward returns, and said it saved the state a lot of money on every return filed through the automated system. Only a small fraction of eligible Californians took advantage of ReadyReturn. Critics say this was because pre-filled returns were rife with errors, and taxpayers feared that the government had no incentive to let filers know about money-saving deductions and credits. On the other hand, lack of participation may primarily be due to ignorance—California had a tiny budget for publicizing the program—and the fact that federal tax returns must still be filed the old-fashioned way. There is also a concern that taxpayers might assume that the information on the government-filled return is accurate, which could increase the incidence of errors and penalties if, in fact, the government's information is flawed. ReadyReturn is no more, having been folded into California's free online filing application, CalFile, which does import information into the tax return that the California tax authority already has on record, such as the W-2 forms, as the ReadyReturn did.

Would simplifying tax compliance be unfair to H&R Block and Intuit?

One of the most peculiar arguments against tax process simplification is that it infringes on the inherent right of tax software makers to profit from the current complex tax system. That's not exactly the way the software companies put it, but that's the gist. They fought tooth and nail against California's ReadyReturn, and have also been implicated in the demise of Virginia's free online system, iFile, for preparing and filing state tax returns.[6] The tax software firms argue that the government has a conflict of interest because it benefits financially if it overstates taxpayers' liability. On the other hand, unlike businesses, the government works for the voters, so it has an incentive to represent their best interest. And, as Joseph Thorndike of Tax Analysts points out, if pre-filled returns have errors, taxpayers can vote with their feet and choose to continue using software and paid preparers.[7]

Joseph Cordes and Arlene Holen argue that "[g]overnment involvement in personal income tax preparation . . . would reduce competition in existing markets. . . . It could also have the unintended effect of reducing innovation in rapidly evolving software markets."[8] But the market only exists because the tax-filing requirement created it. By mitigating the burden of filing, the government is lessening a burden that it imposed itself. And we find it bizarre that the government should maximize taxpayers' compliance burdens as a way to boost innovation in the software industry.

What is a data retrieval platform?

One other process innovation, much less radical than a return-free system, is worth considering. Under a data retrieval system, taxpayers and paid preparers could view, access, and download tax information from a secure database maintained by the federal government, thus relieving them of having to obtain this information from employers, financial institutions, and other third parties, as they do now. Supporters argue that having such a platform would facilitate communication between the IRS, on the one hand, and between taxpayers and return preparers, on the other.[9]

Did the TCJA simplify the income tax?

Yes and no.[10] In the run-up to its passage, the chairman of the House Ways and Means Committee and the Speaker of the House said that, under the new tax system being contemplated, nine of 10 taxpayers could file on a postcard. The rhetorical emphasis on a postcard-sized tax form is more than a bit quaint now that nearly 90 percent of tax returns are filed using software. In any event, a new shrunken Form 1040 was unveiled for tax year 2018. The two-sided form is too large to qualify for the standard postcard rate and would reveal the filer's social security number unless enclosed in an envelope. It would eliminate more than half of the 78 line items on the previous form, but required as many as six new worksheets not on the postcard.[11]

The size of the Form 1040 may be a symbol of tax simplicity, but it is a side issue in assessing the answer to this question. As with the Tax Reform Act of 1986, a substantial simplification was achieved in the 2017 legislation by the near-doubling of the standard deduction, which is predicted to reduce the fraction of itemizing returns from about 26 percent to about 11 percent. Undoubtedly, this will reduce both administrative and compliance costs. To the extent that the itemized deductions should be subtracted from income to obtain a better measure of well-being, as is probably true for most medical expenses, this provision will also erode horizontal equity. Eliminating the corporate alternative minimum tax is certainly a simplification, as is substantially limiting the scope of the individual alternative minimum tax so that it affects many fewer taxpayers.

TCJA also adds some nontrivial complications, especially in certain provisions affecting choice of corporate form and the attempts to block income shifting of corporate taxes. Enforcing the new rules that allow a deduction of up to 20 percent of the income of pass-through entities subject to myriad limits and restrictions is very complex. One newspaper article described the "crack and pack" strategies that businesses are exploring to get around the provision excluding high-income lawyers, doctors, and other professionals from this deduction. One lawyer quoted in the article spoke of splitting his law firm into one entity holding four lawyers and the other holding the 26-person administrative staff, presumably in the hope that the latter could be exempt from the statutory limitation.[12] An even bigger problem might be monitoring the larger incentives now built in to reclassify labor income as business income to gain the 20 percent deduction. In addition, the new rules designed to limit multinational companies' income-shifting in the new world of a modified territorial system, like the BEAT and GILTI mentioned in chapter 3, are labyrinthine.

11

THE BEHAVIORAL ECONOMICS OF TAX POLICY (OR TAX POLICY FOR IMPERFECT HUMANS)

What is behavioral economics?

The standard economic model assumes that individuals and businesses are rational, well informed, and good at math. Individuals make themselves and their families as happy as they can over the course of a lifetime subject to the resources they have at their disposal. Businesses make as much money as they can. The effects of taxes in these models are pretty straightforward—they change prices (for example, a sales tax raises the after-tax price of taxed items) and incomes, but the consumer's or household's basic problem is unchanged. Much of modern economics has tried to make these models more realistic—for example, by looking at what happens when businesses or individuals do not have complete information. But standard economics doesn't account for the fact that people routinely make decisions that look like mistakes in the context of the rational optimization framework.

Behavioral economics draws on lessons from psychology and other social sciences to try to understand and predict the behavior of real humans rather than the ultra-rational "econs" of standard economic theory.[1] Some of the insights come from laboratory experiments where people (often students, because academics find them easy to recruit) are placed in various situations and asked to make choices. Increasingly, governments are drawing on the lessons of behavioral economics to experiment with different ways of implementing policies to see if they can get better outcomes (such as higher participation in public programs or better compliance with tax laws).

Behavioral economics can help explain anomalies that don't fit in the standard model. Understanding these anomalies can help in designing better public policies.

Why does behavioral economics matter for tax policy?

It matters because it offers many examples of low-cost interventions that can help public policy better achieve its objectives. As we noted in chapter 7, the government spends over $1 trillion a year on tax expenditures intended to influence economic decisions. Often the results are disappointing. For example, some of the biggest tax subsidies are aimed at encouraging workers to save for retirement, but there's scant evidence of success. Since the introduction of tax-free IRAs and 401(k) plans, the personal saving rate in the United States has actually fallen. There's a vigorous debate in the economics profession about whether these subsidies increase saving at all, with some economists believing that contributions to tax-free accounts simply replace saving that would otherwise have occurred in taxable accounts. Tax revenues fall, but it's not clear that there's much if any new saving.

In an influential paper, economists Brigitte Madrian and Dennis Shea found that simply enrolling people in retirement plans at the time they start work with an option to *not* participate, rather than requiring them to make a positive election to participate, could have huge effects on participation.[2] Participation rates increased by 20 to 80 percent. Research from around the world shows that most people are passive in their investment decisions.[3] Changing default options can have large and long-lasting effects on individuals' decisions and on the effectiveness of public policy in altering behavior.

Why do sticks (fees) work better than carrots (bonuses) at changing humans' behavior?

One of the key insights of behavioral economics is the phenomenon of "loss aversion." People dislike losses more than they value gains of similar sizes. That is, sticks work better than carrots.

Tatiana Homonoff of the NYU Wagner School found striking evidence of this in a surprising setting. The District of Columbia imposed a tax of five cents per bag on grocery store customers who did not bring their own bags.[4] In pure economic terms, the bag tax should have had the same effect as the five-cent rebate that the grocery store chain Whole Foods offered to customers who brought their own bag. In each case, customers saved five cents for every bag they brought from home, but the rebate had no measurable effect on behavior, whereas shoppers drastically reduced the number of bags they used after the District imposed the five-cent tax.

This could have important policy implications beyond bag usage. Policymakers in the United States have been wary about imposing environmental taxes, instead opting for a variety of tax subsidies. But taxes on gas guzzlers could have much bigger effects on conservation than a comparable subsidy on fuel-efficient vehicles (as exists for electric and hybrid vehicles). There's a standard economic reason—a big tax (as opposed to a bag tax, which is pretty inconsequential) makes the gas guzzler harder to afford. But loss aversion means that people will react more to the tax (regardless of whether they can afford it) than to the subsidy.[5]

Do excise taxes depress spending more than equivalent sales taxes?

A surprising finding for tax nerds like us is that many humans don't notice or respond to taxes unless they are made quite apparent. To better understand this behavior, Raj Chetty, Adam Looney, and Kory Kroft carried out an ingenious experiment.[6]

They added the sales tax to the price labels in some aisles of a grocery store, while leaving them out elsewhere. By comparing people's purchasing decisions before and after this change and between stores with the new labels and those without, they found a significant drop in purchases consistent with the higher tax-inclusive prices. That is, people seemed to ignore the sales tax, which is added at the register, unless effort was made to make the tax salient.[7]

These findings could help policymakers choose between otherwise equivalent taxes. For example, a sales tax has an effect on the price of taxed goods and services similar to that of a value-added tax (VAT) except that the VAT is built into the price, while the sales tax isn't. The evidence from Chetty and his colleagues suggests that humans would make decisions more consistent with their preferences with the salient tax—the VAT—than with the hidden sales tax.

Should we tax internalities like externalities?

As we explained in chapter 4, there's a good reason to tax externalities like pollution because they cause harm to others. But what about things that people do to hurt themselves? Standard economics would argue that people are taking their own interests into account when making decisions and, if nobody else is harmed, government should stay out of the decisions. (Libertarians would argue on philosophical grounds that government intervention is an unwarranted intrusion on liberty even if people are making mistakes.) Donald Marron argues that behavioral biases, such as a tendency to overvalue the present, mean that the present self is not accounting for the preferences of the future self and may thus harm the latter. This intertemporal self-harm is an example of what economists call "internalities."[8]

In that context, it may make sense to tax internalities like externalities if we can identify the activity that causes harm and measure the harm. This argument is sometimes used to justify taxes on sugar-sweetened drinks because their consumption is related to obesity and associated health problems. This is an internality if when people decide how much soda to consume they do not take into account how it will adversely affect their health later in life. However, this is complicated because the drinks can cause health problems for some consumers but not others, so there is no tax rate that is right for everybody.

Also some people may fully understand the risks and decide that their current choice is worth it. And some critics object to the notion of government second-guessing people's decisions. To them, the whole notion of internalities is simply paternalism dressed up as economics.

© John McPherson/Distributed by Universal Uclick via CartoonStock.com

"Instead of passing the fat tax on soda, the government requires that people do 10 chin-ups before the cooler will open."

Source: www.CartoonStock.com.

*The tax on people without health insurance (the "individual
mandate") was the least popular feature of Obamacare. Is it
possible that many who were induced to seek insurance were
made better off?*

The TCJA repealed the tax penalty on those who do not purchase health insurance. It saves the government money
because, without the penalty, many fewer people opt for
subsidized ACA health insurance, and many who are eligible
for Medicaid don't bother to sign up. In the standard economic model, this is a win for rational consumers. They don't
get health insurance because they're better off without it. And,
after the TCJA, they are spared the penalty tax.

But behavioral economics may suggest that many people
who opt not to get coverage might be worse off. Paul Krugman
draws the analogy to the automatic enrollment in retirement
plans we discussed earlier.[9] Some people, prompted by the
penalty tax, went to the ACA exchanges to seek coverage only
to discover that they were eligible for free insurance under
Medicaid in states that had expanded coverage. Some had
been eligible for free insurance under Medicaid all along but
did not know it until they went to sign up at the health insurance marketplace. Krugman argues that if there were automatic enrollment in the Medicaid program, many people who
would not opt to seek coverage absent the penalty tax would
not have opted out. The seemingly coercive penalty tax made
those households better off by prompting them to do what was
clearly in their self-interest.

Whether the gains to those families offset the losses to those
who would have chosen to opt out absent a penalty tax and
those who chose to pay the penalty and forgo coverage is unclear, however.

Does tax complexity cause people to make costly mistakes?

Apparently so. Back in 2002, the General Accounting Office (now
known as the Government Accountability Office) estimated that

over two million taxpayers overpaid their taxes because they failed to itemize their deductions when it would have saved them money to do so; they either didn't understand their options or they judged it wasn't worth the time, money, and energy to itemize. Another study found that receiving personalized advice about the Earned Income Tax Credit induced more eligible people to claim it. And, in a recent lab experiment, subjects presented with an underlying identical, but more complicated-looking tax schedule, were more likely to make mistakes when faced with the same new tax rule, usually by underreacting to it—complexity-induced decision paralysis.[10]

People often misperceive their marginal tax rate, which is the tax applicable to the last dollar of income. That rate should govern decisions to work, save, and engage in tax avoidance or evasion.[11] If they systematically underestimate their marginal tax rate, the tax system distorts behavior less than economists believe. (See page xxx, "Why do economists think that raising funds costs much more than the tax sticker price?") But it also means that tax incentives may be far less effective than policymakers anticipate.

PART III

A TOUR OF THE SAUSAGE FACTORY

12

MISPERCEPTIONS AND REALITY IN THE POLICY PROCESS

What does the public know about taxes?

Not all that much. For example, according to a comprehensive survey done a while back by National Public Radio, Kaiser Family Foundation, and the Kennedy School of Government, only 40 percent of respondents knew that the federal income tax system is progressive.[1] In a 2017 poll, less than half of the respondents knew what tax bracket they're in, or even what a tax bracket is.[2]

Thirty-eight percent of respondents in a 2010 poll guessed that most Americans paid 20 percent or more of their income in federal income taxes.[3] (Table 12.1) The right answer was less than 10 percent.

Self-interest is not enough to move some people to stay informed on taxes. According to the IRS, one in five people eligible for the Earned Income Tax Credit does not receive it because the person failed to claim it or did not file a tax return.[4]

People were unaware that the estate tax only applies to the extremely wealthy people, less than 1 percent of decedents since 2001. One in five people guessed (inaccurately) that the estate tax applies to 40 percent or more of Americans.[5]

The public's ignorance is not limited to federal taxes. Only one in three Californian voters knew the personal income tax was the main source of revenue for California,[6] and only a

Table 12.1 Americans' Perception of Federal Income Tax Burdens on Most Americans

Average tax rate (%)	All Americans (%)	Tea Party Supporters (%)	Actual Distribution (%)
Less than 10	5	11	86.5
10–20	26	25	12.9
20–30	25	26	⎫
30–40	10	14	⎬ 0.6
40–50	2	3	⎭
More than 50	1	1	
Don't know	31	20	
Total	100	100	

Note: The survey question was "On average, about what percentage of their household incomes would you guess most Americans pay in federal income taxes each year—less than 10 percent, between 10 and 20 percent, between 20 and 30 percent, between 30 and 40 percent, between 40 and 50 percent, or more than 50 percent, or don't you know enough to say?"

Source: Bruce Bartlett, "What People Don't Know About Federal Income Taxes," *Wall Street Pit*, April 15, 2010, based on the *New York Times* / CBS News Poll and estimates of the distribution of tax burdens computed by the Joint Committee on Taxation.

third of respondents knew that Proposition 13, the cap on property taxes, applied to both residential and commercial property.

What does the public think about taxes?

The public is unhappy with the tax system, although there's disagreement about what the most pressing problem is. In a poll conducted in April 2017 by the Pew Research Center, 56 percent of respondents said they thought the tax system was not too fair or not at all fair. (Table 12.2) Notably, though, just 42 percent said the tax system was very or moderately fair.[7] Only 40 percent thought they paid more than their fair share in 2017, compared with 55 percent in 2003. When asked what bothers them most, 60 percent said it was that the wealthy did

Table 12.2 The Public's View of Federal Taxes (in percent)

	March 2003	December 2011	April 2017
Federal tax system is . . .			
Very fair / moderately fair	51	43	42
Not too fair / not at all fair	48	55	56
You pay . . .			
More than fair share	55	38	40
Less than fair share	1	5	5
About right amount	41	52	54
What bothers you most . . .			
Amount you pay	14	11	27
Complexity of system	32	28	43
Feel wealthy people don't pay fair share	51	57	60

Source: Pew Research Center, "Top Frustrations with Tax System: Sense That Corporations, Wealthy Don't Pay Fair Share," April 14, 2017, http://www.people-press. org/2017/04/14/top-frustrations-with-tax-system-sense-that-corporations-wealthy-dont-pay-fair-share/.

not pay their fair share (51 percent in 2003), 43 percent thought complexity was the top problem, and 27 percent thought their own tax burden was most troubling, a stark jump from 11 percent in 2011.

The 2017 survey also attempted to gauge the partisan divide between Democrats and Republicans. Members of the two parties had different gripes about the tax system. Forty-nine percent of Republicans said complexity bothered them most, compared with only 40 percent who were upset that the wealthy don't pay their fair share. (Table 12.3) About the same fraction of Democrats complained about complexity, 39 percent, but many more—76 —percent were bothered that the wealthy don't pay their fair share. A similar divergence applied to whether corporations pay their fair share of taxes; 44 percent of Republicans were bothered by this, while 75 percent of Democrats were. This division may explain in part why bipartisan cooperation is so challenging on tax policy.

Table 12.3 Top Complaints about Our Tax System, by Party, April 2017 (in percent)

	Total	Republicans	Democrats
Amount you pay	27	35	21
Complexity of system	43	49	39
Feel wealthy people don't pay fair share	60	40	76
Feel corporations don't pay fair share	62	44	75

Source: Pew Research Center, "Top Frustrations with Tax System: Sense That Corporations, Wealthy Don't Pay Fair Share," April 14, 2017, http://www.people-press.org/2017/04/14/top-frustrations-with-tax-system-sense-that-corporations-wealthy-dont-pay-fair-share/.

How are new taxes enacted?

According to the U.S. Constitution, all tax bills must originate in the House of Representatives: "All bills for raising Revenue shall originate in the House of Representatives; but the Senate may propose or concur with Amendments as on other Bills" (Article 1, Section 7). This would seem to constrain the legislative process, but it does less than you might imagine. In every session of Congress, dozens of bills containing tax provisions pass the House. At that point, the provision allowing the Senate to propose amendments gives senators carte blanche to substitute their own tax bill as a replacement for the House legislation.

In March 2018, the Trump administration floated an idea for a tax change—indexing capital gains, which we discuss on pages 44–45—and suggested that it could be implemented by executive order, thus bypassing Congress. The argument to bypass Congress is that the statute already says that the tax base is an asset's sale price minus its cost, and indexing would clarify, and arguably improve, the cost calculation. Whether bypassing the Congress in this way would pass legal muster is unclear, but it would certainly be a major change in long-standing practice.

Some tax proposals originate in the White House. The president must submit a budget to the Congress on or about the first Monday in February. The budget always includes many tax proposals. Until 2017, the Treasury Department produced an annual accompanying document called "A General Explanation of the Administration's Fiscal Year xx [whatever year applies] Revenue Proposals," which contains a description of current law, reasons for change, and a discussion of each specific revenue proposal, as well as a detailed table of the Treasury Department's Office of Tax Analysis revenue estimates for each proposal and the package as a whole.

Both the House and Senate hold hearings on tax legislation where they hear from administration witnesses, experts, and stakeholders. Generally, when the House and Senate pass different versions of tax bills, the leaders of each body appoint members of a conference committee with the mandate to vote out a conference report—a version that resolves differences in the two bills. If the House and Senate agree on the conference bill, it is sent to the president for approval. If the president vetoes the bill, it can still become law if two-thirds of the members of the House and Senate vote to override the veto.

Was the TCJA like the Tax Reform Act of 1986?

The day after the Tax Cuts and Jobs Act was enacted, House Speaker Paul Ryan (R-WI) was giddy with excitement. "The biggest tax reform in a generation is now the law of the land. As promised, the American people will begin the new year with a new tax code."[8]

Tax reform is clearly a good thing. As this book has illustrated, the tax code in unnecessarily complex, inefficient, and unfair. The TCJA was certainly the biggest change since the Tax Reform Act of 1986. But, as the provenance of the Republican-controlled Congress and President Trump, with little involvement from the minority party, it is perhaps not surprising that there is widespread disagreement about whether or how much it improved the tax code.

By contrast, the Tax Reform Act of 1986 (TRA86) was a bipartisan bill that most observers agreed constituted major reform. Extensive deliberations about every aspect of the code preceded it. The process started in January 1984 when President Ronald Reagan directed his Treasury Department to put together a comprehensive revenue-neutral tax reform plan that the Treasury would release later that year after the presidential election. While many dismissed this as an election-year gambit, nobody told the Treasury analysts who produced an epic three-volume proposal that justified the most sweeping reform in history. (One of us joined the Treasury staff midway through the tax reform process and the other worked on the early stages of tax reform for President Reagan's Council of Economic Advisers.) A revised version reflecting input from the White House released in 1985 provided a comprehensive grounding for serious tax reform.

Prodded by the popular president and his staff's excellent spadework, Congress began to consider every aspect of the tax code and various reform options. The House held 30 hearings and spent 26 days marking up legislation in committee.[9] The Senate held 36 more hearings in 1985 and 1986. The Senate debate in June 1986 lasted a full month. The ultimate bill passed with broad bipartisan support, and President Reagan signed it on October 22, 1986—almost two years after Treasury released its initial plan.

Fast-forward to 2017. There were zero hearings to consider H.R. 1, the TCJA. Treasury's contribution to the debate was a one-page set of bullet points released to great fanfare in April followed by a hardly more detailed "Unified Framework" in September.[10] The Treasury secretary dismissed his own staff's analysis of key elements of the plan.[11]

The House passed a 448-page bill on November 16 after two weeks of deliberations.[12] The Senate also skipped hearings on the TCJA. Finance Committee chair Orrin Hatch (R-UT) introduced a "conceptual mark" (no legislative language) on

November 9, and the panel approved a 515-page amended bill eight days later.[13] The full Senate passed the bill a few weeks later, and the president signed it in mid-December.

Defenders of the TCJA point out that the Senate Finance Committee had earlier held three hearings on broad issues in anticipation of a tax reform push. The Ways and Means Committee passed a comprehensive tax reform bill in 2014 after many hearings and much debate. While that bill never reached the president, some of its elements were included in the TCJA.

Unlike the bipartisan TRA86, the TCJA didn't get a single Democratic vote. And even before the ink dried on the president's signature, observers noted numerous mistakes in the legislation. For example, the new law is not actually called the Tax Cuts and Jobs Act (see chapter 13), but the legislation refers to the non-existent TCJA several places in footnotes. More consequentially, some industries and activities were unintentionally excluded from the new investment incentives.[14] There's even concern that plaintiffs in sexual harassment claims may not be able to deduct their legal fees because of a hastily drafted provision aimed at disallowing deductions for defendants, which could prove to be a significant impediment to holding abusers accountable in the #MeToo era.[15]

TRA86 was designed to be revenue-neutral—neither add nor subtract from federal deficits. Thirty years later, with the debt more than twice as big as a share of GDP, the TCJA was projected at the time to add about $1.5 trillion to the national debt over its first 10 years. President Reagan also insisted that TRA86 not change the distribution of tax burdens. TCJA cut taxes at all income levels, but by the most for those with very high incomes.

One more thing: It's not a "new tax code." The tax law is still called the Internal Revenue Code of 1986 (as amended). And it still contains a lot of baggage of the old code.

Source: Dan Wasserman, Editorial Cartoon / *Boston Globe* / TNS.

What are regulations and why are they important?

Often legislative language is only an outline of Congress's intentions that leaves many details unspecified. The executive branch implements the law via regulations. Sometimes legislation specifically instructs the secretary of the Treasury (or of some other agency in the case of legislation that crosses jurisdictions) to promulgate regulations to implement the law. Other times Treasury writes regulations to provide guidance to taxpayers where the law is unclear. The regulations may be quite lengthy.[16] (See page 219, "How is tax complexity measured, and how should it be measured?")

The Office of the Chief Counsel at the Internal Revenue Service takes the lead on the regulatory process in consultations with lawyers from the Treasury's Office of Tax Policy. The Office of Information and Regulatory Affairs at the Office of Management and Budget reviews major regulations before release.[17] Although critics sometimes complain that the IRS oversteps its authority by redefining the scope of legislation via regulations, the IRS and Treasury are required to implement the intent of the law and nothing more. However, the complexity of tax law often leaves much ground for interpretation. When the statute is unclear, regulators may consult the legislative history as embodied in the General Explanation document published by Congress's Joint Committee on Taxation. The IRS seeks advice from stakeholders and publishes draft versions for feedback before finalizing regulations.

Without regulations, taxpayers would have tremendous uncertainty about the law. Some might avoid taking advantage of murky tax incentives, while others might use the fog to hide sketchy activities. That is, both avoidance and evasion would be more likely without adequate guidance. However, regulators also have to be very careful in interpreting the law. By clearly laying out the tax parameters, regulations may also inadvertently create a roadmap for legal tax avoidance. As in many other areas of government, regulators may profit handsomely passing through the revolving door to work for those who would like to find and exploit loopholes.

How does the tax sausage get made? (House and Senate rules)

Several rules may limit tax (and spending) legislation in Congress. A budget process sets limits for spending and targets for tax revenues. Legislation that would cut taxes below the level specified in the budget resolution may be blocked by any member who raises a "point of order" against it. In the House, this does not much constrain activity, because the leadership-appointed Rules Committee may waive the point of order and the rule may be enacted by a simple majority vote. In the Senate, points of order carry more weight because waiving them requires 60 (out of 100) votes. Thus, a minority of 41 senators can block tax cuts that exceed the budget resolution targets.

"NOW THAT WE'VE AGREED ON THE LOOPHOLES, WHAT SHOULD THE TAX LAWS BE?"

Source: © T- McCracken.

In addition, pay-as-you-go (PAYGO) rules require that all tax cuts and spending increases be offset by other tax increases and spending cuts, respectively. The House let the PAYGO rule lapse in 2011, but it is still in force in the Senate. Tax cuts that are not offset are subject to a point of order and, again, may be blocked by a minority.

Sometimes Congress uses a special procedure called "reconciliation." The TCJA (and the Bush tax cuts) were passed as part of the reconciliation process. Originally intended to facilitate difficult deficit reduction proposals, it has sometimes been used to increase deficits. If Congress opts for reconciliation, the House and the Senate agree to a set of spending and tax targets, and the enacting legislation is "fast-tracked" for approval; it is not subject to points of order or a filibuster (the procedure by which one member may halt all activity in the Senate). The so-called Byrd Rule, named after the late senator Robert Byrd (D-WV), does place some constraints on reconciliation. Members may raise a point of order in objection to the introduction of any provisions that do not affect tax receipts or entitlement spending in the reconciliation bill. Changes in discretionary programs or new regulations would fall afoul of this rule. That effectively would bar the provision unless 60 senators agreed to override the point of order. The Byrd Rule also bars legislation that would increase the deficit outside the 10-year budget window. This is one reason why the Bush tax cuts were designed to expire after 10 years and why most of the TCJA tax cuts (other than the corporate rate reduction) are set to expire after 2025.[18]

Who estimates the revenue impact of tax changes?

The nonpartisan Joint Committee on Taxation (JCT) is the official scorekeeper for changes in tax law. JCT has a staff of 15 to 20 economists, most with Ph.D. degrees, who are charged with providing expert guidance regarding the effects of tax changes on federal revenues.

There are also revenue estimators at the Office of Tax Analysis (OTA) at the Department of the Treasury. They estimate the revenue effects of proposed tax changes used in preparation of the Administration's budget. Treasury revenue estimators also advise on revenue costs of bills as they are being developed. OTA and JCT are also responsible for producing estimates of tax expenditures. (See page 171, "What exactly is a tax expenditure?")

Although the JCT was created to provide an independent source of information for Congress, relations between the professional staffs of the two groups are generally cordial and respectful. Estimators at Treasury and the JCT consult informally about data sources and methods, and it is unusual for the two organizations' estimates to differ by a large amount.

How do they do it? Do they ignore behavioral responses to taxation?

Revenue estimates reflect the estimators' best judgment about the effect of a tax change, subject to some ground rules, which we'll return to. Estimators have large databases of individual, corporate, and estate tax returns and detailed calculators that allow them to estimate tax liability under current law and under alternative policies. Where necessary, they also use data from other sources or draw on evidence from published research.

The estimates account for likely changes in behavior in response to taxation; thus they are not "static," as is sometimes alleged by tax-cut supporters who complain that the JCT methods overstate the likely revenue loss because they understate the positive response of economic activity to the tax cuts. For example, if the JCT was asked to estimate—"score" in Washington-speak—the effect of an increase in taxes on capital gains, it would account for the fact that, based on historical patterns, taxpayers are likely to report fewer capital gains when tax rates increase. Similarly, it accounts for more tax avoidance and evasion when ordinary income tax rates increase. So, for example, if tax rates were to increase by 10 percent across the board, the JCT would estimate a change in tax revenues of less than 10 percent.

The revenue consequences of some provisions are easier to estimate than others. Provisions where eligibility is based entirely on information already reported on tax returns are comparatively simple to measure because those data are in the estimators' database. Forecasting the revenue consequences of new provisions based on information not currently reported to the IRS is more problematic. The estimators must estimate the eligible population, the amounts subject to taxation, deduction, or credit, and the take-up rate for the new provision. All of these elements may be highly uncertain.

In some cases, revenue estimates are very sensitive to projections of the overall level of economic activity. The Congressional Budget Office (CBO) makes those forecasts for the JCT, and the JCT revenue estimates must be consistent with this aggregate economic forecast, which often constrains what kinds of behavioral responses can be built into the revenue estimates. For example, consider a proposal to reinstate an investment tax credit. In this case the estimated response of investment could not be so large that it would imply GDP growth that exceeded the CBO estimate.

However, as we discuss later (See "What is dynamic scoring?"), the JCT estimates the effect of macroeconomic feedback for significant revenue bills. In the case of the investment tax credit, the JCT model would account for induced additional capital investment, which could boost economic growth and thus tax receipts, as well as possible negative effects of additional public debt.

Finally, about those ground rules. Estimators must usually estimate the cost under a "current law baseline." This means that the basic assumption is that all provisions in current law will play out exactly as legislated unless they are modified in the bill under consideration. This technical-sounding rule can make a big difference to revenue estimates. For example, all of the TCJA tax cuts are currently scheduled to expire at the end of 2025. Starting in 2026, the revenue cost of all deduction and exemptions will increase because tax rates will be higher. Also, nonrefundable tax credits will cost more revenue because taxpayers will have more tax liability before credits. If estimators reasonably assumed that most of the tax cuts would be extended because the president and Congress seem to agree on that, these revenue estimates would change markedly. But the JCT is barred from making that judgment.

There are some other potentially important scoring conventions. For one thing, estimators typically must provide their best guess of the most likely outcome, rather than estimate the average expected revenue effect. This can be significant in the case of provisions that only take effect in rare circumstances. For example, there is a tax credit for oil production from relatively unproductive oil wells when oil prices fall below a certain level. Because oil prices are not expected to fall that much, the credit is scored as having zero revenue cost, even though it is a kind of insurance—clearly valuable to the industry when oil prices fall. The problem with this scoring convention is that it treats quasi-insurance programs run through the tax code as if they cost little or no revenue because, except when the insurance is actually needed, they do cost little. The drawback of changing the rule, however, is that JCT revenue estimates would more often turn out to be off the mark.

Another important feature of the revenue estimation process is that estimators do not score the long-run effect of tax policies, even if they are markedly different from the effects within the official 10-year budget window. This can be important for provisions that shift the timing of economic activity. For example, the TCJA includes a one-time tax on unrepatriated profits held by U.S. multinationals in foreign subsidiaries, in exchange for a permanent exemption from tax on foreign profits. JCT scores the provisions as raising substantial tax revenues during the repatriation period, but they will lose even more revenue over ensuing years. JCT can only show the lost revenue to the extent that it occurs over the budget period. Another example is a provision that allowed taxpayers to convert traditional IRAs into Roth IRAs, which increased revenue during the conversion period at the expense of much larger revenue losses over ensuing decades. (See page 127, "Stupid tax tricks: Roth IRA conversions.") A concern is that this rule makes such policies that bring revenue from the future into the 10-year window look more attractive than they really are, exacerbating the large long-term fiscal imbalance the country already faces.[19]

What is dynamic scoring?

Dynamic scoring involves incorporating economic feedback effects into estimates of tax changes. Most economists would agree that a major tax reform in which loopholes were eliminated and tax rates lowered, holding overall revenues constant, would increase economic growth, although there would be a wide range of estimates of how much. And indeed, official scorers were instructed to modify the baseline to account for the salutary effects of the Tax Reform Act of 1986 while it was being debated.

Unfortunately, the vast majority of tax proposals considered by Congress would not fit into this category of likely growth enhancers. While everyone likes lower tax rates, base broadening is a lot more popular with economists than it is with the people who pay higher taxes as a result. Tax cuts enacted since 2001, for example, have lowered marginal tax rates, but they also narrowed the tax base by creating a slew of new targeted tax breaks—including the one for unproductive oil wells mentioned earlier—that are likely to hurt the overall economy rather than help it. This makes assessing the net effect problematic.

The biggest problem, though, is that recent tax bills have produced significant revenue losses with no indication of how those losses will be offset. Without knowing that, it is difficult to assess the economic effects, or even to measure whether the economy will be stronger or weaker in the long run.

Depending on how the increased deficits are closed, there could be dramatically different economic results. The best-case scenario for economic growth is for deficits to be financed by cuts in transfer programs or increases in relatively efficient taxes. That deficits might force spending constraint appears to be the logic behind the "starve-the-beast" rationale for deficit-financed tax cuts discussed in the next chapter, but there is no evidence that this tactic actually works. It is not clear why spending cuts would be politically easier in the future than they are now. Will it be easier to cut Social Security and Medicare 20 years from now when all the baby boomers are retired (and AARP's membership has exploded)?

The worst-case scenario for economic growth is this: years from now, our profligate budgetary policies lead to dramatically higher interest rates as the federal government's solvency comes into doubt, triggering a massive recession. Taxpayers blame this on the tax cuts for the rich and decide to deal with budget problems by raising tax rates on high-income folks. (And they leave in place all the middle-class tax cuts like the child credit, higher standard deduction, and 10 percent bracket.) In the JCT's, the CBO's, and the Treasury's models, such a tax increase would prove most damaging to growth. The net effect would be a much weaker economy than would exist had the tax cuts never been enacted.

To be clear, this long-term risk also means that deficit-financed spending could also be more costly than would appear in either a balanced-budget scenario or one assuming less damaging deficit offsets in the future.

Because it is impossible for official revenue scorers to predict how the deficits will be closed, it is impossible to reliably predict the long-term effect of deficit-financed tax cuts. For related reasons, it is a challenge to predict the short-term effects as well. In the standard Keynesian macroeconomic model, short-term fiscal stimulus (a spending increase or tax cut) boosts the economy during downturns by spurring households to spend and businesses to invest, creating more demand and thus more jobs. When the economy is at full employment, deficit-financed tax cuts can damage the economy by creating inflationary pressure.

The wild card is the Federal Reserve, which tries to stimulate the economy when it is underperforming and slow it down when inflationary pressures arise. Fed policymakers might respond to tax cuts by tightening up monetary policy to prevent inflation. Because monetary policy affects the economy more slowly than fiscal policy, short-term deficits that are larger than the Fed had expected can still have an immediate effect, but the effect beyond that is complicated by the Fed's response. While this is probably more predictable than how future Congresses will deal with the national debt, it significantly complicates forecasting the effects of fiscal policy beyond a year or so.

That said, the same considerations make quantifying the distributional effects of tax cuts difficult. If deficits are closed by tax increases on high-income households, the equity effects are much different than if the deficits lead to cuts in safety-net programs. And advocates for dynamic scoring point out that even if the macroeconomic effects of tax changes are uncertain, they're extremely unlikely to be zero. For that reason, the JCT and CBO are now required to make their best guess of the macroeconomic effects of major legislation and incorporate them into their revenue and spending estimates.

Must taxes be raised?

No. Federal tax revenues at 17.3 percent of GDP in 2017 were at about the postwar average level. CBO projects that the TCJA will cut revenue to 16.5 percent of GDP by 2019 before revenues rebound, assuming the economy continues to grow. After the TCJA expires in 2025, revenues will jump above the historical averages. Over the long run, however, population aging and rising health care costs will put unprecedented pressures on the federal budget. Unless Congress figures out a radical cure for health cost inflation, services would have to be cut drastically from current levels to balance the budget with the tax system of current law.

Figure 12.1 shows CBO projections for spending for Social Security, Medicare, Medicaid, Children's Health Insurance Program, and health care marketplace subsidies assuming recent health care trends continue indefinitely and assuming that health care costs will stop growing faster than GDP after 10 years. Even if we are remarkably successful at controlling health care costs, federal government spending on these

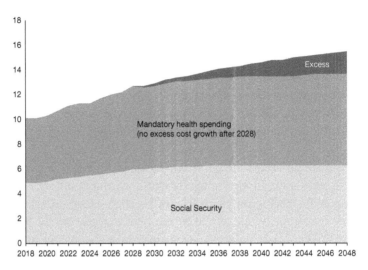

Figure 12.1 Federal Mandatory Spending on Health Care and Social Security, with and without Excess Health Cost Growth after 2028, as Percentage of GDP

Source: CBO Long-Term Budget Outlook, 2018.

programs will amount to nearly 14 percent of GDP by the year 2048, compared to less than 11 percent now. That is only slightly below the current level of total tax revenues.

Either there will have to be unprecedented cuts in public programs or revenues will have to rise significantly. Over the long term, the best solution is probably a mix of higher revenues and spending cuts.

Can we solve the problem by raising tax rates only on those with high incomes?

Not unless spending is cut drastically. A 2012 Tax Policy Center study estimated what top tax rates would need to be to get the deficit down to 2 percent of GDP by 2019 assuming no change in spending patterns. If only the top two tax brackets (applying to married couples with income above $250,000) are adjusted, the top rate would have to increase to almost

Table 12.4 Income Tax Rates Required to Cut Deficit to 2 Percent of GDP in 2019

Current tax rates	Rate required if all rates rise	Rate required if top three rates rise	Rate required if top two rates rise
10.0	14.9	10.0	10.0
15.0	22.3	15.0	15.0
25.0	37.2	25.0	25.0
28.0	41.7	60.8	28.0
33.0	49.1	71.7	85.7
35.0	52.1	76.1	90.9

Source: Rosanne Altshuler, Katherine Lim, and Roberton Williams, "Desperately Seeking Revenue," Tax Policy Center, presented at "Train Wreck: A Conference on America's Looming Fiscal Crisis," January 15, 2010, available at https://www.urban.org/research/publication/desperately-seeking-revenue.

91 percent, if we ignore the likely behavioral responses to such rates. Considering that there would be an enormous amount of avoidance at such high rates, it's clearly not feasible to tame the deficit by simply raising top tax rates. It's probably not even feasible if the top three rates are adjusted. (See table 12.4.)

Another option would be to raise the tax burdens on those with high incomes by paring or eliminating preferences that disproportionately benefit the wealthy, such as the special low tax rates on capital gains and dividends. Unlike increases in tax rates, broadening the tax base actually reduces the scope for tax avoidance. Nonetheless, given the size of our long-term fiscal imbalance, it is likely that spending will need to be cut and taxes raised on more than the highest earners.

13

SNAKE OIL

Wouldn't a flat tax be super simple and efficient?

As discussed in chapter 4, the flat tax is basically a value-added tax with a wrinkle: businesses are allowed a deduction for wages paid, but the employees are subject to a single-rate tax on their wages above an exemption level, typically set at around the poverty level. (See page 117, "What is the flat tax?") Overall, the flat tax would be substantially simpler than a similarly comprehensive income tax. But the same political pressures that riddle the current tax system with deductions and credits would apply to the flat tax. It is not clear that it could stay pristine. Indeed, former Texas governor and current Secretary of Energy Rick Perry proposed to allow deductions for charitable contributions and mortgage interest under his "flat tax" proposal in the 2012 Republican presidential primary campaign. So the comprehensive tax base of the flat tax may not be very durable.

While applauding the simplicity of a flat tax, many economists are even more drawn to the fact that it is a consumption tax and therefore, for reasons explained in chapter 4, does not distort savings and investment decisions.

How about offering a new tax system on an elective basis?

Rick Perry attempted to allay concerns about the regressivity of his flat tax proposal by saying that taxpayers could elect to stay in the current tax system if they so choose. Republican presidential candidate John McCain made a similar proposal in the 2008 campaign.

The main problem with these take-your-pick tax systems is that they would lose an enormous amount of tax revenue. As a general rule, taxpayers will only elect an alternative if they expect to save money. Yes, they might occasionally choose the simpler system to save time and hassle, but they're unlikely to pay much for simplification. You can bet that if Rick Perry's optional alternative flat tax became law, tax software would automatically calculate the alternative that minimizes taxes and select it.

The Tax Policy Center estimated that the Perry plan would reduce revenues by between $600 billion and $1 trillion per year (depending on assumptions unspecified by Perry). John McCain's optional alternative tax plan would have reduced revenues by around $7 trillion over a decade.

Besides being fiscally irresponsible, these optional alternative systems would also add new complexity. They would effectively create an alternative maximum tax—mimicking (and compounding) the complexity of the existing alternative minimum tax. Taxpayers would have the incentive to game the system by switching from one system to the other to minimize tax liability; limiting the ability to switch back and forth would penalize those people whose circumstances change unexpectedly, and provoke serious tax envy among those who are stuck with the less attractive of the two options.

The bottom line is that offering a radical reform plan as an optional system might be good politics, but it's not good tax policy.

What is the "starve-the-beast" theory?

The "starve-the-beast" theory argues that collecting more tax revenues doesn't end up reducing the deficit because it just enables more (wasteful) government spending. The only way to restrain spending is to cut taxes—that is, to starve the beast (i.e., the government).

While this argument is plausible, the evidence does not support it. Indeed, it is hard to imagine that spending could have been higher as tax revenues were slashed by the Bush tax cuts. Government grew much faster from 2001 to 2009 than during the Clinton administration. While some of that was war-related, nondefense discretionary spending also grew, and there was a major expansion in Medicare—the largest expansion of entitlement spending since Medicare was first enacted. It appears that instead of constraining spending, deficit financing was contagious. If deficits don't matter when considering tax cuts, why should they be considered when evaluating a new drug benefit or a "bridge to nowhere?"

The late William Niskanen, former president of the libertarian Cato Institute, posited an intriguing critique of "starve the beast."[1] If deficits finance 20 percent of government spending, he argued, then citizens perceive government services as being available at a discount. Services that are popular at 20 percent off the listed price would garner more support than if offered at full price. So deficit-financed tax cuts induce more government spending, not less.

Niskanen found statistical support for his theory by comparing the time patterns of revenues and changes in spending. He hypothesized that higher—not lower, as suggested by the starve-the-beast theory—revenues could constrain spending and found strong support for that conjecture based on data from 1981 to 2005. Another Cato researcher, Michael New, tested Niskanen's model in different time periods using a more restrictive definition of spending (nondefense discretionary spending) and found the same result as Niskanen did.[2] A careful analysis by two prominent academic economists found "no support for the hypothesis that tax cuts restrain government spending; indeed the point estimates [i.e., their best guess] suggest that tax cuts increase spending." They went on to say that the main effect of tax cuts is to induce subsequent legislated tax increases.[3]

These studies might even have understated the effect of deficits on spending. The message during the last decade seems to have been not that spending and tax cuts were available at a discount, but that they were free. Spending for wars, Medicare expansion, and No Child Left Behind happened at the same time that taxes were falling. Citizens could be forgiven for forgetting that there is *any* connection between spending and taxes.

We surmise that if President Bush had announced a new war surtax to pay for Iraq, or an increase in the Medicare payroll tax rate to pay for the prescription drug benefit, these initiatives would have been less popular. Given that the prescription drug benefit only passed the House of Representatives by one vote after an extraordinary amount of arm-twisting, it seems unlikely that it would have passed at all if accompanied by a tax increase.

More recently, Congress passed a large spending increase within weeks of enacting the TCJA. While the big tax cuts had substantially worsened our already bleak budget outlook, Congress had little appetite for tackling the hard choices involved in cutting—or even limiting the growth in—spending programs. Yes, retiring Republican House Speaker Paul Ryan pushed cuts in entitlement spending, but Democrats countered that those cuts would hurt vulnerable elderly people to pay for tax cuts for millionaires and corporations. Republican Senate majority leader Mitch McConnell and President Trump have promised not to touch Social Security or Medicare. The beast seems to be pretty robust.

Source: Scott Stantis, Editorial Cartoon / *Chicago Tribune* / TNS.

Columnist Bruce Bartlett called starve-the-beast "the most pernicious fiscal doctrine in history."[4] The truth remains that the cost of government is not measured by the taxes in place to fund it, but rather by what it spends.

Does the taxpayer protection pledge protect taxpayers?

Obviously, protecting taxpayers sounds great, but the pledge will do anything but (in our opinion). The pledge is the brain-child of Grover Norquist, president of a group called Americans for Tax Reform that favors a much smaller federal government. The pledge—a promise to never, under any circumstances, raise taxes—has been signed by 253 members of Congress.[5]

The pledge might promote a smaller government if starve-the-beast worked, but it doesn't. And every time legislators vote for a deficit (which is to say, every year since 2001), they implicitly vote for higher future taxes. Over the long run, taxes must equal spending. Spending that is not paid for now must be paid, with interest, in the future. As the auto mechanic in the Fram oil filter commercials used to warn, "You can pay me now, or pay me later." Large-scale cutbacks in entitlement programs could help to complete the square, but the American public has yet to show any appetite for this.

Moreover, the taxpayer protection pledge applies not just to tax rate increases, but also to scaling back tax expenditures, which are more appropriately considered to be spending cuts. Any plan that cuts spending reduces the present value of current and future taxes. The major bipartisan debt reduction plans would protect future taxpayers much more than the status quo, but they are off limits to the tax-pledge signatories because of the cuts in tax expenditures.

What is the "two Santas" theory?

The late conservative writer Jude Wanniski came up with the idea of the two Santas as a way to revive the Republican Party in the 1970s.[6] He argued that the Democratic Party won elections because it always played Santa—promising more and more new government programs without worrying about who would pay for them.

Source: Cagle Cartoons, Inc.

Republicans back then were the party of fiscal responsibility, playing Scrooge to the Democrats' Santa. Mr. Wanniski might have forgotten that Republican President Richard M. Nixon expanded both the social safety net and the military, and that Republican President Dwight D. Eisenhower created the national highway system. But this simple explanation for why the Democrats had controlled Congress for so long resonated with Mr. Wanniski's audience.

He told the Republicans that if the Democrats were going to play Santa, the Republicans had to be Santa, too. When the Democrats promised more spending, the Republicans should promise lower taxes—two Santas. And, for heaven's sake, don't worry about the deficit.

But Mr. Wanniski also thought that if the Republicans cut taxes, tax revenue would rise—that we were on the wrong side of the Laffer Curve. (See page 151, "What is the Laffer Curve?") Tax cuts would pay for themselves, the budget would be balanced, no deficits would ensue, and Republicans would win.

Republicans never really tried Mr. Wanniski's prescription until George W. Bush entered the White House in 2001. True, in 1980 Ronald Reagan ran on a platform of tax cuts, but soon after his election backed off and raised taxes when the deficit exploded and interest rates spiked. In 1990, the first George Bush famously raised taxes in an attempt to tame the deficit—and paid the ultimate political price in the 1992 election.

President Clinton might have wanted to spend more; and the congressional Republicans, led by Newt Gingrich, desperately wanted to cut taxes. Instead of compromising on a giant underfunded government, those two Santas fought to a stalemate and created the first budget surpluses in a generation.

But both parties embraced the two Santas theory in the 2000 presidential election. Al Gore promised lots of new spending and big tax cuts. Mr. Bush promised an expanded role for government in education and much bigger tax cuts than Mr. Gore.

The era of surpluses ended because the younger Mr. Bush was not about to repeat his dad's mistake. His vice president, Dick Cheney, growled that "deficits don't matter." Mr. Bush cut taxes by trillions of dollars while creating a huge prescription drug entitlement program, waging two wars, and increasing nondefense discretionary spending even faster than Mr. Clinton. Mr. Bush left office with a burgeoning deficit and record-low approval ratings, but both sides continued to embrace the two Santas. Candidate Barack Obama criticized Mr. Bush's fiscal profligacy but proposed new spending programs and tax cuts that would have increased the deficit almost as much as Mr. Bush's policies. Candidate John McCain was more restrained on spending, but his huge promised income tax cuts would have led to even larger deficits. Candidate Donald Trump promised large tax cuts while pledging to preserve both Social Security and to increase defense spending, embodying both Santa Clauses. And the Tax Cuts and Jobs Act passed in 2017 will add nearly $2 trillion to deficits over the next decade.

Should we eliminate the IRS?

In 2015, during the Republican presidential nomination campaign, candidate Ted Cruz proposed abolishing the Internal Revenue Service, along with a plan to drastically simplify the tax code so that much less monitoring of the tax process would be needed. He wasn't the first prominent Republican to suggest this, as Rand Paul had mentioned the idea in 2013.[7] Actually, the proposal was to shift the IRS's responsibilities to "some much smaller division" of the Treasury Department, so really Cruz was for downsizing and renaming the IRS. Even natural supporters of the idea were skeptical. Chris Edwards of the libertarian-leaning Cato Institute was among those, saying, "If you're going to have federal taxes, you need an agency to collect them."

The FairTax sounds, well, fair. Is it?

Well, it depends on your definition of fair, but it would be a large tax increase on the middle class, would invite tax evasion, and at the rates advertised would not come close to raising enough revenue to fund the government without massive borrowing. And one more quibble: the advertised rates are misleading.

The FairTax is the name given by supporters to a national retail sales tax. In principle, it's similar to the sales taxes levied by most states, but the FairTax would apply to all goods and services, while most state sales taxes exempt some crucial expenditure items, such as food, medical expenses, and housing, from the tax base. Even advocates recognize that the burden of a sales tax tends to be regressive, and they propose to offset the impact on the poor by providing an annual "prebate"—a payment equal to the sales tax liability of a family at the poverty level if they spend all of their income. FairTax advocates claim that a 23 percent tax would bring in enough revenue to replace all federal taxes plus cover the cost of the prebate.

This sounds really good, but it's misleading. For one thing, state sales taxes are added onto the price of goods, so a 30 percent sales tax would raise the after-tax price of a $1.00 item to $1.30. In the FairTax publicity, the tax rate is expressed as a percentage of the price including tax. So what we would naturally consider to be a 30 percent sales tax is reported by advocates as a 23 percent tax (0.30/1.30). FairTax proponents say this makes the FairTax comparable to income taxes (recall that a 100 percent sales tax rate is akin to a 50 percent income tax rate), which are reported as a share of before-tax income, but it also makes the FairTax rate seem like a smaller sales tax than it is.

A more fundamental problem is that the 23 (or 30) percent tax rate would not come close to replacing the revenue lost from repealing other federal taxes. William Gale of the Brookings Institution shows that the FairTax calculations are based on a set of logically inconsistent assumptions. In particular, when the FairTax designers estimated government revenues under the sales tax, they (implicitly) assumed that consumer prices would rise by the full amount of the sales tax; when they estimated government spending needs, they (implicitly) assumed consumer prices would stay constant. Both of those assumptions cannot be valid at the same time. As a result, the calculation either overstates revenues, understates spending needs, or both.

The FairTax people also assume that there would be no evasion under their plan, which is Pollyannaish at best. A sales tax of 30 percent or more would provide a huge incentive to move sales underground, especially in sectors like grocery stores, where gross margins are often 1 or 2 percent. The income tax is estimated to have a 16 percent "tax gap." It's likely that evasion would be even more of a problem with the FairTax. All told, the actual tax rate would likely have to be more like 50 percent or more to replace all other federal taxes.[8]

But the fatal flaw is probably the effect of such a tax on the middle class. The prebate would protect those with low incomes and, given the clear tax break it provides to high-income families, middle-class people have to make up the lost revenue. President Bush's tax reform panel estimated that replacing just the federal income tax with a national sales tax would on average boost middle-income tax bills by $5,000—and that's after the prebate!

For that reason alone, notwithstanding its appeal to occasional presidential contenders like Mike Huckabee and Ron Paul, the FairTax is not going to ever become law, nor should it.

How did the Tax Cuts and Jobs Act become the law that must not be named?

Almost everyone calls the 2017 law the Tax Cuts and Jobs Act. That's the name its congressional sponsors gave it, and the new law even refers to itself that way in several footnotes. But it is not the Act's official name.

As we explained in chapter 12, the 2017 tax bill was considered under a streamlined parliamentary process called reconciliation. Under reconciliation, bills can pass both the House and the Senate on simple majority votes. There are some limits on reconciliation bills, one of which is called the Byrd Rule. Among other provisions, the Byrd Rule says that any senator may raise an objection (technically called a "point of order") to provisions in a reconciliation bill that do not have any effect on the federal budget. A point of order can only be overruled by a vote of 60 percent of the senators. (See "How does the tax sausage get made? (House and Senate rules)" on page 247.)

The Democratic Senate minority leader raised a Byrd Rule objection to the title of the act, arguing that it was not germane to the budget legislation. This was Senator Schumer's way of expressing objection to a bill that Democrats had no role in crafting and had little prospect of stopping.

All 48 Democrats voted to sustain the point of order and that is why the law informally known as the Tax Cuts and Jobs Act is actually "An Act to provide for reconciliation pursuant to titles II and V of the concurrent resolution on the budget for fiscal year 2018."

An Act

To provide for reconciliation pursuant to titles II and V of the concurrent resolution
on the budget for fiscal year 2018.

(Page 1 of Public Law 115-97, informally known as the Tax Cuts and Jobs Act.)

14

TAX REFORM

Tax reformers talk about a broad base and low rates. What does that mean?

The base refers to the definition of income subject to tax. The broader the base—meaning the fewer the deductions, exclusions, and credits—the lower tax rates can be to raise a given amount of revenue. So a broader base is consistent with lower tax rates. Lower tax rates are more efficient, and fewer deductions, exclusions, and credits make the tax code simpler. Also, a broad base is generally easier for the tax authorities to administer and less prone to tax avoidance and evasion.

Was the so-called Tax Cuts and Jobs Act real tax reform or just a giant tax cut?

A little of the first, and a lot of the second. It did contain several base-broadening measures long favored by tax reform advocates and changed how we tax corporate income in several sensible ways that have significant bipartisan support. But it is also a massive tax cut, to the tune of about $2 trillion over the next decade.[1]

"*I want you to draft the bill with all your usual precision and flair. Explain its purposes, justify its expenditures, emphasize how it fits the broad aims of democratic progress. And one other thing: Can you make it sound like a tax cut?*"

Source: © Ed Fisher / *The New Yorker* Collection.

Is the broadest base always the best base?

No. There are good reasons to allow certain deductions and exclusions. Some deductions, such as for legal expenses in a lawsuit, are necessary to measure income properly. Taxing businesses' gross receipts rather than net income—as some states have recently started doing—would be quite simple, but would distort economic activity on a number of dimensions. Deductions for business costs are necessary to properly measure income. As we have already argued, a deduction for extraordinary medical expenses, which reduce a family's well-being below what their pre-deduction income suggests, narrows the personal income tax base but arguably makes the distribution of tax burdens more equitable.

It also makes sense to run some subsidies, such as the Earned Income Tax Credit and the credit for R&D expenditures, through the tax code. The challenge for reformers is to balance the gains from the subsidy against the costs of complicating the tax base. (See page 177, "How should policymakers decide whether to run a subsidy through the tax system?")

Does the framing of taxes matter?

Sometimes it does, both politically and substantively. For example, the move to scale back or eliminate the estate tax really gained steam about the time that repeal advocates started calling it the "death tax." Polls showed that opposition to the "death tax" was much higher than opposition to the "estate tax," even though the difference is purely semantic.

Another example is the almost ubiquitous state sales tax. As we explained in the previous chapter, many consumers seem to ignore the tax unless it is included in the price shown on grocery shelves. (See page 231, "Do excise taxes depress spending more than equivalent sales taxes?" and page 26, "Are there cases in practice where it does matter who writes the check?")

What is a revenue-neutral tax change?

Revenue-neutral means that the tax change is not expected to add or subtract from the deficit over the budget period, which is typically 10 years. The Tax Reform Act of 1986 was designed to be revenue-neutral over the five-year budget period then used by official scorekeepers, in part to remove deficit politics from the political debate. (It actually turned out to lose revenue because official scorekeepers overestimated the revenue gain from the corporate tax changes.)[2] As we have noted, the Tax Cuts and Jobs Act was not even close to being revenue-neutral, instead adding about $2 trillion to the federal debt over the next decade.

Are there some sensible tax reform ideas?

Sure. President George W. Bush put together a blue ribbon panel to propose fundamental tax reform, and its members came up with two alternative packages that would have each been simpler and more efficient than the existing tax code. One option would have radically simplified the tax code by eliminating many tax expenditures and converting many of the remaining tax deductions to flat credits. One insight of the Bush tax reform panel was that while tax experts view the standard deduction as a simplification—because people who do not itemize don't need to keep records on charitable contributions, mortgage payments, taxes, and so on—most real people think it's unfair that high income people can deduct those items while lower income people can't. The proposal would have dispensed with itemization.

The "simplified income tax" under the Bush panel's scheme would have reduced the number of tax brackets and cut top rates, eliminated the individual and corporate alternative minimum tax, consolidated savings and education tax breaks to reduce "choice complexity" and confusion, simplified the Earned Income and Child Tax Credits, simplified taxation of Social Security benefits, and simplified business accounting. The alternative "growth and investment" tax plan would have lowered the taxation of capital income compared with current law—somewhat similar to Scandinavian dual income tax systems.

As mentioned earlier, the Bipartisan Policy Center (BPC) Debt Reduction Task Force contained a tax reform plan aimed at simplifying the tax code enough so that half of households would no longer have to file income taxes. That plan would create a new value-added tax and use the revenue to substantially cut top individual and corporate income tax rates.[3]

President Obama empaneled another commission, commonly called the Bowles-Simpson Commission (after its two heads), with the mandate to reform the tax code and reduce the deficit. (The Bush panel had been instructed to produce a revenue-neutral plan.) The commission failed to achieve the supermajority required to force legislative consideration, but a majority supported the chairmen's blueprint. Bowles-Simpson would have eliminated even more tax expenditures than the BPC Task Force, allowing substantial tax rate cuts without the need for a new VAT or other revenue source.[4]

Columbia Law School professor Michael Graetz has an even more sweeping proposal.[5] He proposes to raise the income tax exemption level so high that 100 million households would no longer owe income tax. To make up the lost revenue, a new 10 to 15 percent VAT would be enacted. Only families with incomes above $100,000 would have to file an income tax return. The plan would also substantially simplify the income tax for those few who continued to file, but the main simplification would be to take most households off the income tax rolls entirely. (However, households would still have to supply information to claim new refundable tax credits aimed at offsetting the regressivity of the VAT.)

What have we learned?

Tax policy is, and will continue to be, a tremendously contentious issue in the United States. In part this is because taxes come out of our pocketbooks, whether we like it or not. The issue inflamed American revolutionaries at the birth of the nation, and still resonates to this day.

Alas, the stirring call to arms of "No taxation without representation" has devolved considerably so that today the American public debate about taxation rarely goes beyond platitudes and accusations. The rhetoric and misinformation is abetted by the extreme complexity of the tax system, which makes it incomprehensible to all but a handful of experts. On crucial questions that should inform tax policy choices, such as how features of the tax system affect economic growth, the supposed economics experts disagree, and there is little hope that this will change any time soon. Beyond economics, the right tax policy also depends on societal values about equity, privacy, and freedom—perennially contentious issues.

Our hope is that this book has helped to penetrate the fog of tax policy in America by explaining what economists do and do not know so you can evaluate what the sensible alternatives are. Rather than try to summarize all that's come before, we'll close by offering a few lessons.

- There's no such thing as a free lunch. Except in very special circumstances, cutting tax rates does not stimulate the economy enough to increase revenues.
- Taxes collected do not measure the social cost of government; spending is a much better metric. If the government cuts tax collections without restraining spending, all it's done is put off the reckoning of who will bear the cost.
- Tax policy changes create winners and losers, both within and across generations. Talking about this is not class warfare.
- Taxes entail economic cost. They reduce the incentive to work, save, and invest, and encourage taxpayers to engage in unproductive tax shelters. Centuries of experience proves that taxpayers do respond to those incentives, but there is considerable disagreement about how much they respond. Nonetheless, it is apparent that, because of these effects, the all-in economic cost of a dollar of government services is significantly more than a dollar.
- While there are sometimes good reasons for government borrowing—for example, to stimulate the economy

during recessions or to finance long-lived public investments—those arguments do not apply to most government spending most of the time. If we value the services that government provides more than their cost, we should grow up and tax ourselves to pay for them. If not, they should be eliminated.

- A large and growing number of spending programs are now run through the tax system. Policymakers should apply the same scrutiny to those "tax expenditures" as to traditional spending. If they are not worth the cost, they should be eliminated. And if they would work better as a traditional spending program, they should be removed from the tax code.
- The tax code could be made simpler and more efficient by eliminating most preferences and loopholes, and consolidating tax subsidies with similar aims (such as the vast array of education credits and deductions). This is easy for tax policy experts to say and hard for politicians to do, because those preferences and loopholes all have powerful constituencies.
- The Tax Cuts and Jobs Act passed in 2017 addressed some problems with the corporate income tax and sharply reduced the number of taxpayers who will choose to itemize their deductions, but it introduced some byzantine complexities, created a giant new tax shelter generator (the 20 percent deduction for pass-through business income), significantly exacerbated the nation's long-term fiscal imbalance, and did nothing to deal with the growing income inequality in America.

NOTES

Preface

1. Ipsos Poll conducted on behalf of National Public Radio, "United States Tax Policy," April 13, 2017, https://assets.documentcloud.org/documents/3671669/NPR-Ipsos-Tax-Poll.pdf.

Chapter 1

1. This famous quote is from a dissenting opinion by Justice Holmes in the 1927 court case of *Compañía General de Tabacos de Filipinas v. Collector of Internal Revenue*. A slightly edited version of the quote, "Taxes are what we pay for a civilized society," is inscribed on the Internal Revenue Service headquarters in Washington.

2. For popularity of federal agencies, see http://www.theacsi.org/index.php?option=com_content&view=article&id=238&Itemid=298.

3. See Stephen Gad, "Farmers up in Arms over Proposed Methane Tax on Cows," *CPH Post Online*, http://cphpost.dk/news/farmers-up-in-arms-over-proposed-methane-tax-on-cows.html, and John Drennan, "Government Do Not Find Gas-Filled Bovines A-moo-sing and Could Introduce a Tax to Reduce Their CO2 Output," *Irish Sun*, https://www.thesun.ie/news/2822303/government-gas-filled-bovines-introduce-a-tax-to-reduce-their-co2-output/.

4. The reference to the ethanol tax subsidy repeal supported by Senator Tom Coburn of Oklahoma and the subsequent criticism by Grover Norquist is available at http://www.rollcall.com/issues/56_139/grover-norquist-ethanol-tax-206489-1.html?zkMobileView=true.

5. Thomas Garrett and Gary Wagner, "Are Traffic Tickets Countercyclical?," Federal Reserve Bank of St. Louis Working Paper No. 2006-048A (2016), https://papers.ssrn.com/sol3/papers.cfm?abstract_id=923158.

6. The number of nations that have military conscription is from http://www.nationmaster.com/graph/mil_con-military-conscription.

7. The inflation figures for the Weimar Republic are from Hans F. Sennholz, "Hyperinflation in Germany, 1914-1923," Mises Institute (2006), available at https://mises.org/library/hyperinflation-germany-1914-1923.

8. The inflation figures for Zimbabwe are from http://www.nytimes.com/2006/05/02/world/africa/02zimbabwe.html?pagewanted=all.

9. See the Urban Institute's Net Income Change Calculator (NICC) at http://nicc.urban.org/netincomecalculator/calculator.php.

10. In 2014, 53 million people were enrolled in Medicare Part A; 49 million elected to participate in Part B. https://www.ssa.gov/policy/docs/statcomps/supplement/2015/medicare.html.

11. The numbers regarding states with the highest and least burden are drawn from page 1 of "State-Local Tax Burden Rankings: FY 2012," Tax Foundation (2016), available at https://files.taxfoundation.org/legacy/docs/State-Local_Tax_Burden_FY2012.pdf.

12. The figure on the composition of federal taxes for FY 2017 is derived from https://www.cbo.gov/system/files/2018-06/51134-2018-04-historicalbudgetdata.xlsx.

13. The figures on composition of state and local P taxes are taken from the Tax Policy Center's State & Local Government Finance Data Query System: http://slfdqs.taxpolicycenter.org/pages.cfm, U.S. Census Bureau, "Annual Survey of State and Local Government Finances," volume 4, and Census of Governments (1977–2015).

14. The data for tax as a share of GDP are drawn from the OECD's revenue statistics comparative tables at http://stats.oecd.org/Index.aspx?DataSetCode=REV.

15. The official version of the long-term fiscal imbalance is on page 207 of the 2018 Medicare Trustees Report at https://www.cms.gov/Research-Statistics-Data-and-Systems/Statistics-Trends-and-Reports/ReportsTrustFunds/Downloads/TR2018.pdf. Note that the projected sum of the 75-year budgetary impact

of the Hospital Insurance, Supplemental Medical Insurance, and Old-Age, Survivors, and Disability Insurance funds is a shortfall of $53.7 trillion, while the shortfall for the funds themselves is $17.6 trillion over the same period. For some perspective on the problem, read Alan J. Auerbach and William G. Gale, "The Economic Crisis and the Fiscal Crisis: 2009 and Beyond," *Tax Notes* 123, no. 1 (2009): 101–130.

16. On what people think about whether taxes should be reduced or spending cut, see "Taxes," Gallup, http://www.gallup.com/poll/1714/Taxes.aspx and "With Budget Debate Looming, Growing Share of Public Prefers Bigger Government," Pew Research Center, http://www.people-press.org/2017/04/24/with-budget-debate-looming-growing-share-of-public-prefers-bigger-government/.

Chapter 2

1. The principles of tax incidence are explained in Harvey S. Rosen and Ted Gayer, *Public Finance*, 10th ed. (New York: McGraw-Hill, 2017).

2. See Joel Slemrod, "Does It Matter Who Writes the Check to the Government? The Economics of Tax Remittance," *National Tax Journal* 61, no. 2 (June 2008): 251–275.

3. The Tax Protester FAQ, available at http://evans-legal.com/dan/tpfaq.html, dispels the myths about the validity of the income tax in forceful terms. The FAQ first clarifies that it is "not a collection of frequently asked questions, but a collection of frequently made assertions, together with an explanation of why each assertion is false."

4. Tons of income tax statistics are available at https://www.taxpolicycenter.org/statistics. The Tax Policy Center also summarizes the impact of the 2017 tax law in William G. Gale, Hilary Gelfond, Aaron Krupkin, Mark J. Mazur, and Eric Toder, "Effects of the Tax Cuts and Jobs Act: A Preliminary Analysis," Tax Policy Center, 2018, https://www.brookings.edu/wp-content/uploads/2018/06/ES_20180608_tcja_summary_paper_final.pdf.

5. According to the Tax Policy Center, "A tax unit is an individual, or a married couple, that files a tax return or would file a tax return if their income were high enough, along with all dependents of that individual or married couple." In most cases,

tax units are households, and sometimes we might use the term "household" to refer to them. But some households, such as two unmarried people who live together and file separate tax returns, represent multiple tax units. There are more tax units than households, and many more tax units than tax filers.

6. Bradley T. Heim and Yulianti Abbas, "Does Federal Deductibility Affect State and Local Revenue Sources?," *National Tax Journal* 68, no. 1 (March 2015): 33–58.

7. John William Hatfield, "Revenue Decentralization, the Local Income Tax Deduction, and the Provision of Public Goods," *National Tax Journal* 66, no. 1 (March 2013): 97–116.

8. William G. Gale, Hilary Gelfond, Aaron Krupkin, Mark J. Mazur, and Eric Toder, "Effects of the Tax Cuts and Jobs Act: A Preliminary Analysis," Tax Policy Center, 2018, https://www.brookings.edu/wp-content/uploads/2018/06/ES_20180608_tcja_summary_paper_final.pdf.

9. See Roberton Williams, "Why So Few People Pay Income Tax," *TaxVox* blog, February 25, 2010, https:// taxpolicycenter.org/taxvox/why-so-few-people-pay-income-tax/.

10. Net capital loss (losses in excess of gains) deductions are limited to $3,000 per year. Losses that cannot be deducted in the current year may be carried over to later tax years. This prevents wealthy taxpayers from selectively realizing losses to shelter other income, but they can often shelter their realized gains from tax by selling assets with offsetting losses. High-income, high-wealth taxpayers are most likely to do this. Evidence from the 1980s (the most recent available) suggests that taxpayers with net losses in excess of the $3,000 annual deduction limit were usually able to deduct them within a year or two. See Alan J. Auerbach, Leonard E. Burman, and Jonathan Siegel, "Capital Gains Taxation and Tax Avoidance: New Evidence from Panel Data," in *Does Atlas Shrug? The Economic Consequences of Taxing the Rich*, ed. Joel Slemrod (New York: Russell Sage Foundation; Cambridge, Mass.: Harvard University Press, 2000), 355–388.

11. The issue is actually even more complex than we make it out to be here. For a very careful analysis, see Donald Marron, "Goldilocks Meets Private Equity: Taxing Carried Interest Just Right," Tax Policy Center, October 7, 2016.

12. See table T18-0147, Tax Policy Center, https:// www.taxpolicycenter.org/model-estimates/

baseline-alternative-minimum-tax-amt-tables-oct-2018/
t18-0147-characteristics.

13. Howard Gleckman, "The Tax Cuts and Jobs Act
    and the Zombie AMT," *TaxVox* blog, October 2,
    2018, https://www.taxpolicycenter.org/taxvox/
    tax-cuts-and-jobs-act-and-zombie-amt.

14. For an amusing discussion of Warren Buffett's "secretary" and
    her supposed tax status, see Annie Lowrey, "Who Is Warren
    Buffett's Secretary?," *Slate,* September 20, 2011, available at
    http://www.slate.com/articles/business/moneybox/2011/09/
    who_is_warren_buffetts_secretary.html. As of this writing, she
    has not released her tax return.

15. For a critique of the Buffett Rule, see Leonard E. Burman, "The
    Buffett Rule: Right Goal, Wrong Tool," *New York Times*, April
    16, 2012, available at http://www.nytimes.com/2012/04/16/
    opinion/the-buffett-rule-right-goal-wrong-tool.html.

16. The Congressional Budget Office (CBO) study, "For Better or
    for Worse: Marriage and the Federal Income Tax," June 1997,
    although dated, is still the best overview of what generates
    marriage penalties and options to eliminate them. See http://
    www.cbo.gov/ftpdocs/0xx/doc7/marriage.pdf.

17. The GAO count of federal law provisions in which marital status
    is a factor was first done in United States General Accounting
    Office, "Defense of Marriage Act" (GAO/OGC-97-16), January
    31, 1997, available at http://www.gao.gov/archive/1997/
    og97016.pdf. That report was updated in 2004, "Defense of
    Marriage Act: Update to Previous Report" (GAO-04-353R),
    January 23, 2004, available at http://www.gao.gov/new.items/
    d04353r.pdf.

18. See Larry DeWitt, "Research Note #12: Taxation of Social Security
    Benefits," *SSA Historian's Office*, February 2001, https://www.ssa.
    gov/history/taxationofbenefits.html.

19. The tax on Social Security benefits phases in at a 50 percent rate
    starting at a modified adjust gross income (MAGI, which is AGI
    plus tax-exempt interest and half of Social Security benefits)
    of $32,000 for married couples who file jointly and $25,000 for
    everyone else. Starting at MAGI of $44,000 for joint filers and
    $34,000 for others, the phase-in rate increases to 85 percent. The
    phase-in continues until 85 percent of Social Security benefits are
    included in taxable income.

20. The 3.8 percent net investment income tax was also supposed to be dedicated to the Medicare trust fund. It is in the same part of the tax code as payroll taxes, but legislators forgot to include a sentence directing the revenue to the trust fund. So even though it is technically called the "additional Medicare contribution," it is just a tax. (We got this wrong in the first edition.) See Leonard E. Burman, "ACA and the Perils of Reconciliation," Tax Policy Center, March 13, 2017, https://www.taxpolicycenter.org/taxvox/aca-and-perils-reconciliation.

21. See table T18-0054, Tax Policy Center, 2018, https://www.taxpolicycenter.org/model-estimates/distribution-federal-payroll-and-income-taxes-may-2018/t18-0054-distribution-federal.

Chapter 3

1. See Leonard E. Burman, Kimberly A. Clausing, and Lydia Austin, "Is U.S. Corporate Income Double-Taxed?," *National Tax Journal* 70, no. 3 (September 2017): 675–706.

2. The figures about corporations and partnerships come from table 2 of the 2017 IRS Data Book, and the numbers about sole proprietorships are from IRS data presented in https://www.irs.gov/statistics/soi-tax-stats-nonfarm-sole-proprietorship-statistics.

3. The number of shareholders in S corps is drawn from table 6, S Corporation Returns, 2013, https://www.irs.gov/statistics/soi-tax-stats-table-6-returns-of-active-corporations-form-1120s.

4. This poll can be accessed at Frank Newport, "Majority Say Wealthy Americans, Corporations Taxed Too Little," April 18, 2017, https://news.gallup.com/poll/208685/majority-say-wealthy-americans-corporations-taxed-little.aspx.

5. Richard M. Bird provides a well-balanced survey of the arguments for and against a separate tax on corporations in "Why Tax Corporations?," available at http://publications.gc.ca/collections/Collection/F21-4-96-2E.pdf. The majority of Americans support taxing businesses when given a choice between raising taxes on corporations and raising taxes on households making more than $250,000 a year; available at http://www.nytimes.com/2011/05/03/business/economy/03poll.html?_r=2.

6. Value added by corporations can be found in Bureau of Economic Analysis, table 1.14 for FY 2017, https://apps.bea.gov/iTable/iTable.cfm?reqid=19&step=3&isuri=1&1921=survey&1903=55.

7. Value added by businesses and entire economy can be found in Bureau of Economic Analysis, table 1.3.5 for FY 2017, https://apps.bea.gov/iTable/iTable.cfm?reqid=19&step=2&isuri=1&1921=survey#reqid=19&step=2&isuri=1&1921=survey.

8. Walmart's revenue and profits for 2017 are available at Walmart Inc., 2018 Annual Report, January 31, 2018, https://s2.q4cdn.com/056532643/files/doc_financials/2018/annual/WMT-2018_Annual-Report.pdf.

9. Apple's profits come from Jen Wieczner, "The Fortune 500's 10 Most Profitable Companies," June 7, 2017, http://fortune.com/2017/06/07/fortune-500-companies-profit-apple-berkshire-hathaway/.

10. Economic Report of the President, 2018, table B-19.

11. The distribution of corporate ownership based on income and wealth are from tables 3.12a and 3.12b, page 128, from Edward N. Wolff, *A Century of Wealth in America* (Cambridge, Mass.: Belknap Press of Harvard University Press, 2017).

12. The discussion on the incidence of the corporate tax draws from Uwe Reinhardt, "Who Ultimately Pays the Corporate Income Tax?," *New York Times*, July 21, 2010, http://economix.blogs.nytimes.com/2010/07/23/who-ultimately-pays-the-corporate-income-tax/.

13. This controversial assumption is not terribly important to distributional analysis. The corporate income tax is mostly borne by taxpayers with high incomes whether the burden is assumed to be borne by capital or labor. That is because wage and capital income are highly correlated across households. See Benjamin J. Harris, "Corporate Tax Incidence and Its Implications for Progressivity," Tax Policy Center, 2009, available at http://www.taxpolicycenter.org/UploadedPDF/1001349_corporate_tax_incidence.pdf.

14. A more recent argument is that, in the presence of imperfect labor markets, business owners will be induced to "share" some of their tax cut with workers. See, for example, Clemens Fuest, Andreas Peichl, and Sebastian Siegloch, "Do Higher Corporate Taxes Reduce Wages? Micro Evidence from Germany," *American Economic Review* 108, no. 2: 393–418.

15. This report and the estimated effect on wages is discussed in Ylan Mui, "Here's How the White House Wants the GOP to Talk about Tax Reform," *CNBC*, October 16, 2017, https://www.cnbc.com/2017/10/16/white-house-economic-analysis-of-gop-tax-reform-plan.html.

16. For the story of General Electric, see David Kocieniewski, "G.E.'s Strategies Let It Avoid Taxes Altogether," *New York Times*, March 24, 2011, available at http://www.nytimes.com/2011/03/25/business/economy/25tax.html. GE apparently did actually remit a little tax in 2010. See Alan Sloan and Jeff Gerth, "The Truth about GE's Tax Bill," *Fortune*, April 4, 2011, available at https://fortune.com/2011/04/04/the-truth-about-ges-tax-bill/. Nonetheless, its prowess at avoiding income tax is legendary.

17. This report is from the Institute on Taxation and Economic Policy, "The 35 Percent Corporate Tax Myth," March 9, 2017, https://itep.org/the-35-percent-corporate-tax-myth/.

18. In "Book-Tax Conformity for Corporate Income: An Introduction to the Issues," Professor Michelle Hanlon of MIT explains the differences between the tax and financial accounting definition of corporate profits and assesses proposals to conform the two definitions. Her article is in *Tax Policy and the Economy*, vol. 19, ed. James Poterba (Cambridge, Mass.: MIT Press, 2005), 101–134.

19. The difference between income as reported in the financial statements and as reported for tax purposes is drawn from figure 3 of Michelle Hanlon and Terry Shevlin in "Book-Tax Conformity for Corporate Income: An Introduction to the Issues," *Tax Policy and the Economy*, vol. 19, ed. James Poterba (Cambridge, Mass.: MIT Press, 2003), 101–134. See also Mihir A. Desai in "The Divergence between Book Income and Tax Income," *Tax Policy and the Economy*, vol. 17 (Cambridge, Mass.: MIT Press), 169–206.

20. Danielle H. Green and George A. Plesko, "The Relation between Book and Taxable Income since the Introduction of the Schedule M-3," *National Tax Journal* 69, no. 4 (December 2016): 763–784.

21. The survey that reports the proportion of tax executives who rate minimizing the effective tax rate as extremely or very important is discussed in KPMG LLP, "Good, Better, Best: The Race to Set Global Standards in Tax Management. KPMG's 2009 Tax Department Survey," 2010, http://www.kpmg.com.br/publicacoes/tax/goodbetterbest.pdf.

22. See Deborah A. Geier, "Expensing and the Interest Deduction," *Tax Notes,* September 17, 2007, 1069–1071. https://engagedscholarship.csuohio.edu/cgi/viewcontent.cgi?referer=&httpsredir=1&article=1056&context=fac_articles.

23. Tom Neubig's argument that many corporations prefer tax rate cuts to accelerated depreciation is explained in "Where's the Applause? Why Most Corporations Prefer a Lower Tax Rate," *Tax Notes*, April 24, 2006, 483–486.

24. Lily L. Batchelder, "Accounting for Behavioral Considerations in Business Tax Reform: The Case of Expensing," January 24, 2017, https://papers.ssrn.com/sol3/papers.cfm?abstract_id=2904485.

25. The anecdotes about preferential tax treatment for some corporations are taken from Robert Schlesinger, "Targeted Tax Provisions Have a History before AIG Bonus Tax," *U.S. News,* March 20, 2009, http://www.usnews.com/opinion/blogs/robert-schlesinger/2009/03/20/targeted-tax-provisions-have-a-history-before-aig-bonus-tax. The Sonat story is from "U.S. Code: Title 26. INTERNAL REVENUE CODE," http://www.gpo.gov/fdsys/pkg/USCODE-2009-title26/pdf/USCODE-2009-title26-subtitleA-chap1-subchapB-partVI-sec168.pdf.

26. Mark Eichmann, "Delaware's Growing Poultry Industry," August 11, 2014, https://whyy.org/articles/delawares-growing-poultry-industry/.

27. See, for example, "Statement of Alan B. Krueger Assistant Secretary for Economic Policy and Chief Economist, U.S. Department of Treasury Subcommittee on Energy, Natural Resources, and Infrastructure," September 10, 2009, https://www.treasury.gov/press-center/press-releases/Pages/tg284.aspx.

28. The figures on Nike and McDonald's are found, respectively, in http://manufacturingmap.nikeinc.com/# and Matt Rosenberg, "Number of McDonald's Restaurants Worldwide," February 11, 2018, https://www.thoughtco.com/number-of-mcdonalds-restaurants-worldwide-1435174.

29. This argument is made in Mihir A. Desai, C. Fritz Foley, and James R. Hines Jr., "Foreign Direct Investment and the Domestic Capital Stock," *American Economic Review* 95, no. 2 (2005): 33–38.

30. The figures on the ratio of the profits of U.S.-controlled foreign corporations relative to GDP are taken from table 4, on p. 18 of Jane G. Gravelle, "Tax Havens: International Tax Avoidance and

Evasion," Congressional Research Service Report 7-5700, January 15, 2015, available at https://fas.org/sgp/crs/misc/R40623.pdf. An overview of the issues raised by tax havens is in Dhammika Dharmapala, "What Problems and Opportunities Are Created by Tax Havens?," *Oxford Review of Economic Policy* 24, no. 4 (Winter 2008): 661–679.

31. For states within the United States, details on whether they use sales or property or payroll for determining state income tax liability is drawn from Federation of Tax Administrators, "State Apportionment of Corporate Income," February 2018, https://www.taxadmin.org/assets/docs/Research/Rates/apport.pdf.

32. The discussion about corporate tax rates from around the world is drawn from Joel Slemrod, "Are Corporate Tax Rates, or Countries, Converging?," *Journal of Public Economics* 88, no. 6 (June 2004): 1169–1186.

33. For an excellent and accessible discussion of the benefits of trade, see Kimberly A. Clausing, *Open: The Progressive Case for Free Trade, Immigration, and Global Capital* (Cambridge, Mass.: Harvard University Press, 2019).

34. Joel Slemrod presents an overview of these issues in "Competitive Tax Policy," in *Rethinking Competitiveness*, ed. Kevin Hassett (Washington, D.C.: American Enterprise Institute, 2012), 32-67 available at https://www.aei.org/wp-content/uploads/2018/04/Rethinking-Competitiveness.pdf Our discussion draws on the arguments presented there.

Chapter 4

1. The Hobbes quote is from *Leviathan* (London: Andrew Crooke, 1651).

2. Tax rates by state (2018) can be found at "State General Sales Tax Rates 2018," Tax Policy Center, https://www.taxpolicycenter. org/statistics/state-sales-tax-rates.

3. State and local tax rates (2018) can be found at "Local Sales Tax Rates 2018," Tax Policy Center, https://www.taxpolicycenter. org/statistics/local-sales-tax-rates.

4. Of course, retailers in Oregon and Delaware might jack up their prices to take advantage of the sales tax advantage they have, so at least part of the sales tax savings might accrue to retailers rather than consumers.

5. California's compliance statistics are available at Legislative Analyst's Office, "California's Use Tax," February 28, 2011, http://www.lao.ca.gov/handouts/Econ/2011/CA_Use_Tax_2_28_11.pdf, p. 2.
6. The national estimate of uncollected sales tax is available at "Uncollected Sales & Use Tax from Remote Sales: Revised Figures," March 2017, https://www.reit.com/sites/default/files/Sales-Tax-Figure-March-2017-ICSC.pdf.
7. A nice discussion of the telephone excise tax and its history is available at Brian Francis, "Telephone Excise Tax," http://www.irs.gov/pub/irs-soi/99extele.pdf.
8. The website (http://nwtrcc.org/phonetax.php) urges continued resistance to the telephone excise tax to protest war.
9. The Joint Committee on Taxation estimated that a 5 percent VAT with a narrow base would raise $110 billion in 2018, or $22 billion per percentage point; a broader base would raise $180 billion, or $36 billion per percentage point. See Congressional Budget Office, "Options for Reducing the Deficit: 2017 to 2026," December 8, 2016, https://www.cbo.gov/budget-options/2016/52285.
10. The CBO did a comprehensive study of the issues involved in implementing a VAT. See *Effects of Adopting a Value-Added Tax*, February 1992, available at http://www.cbo.gov/sites/default/files/102nd-congress-1991-1992/reports/1992_02_effectsofadloptingavat.pdf.
11. The economic incidence of the VAT is not entirely clear. If the overall price level doesn't change (for example, because the Federal Reserve chooses not to accommodate it via expansionary monetary policy), the tax could ultimately be reflected in lower wages and smaller after-tax returns on capital. See Eric Toder, Jim Nunns, and Joseph Rosenberg, "Implications of Different Bases for a VAT," Tax Policy Center, February 2012, https://www.urban.org/sites/default/files/publication/25086/412501-Implications-of-Different-Bases-for-a-VAT.PDF.
12. The federal rate is 5 percent; most provinces also levy VAT, at rates from 5 percent to 10 percent.
13. The OECD provides VAT rates as of January 2018 in table 2.A2.1, available at https://www.oecd.org/ctp/consumption/Table-2.A2.1-VAT-GST-Rates-2018.xlsx.
14. The average state and local sales tax rate of 7.4 percent is an average of combined state and local tax rates from the Tax

Foundation, weighted by state population. See Jaret Walczak and Scott Drenkard, "State and Local Sales Tax Rates 2018," Tax Foundation, available at https://taxfoundation.org/state-and-local-sales-tax-rates-2018/, and U.S. Census Bureau, "National, State, and Puerto Rico Commonwealth Totals Datasets: Population, Population Change, and Estimated Components of Population Change: April 1, 2010 to July 1, 2017," https://www2.census.gov/programs-surveys/popest/datasets/2010-2017/national/totals/nst-est2017-alldata.csv.

15. Alan Viard of the American Enterprise Institute has an excellent explanation of this somewhat complex issue. See "Border Tax Adjustments Won't Stimulate Exports," March 2, 2009, available at http://www.aei.org/article/economics/fiscal-policy/border-tax-adjustments-wont-stimulate-exports/.

16. This section is adapted from Leonard Burman, "What Markets Tell Us about the Prospects for a BAT," *TaxVox* blog, February 27, 2017, https://www.taxpolicycenter.org/taxvox/what-markets-tell-us-about-prospects-bat.

17. See Howard Gleckman, "In Praise of the Debate over the Border Adjustable Tax," *TaxVox* blog, February 23, 2017, https://www.taxpolicycenter.org/taxvox/praise-debate-over-border-adjustable-tax.

18. Kenneth Rogoff, "The Purchasing Power Parity Puzzle," *Journal of Economic Literature* 34, no. 2 (June 1996): 647–668, http://dept.ku.edu/~empirics/Courses/Econ850/Papers/The%20Purchasing-Power%20Parity%20Puzzle.pdf.

19. Caroline Freund and Joe Gagnon were on a panel at an event titled "Border Tax Adjustment and Corporate Tax Reforms," conference, Peterson Institute for International Economics, Washington, February 1, 2017, https://www.piie.com/events/border-tax-adjustment-and-corporate-tax-reforms.

20. Joseph Lawler, "Yellen Not Sure GOP Tax Plan Would Boost the dollar," *Washington Examiner,* February 15, 2017, http://www.washingtonexaminer.com/yellen-not-sure-gop-tax-plan-would-boost-the-dollar/article/2614918.

21. Robert E. Hall and Alvin Rabushka are the intellectual fathers of the flat tax. They updated their book, *The Flat Tax*, 2nd ed. (Stanford, Calif.: Hoover Institution Press, 2007) and have made it available free online: http://www.hoover.org/publications/books/8329.

22. David Bradford explained how to make the flat tax more progressive in *Untangling the Income Tax* (Cambridge, Mass.: Harvard University Press, 1986), 329–334. At that time he hadn't yet dubbed the tax scheme the "X tax."

23. The Treasury analysis of the progressive consumption tax is discussed in President's Advisory Panel on Federal Tax Reform, *Simple, Fair, and Pro-growth: Proposals to Fix America's Tax System* (2005), chapter 7, available at https://www.treasury.gov/resource-center/tax-policy/Documents/Report-Fix-Tax-System-2005.pdf

24. Robert Carroll and Alan Viard have an excellent book on the subject of progressive versions of consumption taxes such as the X tax and the consumed income tax; see *Progressive Consumption Taxation: The X Tax Revisited* (Washington, D.C.: AEI Press, 2012).

25. This section is adapted from Leonard E. Burman, "We Are All Keynesians Now (Heaven Help Us!)," *TaxVox* blog, December 31, 2007, available at https://www.taxpolicycenter.org/taxvox/we-are-all-keynesians-now-heaven-help-us.

26. For a discussion of how the VAT (and other consumption taxes) would affect the elderly and other groups, see Eric Toder, Jim Nunns, and Joseph Rosenberg, "Methodology for Distributing a VAT," Tax Policy Center, April 2011, available at https://www.taxpolicycenter.org/sites/default/files/alfresco/publication-pdfs/1001533-Methodology-for-Distributing-a-VAT.PDF.

Chapter 5

1. An accessible treatment of the pros and cons of the U.S. estate tax is found in William G. Gale and Joel Slemrod, "Overview," in *Rethinking Estate and Gift Taxation*, ed. William G. Gale, James R. Hines Jr., and Joel Slemrod (Washington, D.C.: Brookings Institution Press, 2001), 1–64.

2. Wojciech Kopczuk and Joel Slemrod won an Ig Nobel Prize in Economics for reporting evidence that the timing of death of people subject to the estate tax is tax-sensitive in the United States (see "Dying to Save Taxes"). Others have found similar responses in Australia and Sweden. ("The Ig Nobel Prizes honor achievements that first make people laugh, and then make them think." See http://improbable.com/ig/).

3. For the value of farm and business estate tax provisions, see Justin Ransome and Vinu Satchit, "Valuation Discounts for Estate

and Gift Taxes," July 1, 2009, *Journal of Accountancy,* http://www.journalofaccountancy.com/Issues/2009/Jul/20091463.

4. For estimates of the distribution of the estate tax burden, see "Tax Policy Center Briefing Book: Who Pays the Estate Tax?," https://www.taxpolicycenter.org/briefing-book/who-pays-estate-tax.

5. Leonard E. Burman, Robert McClelland, and Chenxi Lu, "The Effects of Estate and Inheritance Taxes on Entrepreneurship," Tax Policy Center, March 5, 2018, https://www.taxpolicycenter.org/sites/default/files/publication/153466/2018.03.05_estate_tax_and_entrepreneurship_final_1_0.pdf.

6. For a capsule history of Margaret Thatcher's rise and fall, see John Simkin, "Margaret Thatcher," September 1997, http://www. https://spartacus-educational.com/COLDthatcher.htm.

7. Greg Mankiw argues that the rejection of this idea suggests that the rationale behind a progressive tax system is fundamentally flawed. See Greg Mankiw, "The Optimal Taxation of Height," Greg Mankiw's blog, April 17, 2007, http://gregmankiw.blogspot.com/2007/04/optimal-taxation-of-height.html. We think the problem is that height is a very imperfect predictor of income. So while it might improve fairness on average, it would create large and inexplicable inequities. (Disclosure: Both of us are over six feet tall.)

8. For the science fiction buffs out there, Kyle Logue and Joel Slemrod speculate on the tax implications of easily available information about one's genomes and its probabilistic consequences for one's standard of living. This article is "Genes as Tags: The Tax Implications of Widely Available Genetic Information," published in the *National Tax Journal* special issue on taxes and technology (December 2008): 843–863.

Chapter 6

1. Claudia Sahm, Matthew Shapiro, and Joel Slemrod present evidence from consumer surveys that suggest that for only 20 percent of people did the rebates lead people to mostly spend more. See "Household Response to the 2008 Tax Rebate: Survey Evidence and Aggregate Implications," in *Tax Policy and the Economy,* vol. 24, ed. Jeffrey R. Brown (Chicago: University of Chicago Press, 2010), 69–110. The research of Jonathan Parker and his co-authors suggest higher spending out of the tax cuts. See, e.g., David S. Johnson, Jonathan Parker, and Nicholas Souleles,

"Household Expenditure and the Income Tax Rebates of 2001," *American Economic Review* 96, no. 5 (December 2006): 1589–1610.

2. Victor Fuchs, Alan Krueger, and James Poterba, "Economists' Views about Parameters, Values, and Politics: Survey Results in Labor and Public Economics," *Journal of Economic Literature* 36, no. 3 (September 1998): 1387–1425.

3. The evidence is discussed at more length in chapter 4 of Joel Slemrod and Jon Bakija, *Taxing Ourselves: A Citizen's Guide to the Debate over Taxes*, 5th ed. (Cambridge, Mass.: MIT Press, 2017), 145–228.

4. Economists Julie Berry Cullen and Roger Gordon argue that there are many other implicit subsidies to entrepreneurship, including the ability to deduct many expenses that are nondeductible for wage earners and the option to incorporate and pay a 21 percent corporate tax rate if the business prospers (while deducting losses at higher individual rates if the business fails). See Julie Berry Cullen and Roger H. Gordon, "Taxes and Entrepreneurial Risk-Taking: Theory and Evidence for the U.S.," *Journal of Public Economics* 91, nos. 7–8 (2007): 1479–1505.

5. The study cited is Nick Bloom, Rachel Griffith, and John Van Reenen, "Do R&D Tax Credits Work? Evidence from a Panel of Countries 1979–1997," *Journal of Public Economics* 85, no. 1 (July 2002): 1–31.

6. The analysis of trickle-down economics is taken from Thomas Piketty, Emmanuel Saez, and Stefanie Stantcheva, "Optimal Taxation of Top Labor Incomes: A Tale of Three Elasticities," *American Economic Journal: Economic Policy* 6, no. 1 (February 2014): 230–271.

7. For a very comprehensive and clear analysis of the economics of deficits, see Doug Elmendorf and Greg Mankiw, "Government Debt," in *Handbook of Macroeconomics*, vol. 1, ed. John B. Taylor and Michael Woodford (Amsterdam: Elsevier, 1999), 1615–1669.

8. This estimate comes from Jonathan Huntley, "The Long-Run Effects of Federal Budget Deficits on National Saving and Private Domestic Investment," Congressional Budget Office Working Paper Series 1(2), 2014.

9. Congressional Budget Office, *The Budget and Economic Outlook: 2018 to 2028*, p. 127.

10. William G. Gale and Andrew A. Samwick, "Effects of Income Tax Changes on Economic Growth," chap. 2 in *The Economics*

of Tax Policy, ed. Alan J. Auerbach and Kent Smetters (New York: Oxford University Press, 2016), 13–39.

11. For more on this cheery scenario, see Leonard E. Burman, Jeffrey Rohaly, Joseph Rosenberg, and Katherine C. Lim, "Catastrophic Budget Failure," *National Tax Journal* 63, no. 3 (September 2010): 561–584. For a comprehensive analysis of the effects of debt and deficits, see William G. Gale, *Fiscal Therapy: Curing America's Debt Addiction and Investing in the Future* (Oxford: Oxford University Press, 2019).

12. The revival of the Ricardian view of deficits is due to the article by Robert Barro, "Are Government Bonds Net Wealth?," *Journal of Political Economy* 82, no. 6 (November–December 1974): 1095–1117. Doug Bernheim extended the idea to its logical extreme in "Is Everything Neutral?," *Journal of Political Economy* 96, no. 2 (April 1988): 308–338.

13. See Robert Barro et al. to Steven Mnuchin, November 25, 2017, https://www.treasury.gov/press-center/press-releases/Documents/Economist_Letter_STM_11252017.pdf.

14. For a range of possible outcomes, see William Gale, Surachai Khitatrakun, and Aaron Krupkin, "Winners and Losers after Paying for the Tax Cuts and Jobs Act," Tax Policy Center, December 8, 2017, https://www.taxpolicycenter.org/sites/default/files/publication/150211/winners_and_losers_after_paying_for_the_tax_cuts_and_jobs_act_12.8.pdf.

Chapter 7

1. The title for this chapter is borrowed from the excellent book by political scientist Christopher Howard, *The Hidden Welfare State: Tax Expenditures and Social Policy in the United States* (Princeton: Princeton University Press, 1997).

2. See Stanley S. Surrey and Paul R. McDaniel, *Tax Expenditures* (Cambridge, Mass.: Harvard University Press, 1985), 3.

3. See Donald Marron and Eric Toder, "Measuring Leviathan: How Big Is the Federal Government?," Tax Policy Center, presentation at "Starving the Hidden Beast: New Approaches to Tax Expenditure Reform," Loyola Law School, Los Angeles, January 14, 2011.

4. See also John L. Buckley, "Tax Expenditure Reform: Some Common Misconceptions," *Tax Notes* 132 (July 18, 2011): 255–259.

5. See Eric Toder, Daniel Berger, and Yifan Zhang, "Distributional Effects of Individual Income Tax Expenditures: An Update," September 26, 2016, available at https://www.taxpolicycenter. org/sites/default/files/publication/134396/2000945-distributional-effects-of-individual-income-tax-expenditures-an-udate.pdf, which updates earlier estimates from Leonard E. Burman, Christopher Geissler, and Eric J. Toder, "How Big Are Total Individual Income Tax Expenditures, and Who Benefits from Them?," *American Economic Review Papers and Proceedings* 98, no. 2 (May 2008): 79–83.

6. See Joint Committee on Taxation, "Background Information on Tax Expenditure Analysis and Historical Survey of Tax Expenditure Estimates" (JCX-15-11), February 28, 2011, p. 16, for a count of tax expenditures from 1987 to 2007. JCT's list of tax expenditures for 2018 can be found at Joint Committee on Taxation, "Estimates of Federal Tax Expenditures for Fiscal Years 2018–2022" (JCX-81-18), October 4, 2018.

7. William Gale, Jonathan Gruber, and Seth Stephens-Davidowitz, "Encouraging Homeownership through the Tax Code," *Tax Notes* 115, no. 12 (June 2007): 1171–1189.

8. See Kaiser Family Foundation, "Average Annual Single Premium per Enrolled Employee for Employer-Based Health Insurance," 2017, https://www.kff.org/other/state-indicator/single-coverage/?currentTimeframe=0&sortModel=%7B%22colId%22:%22Location%22,%22sort%22:%22asc%22%7D .

9. Chief Justice Roberts is quoted in Mike Sacks, "Supreme Court Health Care Decision: Individual Mandate Survives," *Huffington Post*, June 28, 2012, https://www.huffingtonpost.com/2012/06/28/supreme-court-health-care-decision_n_1585131.html.

10. Gordon B. Mermin, "The Big Tax Changes in the House GOP Health Plan," *TaxVox* blog, March 8, 2017, https://www.taxpolicycenter.org/taxvox/big-tax-changes-house-gop-health-plan.

11. For the income and payroll tax expenditures attributable to the tax exclusion for health insurance, see Analytical Perspectives, Budget of the United States Government, Fiscal Year 2019, Section 13, https://www.whitehouse.gov/wp-content/uploads/2018/02/spec-fy2019.pdf.

12. See Bruce F. Davie, "Tax Expenditures in the Federal Excise Tax System," *National Tax Journal* 47, no. 1 (March 1994): 39–62.

13. The quotes are from Neil Brooks, "Review of Surrey and McDaniel (1985)," *Canadian Tax Journal* 34, no. 3 (May–June 1986): 681–694.

14. Dan Shaviro argues compellingly that a big problem is that our "fiscal language" is very imprecise and sometimes misleading. See Daniel Shaviro, "Rethinking Tax Expenditures and Fiscal Language," *Tax Law Review 57*, no. 2 (2004): 187–231.

Chapter 8

1. TPC's estimates of the distribution of federal tax burdens are available at "T18-0083—Average Effective Federal Tax Rates—All Tax Units, by Expanded Cash Income Percentile, 2018," https://www.taxpolicycenter.org/model-estimates/baseline-average-effective-tax-rates-august-2018/t18-0083-average-effective-federal.

2. See Julie-Anne Cronin, "U.S. Treasury Distributional Analysis Methodology," U.S. Department of the Treasury, OTA Paper 85 (September 1999).

3. TPC Staff, "Distributional Analysis of the Tax Cuts and Jobs Act as Passed by the Senate," Tax Policy Center, December 4, 2017, https://www.taxpolicycenter.org/publications/distributional-analysis-tax-cuts-and-jobs-act-passed-senate/full.

4. Chris Edwards, "Senate Tax Bill Increases Progressivity," CATO Institute, December 11, 2017, https://www.cato.org/blog/senate-tax-bill-increases-progressivity.

5. See William Gale, Surachai Khitatrakun, and Aaron Krupkin, "Winners and Losers after Paying for the Tax Cuts and Jobs Act," Tax Policy Center, December 8, 2017, https://www.taxpolicycenter.org/publications/winners-and-losers-after-paying-tax-cuts-and-jobs-act/full for a discussion of how paying for tax cuts can affect distributional conclusions.

Chapter 9

1. The IRS budget for Fiscal Year 2017 can be found at Internal Revenue Service, "IRS Budget and Workforce," https://www.irs.gov/statistics/irs-budget-and-workforce.

2. The assertion that the IRS is one of the most efficient tax administrators can be found at Internal Revenue Service, "The Whys of Taxes," https://apps.irs.gov/app/understandingTaxes/student/whys.jsp.

3. A ProPublica report concluded that the IRS has far less resources than it needs to effectively enforce the tax system. They also report that morale at the IRS is very low and experienced auditors are fleeing, suggesting that enforcement might not rebound for years even if adequate funding is restored. Paul Kiel and Jesse Eisinger, "How the IRS Was Gutted," *ProPublica,* December 11, 2018, https://www.propublica.org/article/how-the-irs-was-gutted.

4. The compliance cost estimate is detailed in Testimony Submitted to the Committee on Ways and Means, Subcommittee on Oversight, Hearing on Tax Simplification, Washington, D.C., June 15, 2004.

5. The data about the percentage of returns that are audited in broad classes of taxpayers are taken from table 9a of the 2017 IRS Data Book, available at https://www.irs.gov/pub/irs-soi/17databk.pdf.

6. There is also a UIDIF score (Unreported Income DIF), based on the IRS's estimate of the potential that a taxpayer has unreported income.

7. The data about the number of information returns, number of contacts generated, and amount collected in additional assessments can be found in table 14 of the IRS Data Book, Fiscal Year 2017, https://www.irs.gov/pub/irs-soi/17databk.pdf.

8. The states offering vendor discounts are listed in "State Sales Tax Rates and Vendor Discounts," Federation of Tax Administrators, January 2019, https://www.taxadmin.org/assets/docs/Research/Rates/vendors.pdf.

9. For an overview of the facts and policy issues regarding tax evasion, see Joel Slemrod, "Cheating Ourselves: The Economics of Tax Evasion," *Journal of Economic Perspectives* 21, no. 1 (Winter 2007): 25–48. Our text draws on this article.

10. The 63 percent figure refers to the IRS estimate for tax years 2008 to 2010, and actually refers to all income subject to little or no information reporting, which includes nonfarm proprietor income as well as rents and royalties, farm income, and sales of business property, but self-employment income is the largest component. The estimate can be found on figure 1 of the IRS publication "Tax Gap Estimates for Tax Years 2008–2010," which can be accessed at https://www.irs.gov/pub/newsroom/

tax%20gap%20estimates%20for%202008%20through%202010. pdf.

11. The story of the day-care experiment in Israel is related in Uri Gneezy and Aldo Rustichini, "A Fine Is a Price," *Journal of Legal Studies* 29, no. 1 (January 2000): 1–17.

12. "Henry David Thoreau: A War Tax Resistance Inspiration," National War Tax Resistance Coordinating Committee, July 2014, https://nwtrcc.org/2014/07/10/henry-david-thoreau-a-war-tax-resistance-inspiration/.

13. The discussion on the effect of war on compliance draws on the work of Naomi Feldman and Joel Slemrod, "War and Taxation: When Does Patriotism Overcome the Free-Rider Impulse?," in *The New Fiscal Sociology*, ed. Isaac William Martin, Ajay K. Mehrotra, and Monica Prasad (Cambridge: Cambridge University Press, 2009), 138–154.

14. How tax cheating varies by demographic and other characteristics is based on information in pages 30 and 31 of Joel Slemrod, "Cheating Ourselves: The Economics of Tax Evasion," *Journal of Economic Perspectives* 21, no. 1 (Winter 2007): 25–48. The original sources vary and are mentioned in the paper.

15. The variation in the percentage of true income not reported and tax liability with income can be found in Andrew Johns and Joel Slemrod, "The Distribution of Income Tax Noncompliance," *National Tax Journal* 63, no. 3 (September 2010): 397–418.

16. The tax gap numbers come from the IRS publication "Tax Gap Estimates for Tax Years 2008–2010," referenced earlier.

17. The amount of underreporting based on type of income is again taken from the 2008–2010 IRS tax gap estimates: https://www.irs.gov/pub/newsroom/tax%20gap%20estimates%20for%20 2008%20through%202010.pdf.

18. The fraction of Michigan's use tax liability that is remitted by taxpayers is available at "Michigan's Sales and Use Taxes 2010," Michigan Department of Treasury, August 2011, http://www.michigan.gov/documents/treasury/Sales__Use_Tax_Report_ 2010_August_2011_360206_7.pdf.

19. This range is cited on page 2 of the opinion of the Supreme Court in *South Dakota v. Wayfair, Inc.*, available at https://www.supremecourt.gov/opinions/17pdf/17-494_j4el.pdf.

20. The number and amount of civil penalties assessed and number of criminal investigations initiated are from p. 42 of the IRS 2017 Data Book.

21. The proportion of criminal investigations that led to convictions and sentences are from table 18, "Criminal Investigation Program, by Status or Disposition, Fiscal Year 2017" of the IRS 2017 Data Book.

22. The passport initiative is discussed in Laura Saunders, "Thousands of Americans Will Be Denied a Passport Because of Unpaid Taxes," *Wall Street Journal*, July 6, 2018, https://www.wsj.com/articles/thousands-of-americans-will-be-denied-a-passport-because-of-unpaid-taxes-1530869401.

23. The extent of fraud in the EITC program can be found in Steve Holt, "The Earned Income Tax Credit at Age 30: What We Know," Brookings Institution Research Brief, February 2006. The original source is George K. Yin, John Karl Scholz, Jonathan Barry Forman, and Mark J. Mazur, "Improving the Delivery of Benefits to the Working Poor: Proposals to Reform the Earned Income Tax Credit Program," *American Journal of Tax Policy* 11, no. 2 (Fall 1994): 225–298.

24. Figures regarding number of tax refunds, number of tax returns, and amount of tax refunds are from tables 7, 4, and 8, respectively, of the 2017 IRS Data Book.

25. On the reasons why most individuals settle for getting a tax refund, see Damon Jones, "Inertia and Overwithholding: Explaining the Prevalence of Income Tax Refunds," *American Economic Journal: Economic Policy* 4, no. 1 (February 2012): 158–185.

26. The number of tax preparers is from Internal Revenue Service, "Return Preparer Review Leads to Recommendations for New Requirements of Paid Tax Return Preparers," January 2010, https://www.irs.gov/pub/irs-news/fs-10-01.pdf .

27. The percentage of each type of individual return filed by a paid preparer can be calculated using data from Internal Revenue Service, "Individual Income Tax Returns: Line Item Estimates, 2016," https://www.irs.gov/pub/irs-soi/16inlinecount.pdf.

28. The percentage of EITC filers using paid preparers in 2015 is found on page 2 of this report from the Treasury Inspector General for Tax Administration: "Improvements Are Needed to Better Document the Return Preparer Refundable Credit

Compliance Treatment Identification and Selection Process,"
October 19, 2017, https://www.treasury.gov/tigta/auditreports/
2018reports/201840001fr.pdf.

29. See "Chart 4: Individuals—Returns by Lodgment Type, 2015–16
Income Year," Australian Tax Office, 2017, https://www.ato.gov.
au/About-ATO/Research-and-statistics/In-detail/Taxation-
statistics/Taxation-statistics---previous-editions/Taxation-
statistics-2015-16/?page=6.

Chapter 10

1. The poll results are available at Seth Motel, "5 Facts on How
Americans View Taxes," Pew Research Center, April 10, 2015,
http://www.pewresearch.org/fact-tank/2015/04/10/5-facts-on-
how-americans-view-taxes/.

2. The number of words in the IRS code and federal tax regulations
is taken from "Number of Words in Internal Revenue Code and
Federal Tax Regulations, 1955–2005," Tax Foundation, https://
taxfoundation.org/number-words-internal-revenue-code-and-
federal-tax-regulations-1955-2005/. See also Scott Greenberg,
"Federal Tax Laws and Regulations Are Now Over 10 Million
Words Long," Tax Foundation, October 8, 2015, https://
taxfoundation.org/federal-tax-laws-and-regulations-are-now-
over-10-million-words-long/.

3. These figures come from the 2017 IRS Data Book, tables 3 and 4.

4. The quote by Charles McLure of Stanford University is from
Lawrence Zelenak, "Complex Tax Legislation in the TurboTax
Era," *Columbia Journal of Tax Law* 1, no. 1 (2010): 91–119.

5. See Joseph Cordes and Arlene Holen, "Should the Government
Prepare Individual Income Tax Returns?," Technology Policy
Institute, September 2010, https://techpolicyinstitute.org/wp-
content/uploads/2010/09/should-the-government-prepare-
2007495.pdf.

6. The Virginia story is told in Jim Nolan, "State to End Free Online
Tax-Filing Service," *Richmond Times-Dispatch*, April 4, 2010,
available at https://www.richmond.com/news/state-to-end-
free-online-tax-filing-service/article_6e7afbc1-8067-5b76-a013-
90b90f614fc7.html.

7. Joseph J. Thorndike, "Why Everyone Should Like
ReadyReturn—Even the Tax Foundation," October 8, 2009,

http://www.taxhistory.org/taxcom/taxblog.nsf/Permalink/
JTHE-7WMJ94?OpenDocument.

8. See Cordes and Holen, "Should the Government Prepare
   Individual Income Tax Returns?".

9. The argument for a data retrieval platform is made in Dennis
   Ventry, "Americans Don't Hate Taxes, They Hate Paying Taxes,"
   University of British Columbia Law Review 44, no. 3 (2011): 835–889.

10. The answer to this question draws on an article by one of
    this book's co-authors (Slemrod), "Is This Tax Reform, or
    Just Confusion?," which appears in the *Journal of Economic
    Perspectives*, 32, no. 4 (Fall, 2018): 73–95.

11. See Jim Tankersley, "The New Tax Form Is Postcard-Size, but
    More Complicated Than Ever," *New York Times*, June 25, 2018,
    https://www.nytimes.com/2018/06/25/your-money/1040-
    income-tax-postcard.html.

12. Ruth Simon and Richard Rubin, "Crack and Pack: How
    Companies Are Mastering the New Tax Code," *Wall Street
    Journal*, April 3, 2018, https://www.wsj.com/articles/crack-
    and-pack-how-companies-are-mastering-the-new-tax-code-
    1522768287.

Chapter 11

1. Richard Thaler and Cass Sunstein, *Nudge: Improving Decisions
   about Health, Wealth, and Happiness* (New Haven: Yale University
   Press, 2008).

2. Brigitte C. Madrian and Dennis F. Shea, "The Power of
   Suggestion: Inertia in 401(k) Participation and Savings Behavior,"
   Quarterly Journal of Economics 116, no. 4 (2001): 1149–1187.

3. See Raj Chetty, John N. Friedman, Søren Leth-Petersen, Torben
   Heien Nielsen, and Tore Olsen, "Active vs. Passive Decisions
   and Crowd-Out in Retirement Savings Accounts: Evidence
   from Denmark," *Quarterly Journal of Economics* 129, no. 3
   (2014): 1141–1219.

4. "Can Small Incentives Have Large Effects? The Impact of Taxes
   versus Bonuses on Disposable Bag Use," *Proceedings of the
   105th National Tax Association Annual Conference on Taxation*, vol.
   105, 64–90.

5. For more on loss aversion and behavioral nudges, see Alex Rees-
   Jones, "Quantifying Loss-Averse Tax Manipulation," *Review
   of Economic Studies* 85, no. 2 (April 2018): 1251–1278; and Per

Engström, Katarina Nordblom, Henry Ohlsson, and Annika Persson, "Tax Compliance and Loss Aversion," *American Economic Journal: Economic Policy* 7, no. 4 (November 2015): 132–164.

6. Raj Chetty, Adam Looney, and Kory Kroft, "Salience and Taxation: Theory and Evidence," *American Economic Review* 99, no. 4 (2009): 1145–1177.

7. The salience research also has implications for the design of tax subsidies. See Caroline Hoxby and George Bulman, "The Effects of the Tax Deduction for Postsecondary Tuition: Implications for Structuring Tax-Based Aid," NBER Working Paper 21554, National Bureau of Economic Research, September 2015, https://www.nber.org/papers/w21554.pdf.

8. Donald Marron, "Should We Tax Internalities like Externalities?," Tax Policy Center, 2015, available at https://www.urban.org/sites/default/files/publication/72891/2000508-should-we-tax-internalities-like-externalities.pdf.

9. See Paul Krugman, "Choice and the Insurance Mandate," *New York Times* blog, November 27, 2017, https://krugman.blogs.nytimes.com/2017/11/27/choice-and-the-insurance-mandate/.

10. Johannes Abeler and Simon Jäger, "Complex Tax Incentives," *American Economic Journal: Economic Policy* 7, no. 3 (2015): 1–28.

11. See Jeffrey B. Liebman and Richard J. Zeckhauser, "Schmeduling," working paper, Harvard University and NBER (April 2003), http://www.people.hbs.edu/bhall/NOMTalks/papers/schmeduling_apr62003.pdf; and Alex Rees-Jones and Dmitry Taubinsky, "Measuring 'Schmeduling,' " NBER Working Paper 22884, National Bureau of Economic Research, June 2018, https://www.nber.org/papers/w22884.

Chapter 12

1. The NPR poll is available at "National Survey of Americans' Views on Taxes," National Public Radio, Kaiser Family Foundation, and Kennedy School of Government, April 2003, http://www.npr.org/news/specials/polls/taxes2003/20030415_taxes_survey.pdf.

2. The poll results are available at Tina Orem, "Americans Don't Know Much about Taxes—or That They Might Get Them Done for Free," Nerdwallet, February 15, 2017, https://www.nerdwallet.com/blog/taxes/americans-dont-know-much-about-taxes-or-that-they-might-get-them-done-for-free/.

3. See also Bruce Bartlett, "What People Don't Know about Federal Income Taxes," *Wall Street Pit* blog, April 15, 2010, available at https://wallstreetpit.com/23468-what-people-dont-know-about-federal-income-taxes/.

4. The IRS estimates of EITC take-up are available at https://www.eitc.irs.gov/eitc-central/participation-rate/eitc-participation-rate-by-states.

5. Perceptions of the estate tax from the 2007 and 2008 Cooperative Congressional Election Surveys are reported in John Sides, "Stories, Science, and Public Opinion about the Estate Tax," George Washington University, July 2011.

6. The California data are reported in "What Do You Know?," *The Economist*, April 20, 2011, http://www.economist.com/node/18563612.

7. This data are from Pew Research Center, "Top Frustrations with Tax System: Sense That Corporations, Wealthy Don't Pay Fair Share," April 14, 2017, http://www.people-press.org/2017/04/14/top-frustrations-with-tax-system-sense-that-corporations-wealthy-dont-pay-fair-share/.

8. Paul Ryan, December 22, 2018, "The Biggest Tax Reform in a Generation Is Now Law," Press Release.

9. "The Tax Reform Act of 1986," American Institute of Certified Public Accountants, https://www.aicpa.org/content/dam/aicpa/advocacy/tax/downloadabledocuments/the-tax-reform-act-of-1986-qa.docx.

10. The bullet points can be found here: "2017 Tax Reform for Economic Growth and American Jobs," http://newsletters.usdbriefs.com/2017/Tax/TNV/170426_1suppA.pdf. The unified framework released by the Treasury is here: "Unified Framework for Fixing Our Broken Tax Code," September 27, 2017, https://www.treasury.gov/press-center/press-releases/Documents/Tax-Framework.pdf.

11. Yuval Rosenberg, "Treasury Pulls a Paper That Contradicts Mnuchin's Corporate Tax Argument," *Fiscal Times*, September 29, 2017, http://www.thefiscaltimes.com/2017/09/29/Treasury-Pulls-Paper-Contradicts-Mnuchin-s-Corporate-Tax-Argument.

12. U.S. Congress, House, An Act to provide for reconciliation pursuant to titles II and V of the concurrent resolution on the budget for fiscal year 2018, HR 1, 115th Congress, 1st session, https://www.congress.gov/115/bills/hr1/BILLS-115hr1eh.pdf.

13. For a discussion of the "conceptual mark," see "Senate Finance Committee Releases 'Chairman's Mark' of Tax Reform Legislation; Mark Up Begins," Baker McKenzie, November 13, 2017, https://www.bakermckenzie.com/en/insight/publications/2017/11/senate-finance-committee-releases/. The 515-page Senate Finance Committee's document can be found here: U.S. Congress, Senate Finance Committee, https://www.finance.senate.gov/imo/media/doc/11.20.17%20Tax%20Cuts%20and%20Jobs%20Act.pdf.

14. For a discussion of some of the mistakes made in the TCJA, see "Lawmakers Explain TCJA Errors & Request IRS Guidance Reflect Congressional Intent Pending Corrections," *Thomson Reuters,* August 20, 2018 https://tax.thomsonreuters.com/news/lawmakers-explain-tcja-errors-request-irs-guidance-reflect-congressional-intent-pending-corrections//.

15. See Robert Wood, "Sexual Harassment Tax Law That Double-Taxes Victims Needs Fixing," *Forbes,* June 6, 2018, https://www.forbes.com/sites/robertwood/2018/06/06/sexual-harassment-tax-law-that-double-taxes-victims-needs-fixing/#2e1f806c6d59.

16. For more information on the regulatory process, see Internal Revenue Service, "Overview of the Regulations Process," available at http://www.irs.gov/irm/part32/irm_32-001-001.html.

17. See Leonard Burman, "OMB Review of Tax Regulations: A 'Dispassionate Second Opinion' or Needless Sand in the Gears?," *TaxVox* blog, September 17, 2018, https://www.taxpolicycenter.org/taxvox/omb-review-tax-regulations-dispassionate-second-opinion-or-needless-sand-gears for a brief summary of the OMB regulation process and some issues.

18. This section draws heavily from the Center on Budget and Policy Priorities, "Policy Basics: Introduction to the Federal Budget Process," December 6, 2010, available at http://www.cbpp.org/files/3-7-03bud.pdf.

19. For more on the JCT's role in the revenue-estimating process, see Joint Committee on Taxation, "Joint Committee Revenue Estimation Process," http://www.jct.gov/about-us/revenue-estimating.html.

Chapter 13

1. See William A. Niskanen, "Limiting Government: The Failure of 'Starve the Beast,' " *Cato Journal* 26, no. 3 (Fall 2006): 553–558.

2. See Michael J. New, "Starve the Beast: A Further Examination," *Cato Journal* 29, no. 3 (Fall 2009): 487–495.

3. Christina D. Romer and David H. Romer, "Do Tax Cuts Starve the Beast? The Effect of Tax Changes on Government Spending," *Brookings Papers on Economic Activity* (Spring 2009): 139–200.

4. See Bruce Bartlett, "Tax Cuts and 'Starving the Beast,' " *Forbes. com,* May 7, 2010, http://www.forbes.com/2010/05/06/tax-cuts-republicans-starve-the-beast-columnists-bruce-bartlett. html.

5. Americans for Tax Reform reports that 44 senators and 209 House members had signed the pledge as of December 14, 2018. See the "Taxpayer Protection Pledge Database," available at https:// www.atr.org/pledge-database.

6. This is adapted from Leonard E. Burman, "We Need to Ban the Evil Santas," *Washington Times*, December 22, 2009, available at http://www.washingtontimes.com/news/2009/dec/22/we-need-to-ban-the-evil-santas/.

7. See Philip Elliott, "Ted Cruz's Plan to Abolish the IRS Is Unlikely to Ever Happen," *Business Insider / Associated Press,* March 25, 2015, https://www.businessinsider.com/ted-cruzs-plan-to-abolish-the-irs-is-unlikely-to-ever-happen-2015-3.

8. See William G. Gale, "The National Retail Sales Tax: What Would the Rate Have to Be?" *Tax Notes* (2006): 889–911.

Chapter 14

1. For a longer assessment of TCJA by one of us, see Joel Slemrod, "Is This Tax Reform, or Just Confusion?" in the Fall 2018 issue of the *Journal of Economic Perspectives*, 73–95.

2. For the corporate tax shortfall after the Tax Reform Act of 1986, see James M. Poterba, "Why Didn't the Tax Reform Act of 1986 Raise Corporate Taxes?," in *Tax Policy and the Economy*, vol. 6, ed. James M. Poterba (Cambridge, Mass.: MIT Press, 1992), 43–58.

3. See Bipartisan Policy Center, *Restoring America's Future*, available at https://bipartisanpolicy.org/report/restoring-americas-future/.

4. See the National Commission on Fiscal Responsibility and Reform, *The Moment of Truth*, December 2010, available at https://www.senate.gov/reference/resources/pdf/NationalCommissiononFiscalResponsibilityandReform_Dec012010.pdf.

5. See Michael Graetz, *100 Million Unnecessary Returns* (New Haven: Yale University Press, 2008).

GLOSSARY

This glossary is an edited and abridged version of the one that appears in the Tax Policy Center's excellent *BriefingBook*, available at http://www.taxpolicycenter.org/briefing-book. Used with permission.

A

accelerated depreciation. See **depreciation**.

adjusted gross income (AGI). A measure of income used to determine a tax filing unit's tax liability (before subtracting **personal exemptions** and the **standard deduction** or **itemized deductions**). AGI excludes certain types of income received (e.g., municipal bond interest, most Social Security income, some alimony), and some expenses are deducted from AGI (e.g., **IRA** deductions, some educational expenses, and health insurance premiums for self-employed). (See also **taxable income**.)

alternative minimum tax (AMT). The individual alternative minimum tax applies an alternative tax rate schedule to an expanded measure of taxable income and, if the resulting "tentative AMT" exceeds ordinary income tax, the difference is added to tax liability. It was intended to ensure that high-income filers not take undue advantage of tax preferences to reduce or eliminate their tax liability, but prior to passage of the TCJA, many upper-middle-income taxpayers were subject to the AMT. The TCJA limited or repealed many middle-class AMT "preference items" and raised the AMT exemption, but only through 2025. The TCJA eliminated a parallel corporate alternative minimum tax.

American Taxpayer Relief Act of 2012 (ATRA). Permanently extended most provisions of the 2001 and 2003 tax acts (**EGTRRA** and **JGTRRA**) but generally allowed both acts to expire for taxpayers with the highest incomes. ATRA maintained most reduced tax rates, expansion of the Child Tax Credit and EITC, and the American Opportunity Tax Credit for higher education. It also made permanent reductions to the AMT and the estate tax.

average effective tax rate (ETR). A widely used measure of tax burdens, equal to tax paid divided by some measure of income. ETRs may be calculated with respect to a single tax, such as the individual income tax, or with respect to all taxes together (i.e., including payroll taxes, corporate income taxes, and estate taxes). However, the ETR may differ substantially from the economic incidence of tax. (See also **tax incidence**.)

B

base broadening. A term applied to efforts to expand the tax base, usually by eliminating deductions, exclusions, and other preferences from the tax base. A broader base allows more revenue to be raised without increasing tax rates or for rates to be cut without sacrificing revenues.

base erosion and anti-abuse tax (BEAT). This is a minimum tax on U.S. corporations that make deductible payments, such as interest, royalties, and certain service payments, to a related foreign subsidiary. The U.S. firm pays the higher of its regular corporate income tax or the BEAT.

BEAT. See **Base erosion and anti-abuse tax**.

bonus depreciation. The policy of accelerating depreciation by allowing firms to deduct immediately—expense—some fraction of the cost of most capital goods while depreciating the remaining fraction over time. Bonus depreciation was enacted as a temporary economic stimulus in 2002, but has remained in the law since then The fraction has varied between 30, 50, and 100 percent. (See **depreciation** and **expensing**.)

bracket creep. The movement of taxpayers into higher tax brackets caused by inflation. Under a progressive tax system, rising nominal income can move taxpayers into higher tax brackets, even if their real income (after adjusting for inflation) remains constant. Congress indexed tax rate schedules for inflation in the early 1980s to prevent general increases in the price level from causing bracket creep. (See **indexation of the tax system**.)

budget baseline. The baseline is the level of revenue (or spending) expected under a given set of assumptions. Traditionally, Congress and the administration have used a "current law baseline" that assumes that discretionary spending grows at the rate of inflation and mandatory spending and tax revenues are determined by current law. In particular, temporary tax provisions expire as scheduled. However, the Obama administration advocated using a "current policy baseline," which assumes that the **Bush tax cuts**, which were scheduled to expire, would be extended indefinitely (and that a politically unpopular Medicare provision that was temporarily suspended would never be allowed to take effect).

budget scoring. The process of estimating the budgetary effects of proposed changes in tax and expenditure policies and enacted legislation. The budget score represents the difference from baseline revenues or spending.

Bush tax cuts. A set of tax provisions that were originally enacted in the administration of President George W. Bush—most in 2001 and 2003. The first installment, the **Economic Growth and Tax Relief Reconciliation Act of 2001** (EGTRRA), cut individual income tax rates, phased out the estate and gift tax, doubled the Child Tax Credit, provided marriage penalty relief, expanded retirement tax incentives, and temporarily raised the threshold for taxation under the individual **alternative minimum tax** (AMT). The provisions of EGTRRA phased in slowly and were all set to expire at the end of 2010. Subsequent legislation in 2003, the **Jobs and Growth Tax Relief Reconciliation Act of 2003**, sped up many of the 2001 tax cuts, added cuts in the tax rates on long-term capital gains and dividends, and temporarily indexed the AMT, but preserved the 2010 expiration date. The Pension Protection Act of 2006 made the retirement savings provisions of EGTRRA permanent and indexed the AMT through 2010. In 2010, President Obama signed legislation extending the Bush income tax cuts and restoring the estate and gift tax, as well as adding several new tax cuts through 2012. In 2012, most of the Bush income tax cuts, except those affecting the highest-income taxpayers, and the Obama estate tax parameters were made permanent.

C

capital cost recovery. Income tax features intended to allow businesses to deduct over time the costs of tangible capital assets that are used to produce income. It is similar to a depreciation allowance, except that "depreciation" in principle relates the timing of the deductions to changes in asset value over time. (See **depreciation**.)

capital gains. The difference between the sale price and purchase price of capital assets net of brokers' fees and other costs. Capital gains are generally taxable upon sale (or "realization"). Long-term gains, those realized after holding the asset for a year or longer, face lower tax rates (no more than 20 percent) than short-term gains, which are taxed the same as earned income. Taxpayers can deduct up to $3,000 of net losses (losses in excess of gains) each year against other income; taxpayers can carry over losses above that amount and subtract them from future gains.

capitalization. An increase or decrease in the value of an asset arising from a tax or subsidy provision. For example, the mortgage interest deduction may increase demand for housing and push up its price. That is, part of the subsidy is capitalized into home prices.

charitable deductions. Deductions allowed for gifts to charity. Subject to certain limits, individual taxpayers who itemize deductions and corporations are allowed to deduct gifts to charitable and certain other nonprofit organizations. In part, the deduction is intended to subsidize the activities of private organizations that provide viable alternatives to direct government programs. (See **itemized deductions**.)

Child and Dependent Care Tax Credit (CDCTC). A tax credit based on eligible child care expenses incurred by taxpayers who are employed or in school. The credit varies with the expenses incurred, the number of eligible children, and the taxpayer's **AGI**. A separate exclusion is available for some employer-provided childcare.

Child Tax Credit (CTC). A tax credit of $2,000 per qualifying child. The credit is partially refundable for filers with earnings over a threshold ($2,500). The refundable portion is limited to 15 percent of earnings above the threshold up to $1,400 per child. The maximum refundable credit is indexed for inflation. (See **refundable tax credit**.)

consumer price index (CPI). A measure of the average level of prices, inclusive of sales and excise taxes. Until 2017, adjustments to tax parameters (see **indexation of the tax system**) were based on the cost of a fixed basket of goods and services called the Consumer Price Index for all Urban Consumers, or CPI-U. The TCJA changed the index to the chained CPI, a measure that accounts for the ability of consumers to purchase substitutes when some prices rise more than others. When prices rise unevenly, the chained CPI rises more slowly than the CPI-U, which is why the switch to the new index raises tax receipts over time.

consumption tax. Tax on goods or services. In the United States, most consumption taxes are levied by states and local governments (as retail sales taxes), although the federal government does levy some selective consumption taxes, called **excise taxes**. The **value-added tax (VAT)** is a consumption tax that is common in the rest of the world.

corporate income tax. A tax levied on corporate profits. A corporation's taxable income is its total receipts minus allowable expenses, including capital depreciation.

D

deduction. A reduction in **taxable income** for certain expenses. Some deductions, such as that for contributions to an **Individual Retirement Account (IRA)**, reduce **AGI**. Most deductions, such as those for home mortgage interest and state and local taxes, are only available to those who **itemize deductions**. Most taxpayers choose not to itemize and instead claim the **standard deduction** because it provides a greater tax benefit. Because tax rates increase with taxable income, a dollar of deductions generally benefits a high-income taxpayer more than a low-income taxpayer. Deductions cannot reduce taxable income below zero.

depreciation. A measurement of the declining value of assets over time because of physical deterioration or obsolescence. The actual rate at which an asset's value falls is called economic depreciation, which depends on wear and tear and the rate of technological obsolescence. In practice, tax depreciation is calculated by a schedule of deductions, usually over the asset's "useful life" specified in the tax code through which the full cost of an asset can be written off. Accelerated depreciation refers to a depreciation schedule that allows larger deductions in early years than would be expected due to economic depreciation.

distortion. The economic cost of changes in behavior due to taxes, government benefits, monopolies, and other forces that interfere with the otherwise-efficient operation of a market economy. For example, employees might choose to work fewer hours because taxes reduce their after-tax wage.

distribution table. A table that details how a proposal or policy is estimated to affect the distribution of tax burdens across income categories, demographic groups, or sets of taxpayers defined by other characteristics.

dividends. Profits distributed by a corporation to its shareholders. Most dividends are taxed at the same lower tax rates that apply to **capital gains**.

double taxation of dividends. Most tax systems that have both corporate and individual income taxes levy tax on corporate profits twice, once at the corporate level and again at the individual level when shareholders receive profits in the form of dividends or capital gains. The reduced tax rates on capital gains and dividends are intended in part as an offset to double taxation.

dynamic modeling. Computer-based simulation of how tax policy or tax reform affects the economy taking into account how individuals, households, or firms alter their work, saving, investment, or consumption behavior, and how those effects feed back to affect tax revenues.

dynamic scoring. An approach to calculating how a tax proposal would affect the economy in the short and long run by determining the policy's macroeconomic effects. Unlike conventional ("static") scoring, which holds economic inputs and outputs constant, dynamic scoring predicts how a policy would affect macroeconomic factors, such as consumption, investment, saving, and labor supply, and uses those factor changes to forecast GDP and government revenues over a period of time. Dynamic scoring can also be used for proposals affecting government spending and regulation.

E

earmarked tax. A tax that is dedicated to fund a particular spending program. The most prominent earmarked taxes are the **payroll taxes** that are dedicated to fund Social Security and Medicare, and motor fuels excise taxes, which are dedicated to the Highway Trust Fund and the Leaking Underground Storage Tank Trust Fund.

Earned Income Tax Credit (EITC). A refundable tax credit that supplements the earnings of low-income workers. The credit is a fixed percentage of earnings up to a maximum level, remains constant over a range above that level (the "plateau"), and then phases out as income rises further. Those income ranges depend on both the taxpayer's filing status and the number of children in the taxpayer's family. In contrast, the credit rate depends only on the number of children. Married couples with three or more children receive the largest credit, a maximum of $6,431 in 2018. Childless workers get the smallest credit, no more than $519 in 2018. Originally enacted in 1975, the EITC is now the largest federal means-tested cash transfer program.

Economic Growth and Tax Relief Reconciliation Act of 2001 (EGTRRA). A tax bill passed under the presidency of George W. Bush (see **Bush tax cuts**) that reduced most tax rates, increased the **Child Tax Credit** and made it partially refundable, expanded tax-free retirement savings, reduced **marriage penalties,** increased the **Child and Dependent Care Tax Credit,** and phased out the **estate tax**. Most provisions were scheduled to phase in slowly between 2001 and 2010, and then expire at the start of 2011. **JGTRRA** accelerated some of the EGTRRA tax cuts and added others.

economic income. A very broad income concept that includes cash income from all sources, fringe benefits, net realized capital gains, both cash and in-kind transfers, the employer's share of payroll taxes, and corporate income tax liability. The Treasury Department's Office of Tax Analysis developed a similar measure in the 1980s and used it for distribution tables until 2000.

Economic Recovery Tax Act (ERTA). Tax legislation enacted in 1981 (and often referred to as the "Reagan tax cut") that significantly reduced income taxes on individuals and businesses. The Tax Equity and Fiscal Responsibility Act (TEFRA) scaled back the cuts in 1982.

EGTRRA. See **Economic Growth and Tax Relief Reconciliation Act of 2001**.

employer-sponsored health insurance. Health insurance offered by an employer to some or all employees. Employer contributions to health insurance plans are exempt from both income and payroll taxes. Economists believe that workers receive lower wages in exchange for the valuable tax-free fringe benefit. The exclusion from tax of employer-sponsored health insurance is the single biggest **tax expenditure**.

entitlements. Payments to individuals, governments, or businesses that, under law, must be made to all those eligible and for which funds do not have to be appropriated in advance. The largest entitlement programs are Social Security, Medicare, and Medicaid.

ERTA. See **Economic Recovery Tax Act**.

estate tax. A tax levied on a person's estate at the time of his or her death. The federal estate tax applies only to large estates, those worth over $11.2 million for people dying in 2018. No tax is owed on transfers to spouses or to charities, and special provisions apply to farms and small businesses. (See also **gift tax**.)

excise tax. A tax on specific goods and services, levied at federal, state, and local levels. The most common excise taxes are on gasoline, alcohol, and tobacco products.

expensing. Allows businesses to immediately deduct the entire cost of a capital asset, rather than claiming depreciation deductions over the useful life of the asset. (See also **depreciation**.)

externality. The effects of private consumption and production activities on others that are not reflected in market prices. For example, some manufacturing activities may produce pollution and, absent taxation or regulation (or a costless way for those injured by pollution to seek legal recourse for damages), the manufacturer will ignore those costs in making production decisions and there will be an inefficiently high level of pollution. A **Pigouvian tax** may be imposed so that prices reflect the cost of externalities.

F

FDII. See **foreign-derived intangible income**.

filing status. Tax filers fall into one of five categories, depending on their marital status and family structure. A single person without children files as a single; a single parent with dependent children files as a head of household; a married couple, with or without children, files either as married filing joint or married filing separate; and a recent widow(er) may file as a qualifying widow(er), which is the same, in effect, as married filing joint. The standard deductions, bracket widths, and qualification criteria for certain credits and deductions vary by filing status.

fiscal year (FY). A government's accounting period designated by the calendar year in which it ends. The federal government's 2019 fiscal year begins on October 1, 2018 and ends on September 30, 2019. The fiscal year in most states ends on June 30.

flat tax. A proposal for tax reform that would replace the income tax system with a single-rate (or flat-rate) tax on businesses and on individuals after an exempt amount. Many flat-tax proposals are designed to be consumption rather than income taxes (see **VAT**), many would retain politically sensitive deductions such as for mortgage interest payments, and most are really not "flat" because they grant an exemption for a certain amount of earnings.

foreign-derived intangible income (FDII). U.S. corporations can take a deduction for **foreign-derived intangible income**, which is income from the sale of goods and services abroad that is attributable to intangible assets, such as patents, trademarks, and copyrights, held in the United States.

foreign tax credit. A credit that allows U.S. residents to subtract foreign income taxes paid from the U.S. income tax due on income earned abroad.

G

gift tax. A tax levied on gifts in excess of a specified threshold. In 2018, no tax was levied on annual gifts of up to $15,000 per donor, per recipient; gifts in excess of the limit are taxable, but no tax is due until lifetime taxable gifts total more than $11.2 million. Any tax still due must be remitted when the donor dies and is incorporated into the decedent's estate tax. (See also **estate tax**.)

GILTI. See **global intangible low-taxed income**.

global intangible low-taxed income (GILTI). This is the income earned by foreign affiliates of U.S. companies from intangible assets such as patents, trademarks, and copyrights. A U.S. corporation must include half of the GILTI earned by its foreign affiliates in its gross income subject to the U.S. corporate income tax, but it can deduct 80 percent of the foreign tax paid on GILTI.

H

health savings account (HSA). A special tax-favored account for deposits made to cover current and future health care expenses paid by the individual. As with defined contribution retirement plans, contributions to HSAs and any earnings are generally deductible (or excluded from income if made by an employer). Unlike defined contribution retirement plans, withdrawals from the account are also tax-free as long as they are used to pay for medical expenses. Enacted in 2003 as part of legislation providing prescription drug benefits under Medicare, the tax preference is only available if the individual purchases a high-deductible health insurance policy.

horizontal equity. (See also **vertical equity**.) The concept that people of equal well-being should have the same tax burden.

human capital. Knowledge and skills that people acquire through education, training, and experience.

I

indexation of the tax system. Annual adjustments to various parameters in the tax code to account for inflation and prevent **bracket creep**. Since 1981, many features of the federal individual income tax, including tax brackets, the standard deduction, and certain credits, have been automatically indexed for inflation based on a

consumer price index. For instance, after a year with 5 percent inflation, a $12,000 standard deduction would increase to $12,600. More broadly, the term applies to all efforts to adjust measures of income to account for the effects of price inflation.

inheritance tax. A tax imposed on the bequests a taxpayer receives from a person who dies. Currently the United States has no federal inheritance tax, but several states do. Inheritance tax rates can differ, depending on the relationship of an heir to the decedent, with the lowest rates generally applying to closer relatives such as spouses and children. (See also **estate tax** and **gift tax**.)

IRA (Individual Retirement Account). Retirement accounts funded by individuals through their own contributions or by rolling over benefits earned under an employee-sponsored plan. An IRA is a kind of defined contribution retirement account. In traditional IRAs, contributions and earnings are tax-free, but withdrawals are taxable. In Roth IRAs, contributions are not deductible, but withdrawals are exempt from income tax.

itemized deductions. Particular kinds of expenses that taxpayers may use to reduce their taxable income. The most common itemized deductions are for state and local taxes, mortgage interest payments, charitable contributions, and large medical expenses. Individuals may opt to deduct these expenses or claim a **standard deduction**.

J

JGTRRA. See the **Jobs and Growth Tax Relief Reconciliation Act of 2003**.

Jobs and Growth Tax Relief Reconciliation Act of 2003 (JGTRRA). The 2003 tax act that accelerated the phase-in of tax rate reductions scheduled under **EGTRRA**, reduced the taxation of **capital gains** and **dividends**, accelerated increases in the **Child Tax Credit** amount, and temporarily raised the exemption for the **alternative minimum tax (AMT)**. Most provisions were set to expire at the end of 2010, but were then extended through 2012. (See also **Bush tax cuts**.)

Joint Committee on Taxation (JCT). A nonpartisan committee of the United States Congress charged with assisting members of Congress on tax legislation and related issues. The committee helps draft legislative proposals, estimates the revenue effects of all tax legislation considered by Congress, and examines various aspects of U.S. federal taxes.

L

low-income housing tax credit. A tax credit given to investors for the costs of constructing and rehabilitating low-income housing. The credit is intended to encourage the acquisition, construction, and/ or rehabilitation of housing for low-income families. Credits are allocated to state housing agencies based on state population. The agencies select qualifying projects and authorize credits subject to statutory limits.

M

marginal tax rate. The additional tax liability due on an additional dollar of income. It is a measure of the effect of the tax system on incentives to work, save, and shelter income from tax. Provisions such as the phase out of tax credits can cause marginal tax rates to differ from statutory tax rates.

marriage bonus. The reduction in the tax liability of some married couples that arises from filing as married rather than as single filers. Marriage bonuses result from the combination of treating a family as a single tax unit and progressive tax rates. In general, couples in which spouses have quite different incomes receive marriage bonuses. (See also **marriage penalty**.)

marriage penalty. The additional tax that some married couples pay because they must file as married rather than as single filers. Marriage penalties result from the combination of treating a family as a single tax unit and progressive tax rates. In general, couples in which spouses have similar incomes incur marriage penalties. (See also **marriage bonus**.)

Medicaid. A federal entitlement program that reimburses states for a portion of the costs associated with providing acute and long-term care services to certain low-income individuals. States determine which services and categories of people, beyond the minimum required by federal law, to cover. States also establish payment rates for providers and administer the program.

Medicare Part A. The part of Medicare that covers hospital services, skilled nursing facility services, and some home health care. Anyone over age 65 who is eligible for Social Security and persons under age 65 who have received Social Security disability payments for two years are eligible. Participants pay no premiums for Part A coverage.

Medicare Part B. Supplementary medical insurance for Medicare beneficiaries that provides physician services and other ambulatory care (such as outpatient hospital services and tests). Beneficiaries must pay a premium to join; premiums cover about one-fourth program costs. All persons over the age of 65 and other Medicare beneficiaries can enroll.

N

nominal income. A measure of income that is not adjusted for inflation. That is, nominal income is expressed in current dollars. (See also **real income.**)

non-filer. A person or household who does not file an individual income tax return. Most non-filers are not employed; many are elderly.

O

OASDI (Old Age, Survivors, and Disability Insurance). The Social Security programs that pay monthly benefits to retired workers and their spouses and children, to survivors of deceased workers, and to disabled workers and their spouses and children.

Omnibus Budget Reconciliation Act of 1987. Legislation that attempted to decrease the budget deficit through tax increases and expenditure decreases.

Omnibus Budget Reconciliation Act of 1990 (OBRA90). This act increased excise and payroll taxes, added a 31 percent income tax bracket, and introduced temporary high-income phase-outs for personal exemptions and itemized deductions. OBRA93 made these changes permanent.

Omnibus Budget Reconciliation Act of 1993 (OBRA93). This act introduced 36 percent and 39.6 percent income tax brackets, repealed the wage cap on Medicare payroll taxes, increased the portion of Social Security benefits subject to income taxation for those with higher incomes, made more workers with children eligible for the **Earned Income Tax Credit** and increased their benefits, and made permanent the temporary high-income phase-outs of the personal exemption and itemized deductions. Overall, the bill was focused on deficit reduction.

P

pass-through business. Businesses organized as S corporations, partnerships, and sole proprietorships that pass through any taxable profit or loss directly to the owners, who report it on individual income tax returns. Pass-through businesses are not subject to the corporate income tax that applies to most large corporations and many small ones.

pass-through business deduction. The TCJA introduced a new provision allowing pass-through businesses to deduct up to 20 percent of qualified business income (QBI) from **taxable income**.

payroll taxes. Taxes imposed on employers, employees, or both that are levied on some or all of workers' earnings. Employers and employees each remit Social Security taxes equal to 6.2 percent of all employee earnings up to a cap ($128,400 for 2018) and Medicare taxes of 1.45 percent on all earnings with no cap. Those taxes are referred to by the names of their authorizing acts: FICA (Federal Insurance Contributions Act) or SECA (Self-Employment Contributions Act), depending on the worker's employment status. Employers also remit State and Federal Unemployment Taxes (SUTA and FUTA) that cover the costs of unemployment insurance.

personal exemption. A per-person amount of income that is shielded from income tax. In calculating taxable income, tax filers may subtract the value of the personal exemption times the number of people in the tax unit. The personal exemption is indexed for inflation. The TCJA eliminated personal exemptions through 2025.

Pigouvian tax. A consumption tax designed to reflect the cost of negative **externalities**. Some spending imposes costs on others. The classic example is pollution—when I drive my car, for example, the tailpipe emissions include greenhouse gases that contribute to climate change as well as pollutants that degrade the environment and may contribute to health problems. Absent a tax, the price of gasoline does not reflect the environmental damage and I will thus ignore those costs in making decisions about what kind of car to buy or how much to drive. A Pigouvian tax adds an estimate of the marginal social damage costs to the price of a good or service and improves market efficiency as it induces consumers and businesses to account for all costs when making economic decisions.

pre-filled (or pre-populated) return. A tax return supplied by the tax authority with many items pre-filled based on information reported by third parties. For example, the IRS could send taxpayers a 1040 form with wages and salaries as reported by employers, and interest, dividends, and some capital gains as reported by financial institutions. The taxpayer must correct any errors and add missing information before certifying the return as accurate and submitting it. The state of California's ReadyReturn program provided pre-filled tax returns until objections from the tax preparation industry killed the program.

progressive tax. A tax that levies a larger percentage of the income of higher-income households than from lower-income households. (See also **regressive tax**.)

progressivity. A measure of how tax burdens increase with income. A progressive tax claims a proportionately larger share of income from higher-income than from lower-income taxpayers. Conversely, a **regressive tax** levies a larger share of income from lower-income households than from higher-income ones. Taxes that claim the same percentage of income from all taxpayers are termed "proportional."

property tax. A tax based on the value of property owned by an individual or household. In the United States, most property taxes are levied by local governments.

R

real income. The value of income after accounting for inflation. Real income is typically converted in terms of a particular year's prices—for example, a table may show income in 2010 dollars, meaning that the incomes are shown in terms of purchasing power in 2010. (See also **nominal income**.)

refundable tax credit. A tax credit that is payable even when it exceeds an individual's tax liability. Tax credits generally may be used only to reduce positive tax liability and are therefore limited to the amount of tax the individual otherwise would owe. Unlike other tax credits, the refundable portion of a tax credit is scored as an outlay in government budget accounts—that is, it is treated the same as direct spending. (See, e.g., **Earned Income Tax Credit**.)

regressive tax. A tax that claims a larger percentage of the income of lower-income households than of higher-income households. (See also **progressive tax**.)

revenue-neutral. A term applied to tax proposals in which provisions that raise revenues offset provisions that lose revenues so the proposal in total has no net revenue cost or increase.

S

SSDI (Social Security Disability Insurance). Social insurance that provides benefits to the disabled who qualify on the basis of years of work covered by Social Security. (See also **OASDI**.)

standard deduction. A deduction that taxpayers may claim on their tax returns in lieu of itemizing deductions such as charitable contributions, mortgage interest, or state and local taxes. Typically, taxpayers with modest deductible amounts that could be itemized choose to take the standard deduction. Single filers, heads of household, and married couples filing jointly have different standard deductions. Almost 90 percent of tax filers will claim a standard deduction in 2018. (See also **itemized deductions**.)

sunset. Provision of a tax act that terminates or repeals parts of the act on a certain date unless legislation is passed to extend them.

surtax. A tax added on top of another tax.

T

taxable income. The final income amount used to calculate tax liability. Taxable income equals adjusted gross income (**AGI**) less either the **standard deduction** or **itemized deduction** and, starting in 2018, the deduction for qualified business income.

Tax after credits. A filer's calculated, final tax liability after all credits (e.g., the **Earned Income Tax Credit**, the **Child Tax Credit**, the **Child and Dependent Care Tax Credit**, and the **foreign tax credit**) have been applied. If this amount is less than taxes paid via withholding or estimated tax payments, the taxpayer receives the difference as a refund. If the amount exceeds taxes paid, the taxpayer must remit the difference as a final payment.

tax burden. The total cost of taxation borne by a household or individual. The burden accounts not only for taxes remitted directly but also for burden incurred indirectly through lower wages or a reduced return on an investment and for **distortions** due to tax-induced changes in behavior. For example, in addition to the employee portion of payroll taxes, a worker may also bear the employer's share in the form of lower compensation.

tax credit. A reduction in tax liability for specific expenses such as for childcare or retirement savings. Unlike deductions, which reduce taxable income, a tax credit reduces tax liability dollar for dollar. Nonrefundable credits may only offset positive tax liability; in contrast, if a refundable credit exceeds the taxpayer's tax liability, the taxpayer receives the excess as a refund. (See also **refundable tax credit**.)

Tax Cuts and Jobs Act (TCJA). A major overhaul of the tax law enacted in 2017 that cut individual and especially corporate income tax rates, allowed businesses to immediately deduct (expense) the cost of non-real-estate investments, exempted much foreign business income from U.S. taxation, created a new deduction for pass-through business income, raised the standard deduction, doubled the child tax credit and eliminated the personal exemption, eliminated or curtailed many itemized deductions (including capping the deduction for state and local taxes), changed the price index used for inflation adjustments, and doubled the threshold for estate taxation. To limit the budgetary cost, expensing phases out starting in 2023 and most of the individual provisions are set to expire at the end of 2015, but the lower corporate tax rate and revised price index are permanent.

tax expenditure. A revenue loss attributable to a provision of federal tax laws that allows a special exclusion, exemption, or deduction from gross income or provides a special credit, preferential tax rate, or deferral of tax liability. Tax expenditures often result from tax provisions used to promote particular activities in place of direct subsidies.

tax filing threshold. The level of income at which filing units of specific size and filing status first owe a tax before considering tax credits. The amount varies with filing status, allowable adjustments, deductions, and exemptions. Tax credits can further increase the amount of untaxed income.

tax haven. A country that assesses little or no tax on the income of foreign multinationals. Many are small island nations such as the Cayman Islands and Bermuda.

tax incidence. A measure of the actual burden of a tax. Tax incidence may deviate from statutory tax liability because the imposition of a tax may change pre-tax prices. For example, retailers remit sales taxes, but those taxes raise the prices faced by consumers, who ultimately bear much of the burden of the tax.

tax liability. The amount of total taxes owed after application of all tax credits.

Taxpayer Relief Act of 1997 (TRA97). Tax legislation passed in 1997 that reduced capital gains tax rates, introduced the child credit, created education credits, raised the estate tax exemption level, created Roth IRAs, and increased the contribution limit for traditional IRAs.

Tax Reform Act of 1986 (TRA86). Revenue-neutral legislation passed in 1986 that simplified the tax code, lowered marginal tax rates, and closed corporate loopholes.

territorial taxation. A business tax system that exempts most active foreign income of multinational businesses from domestic taxation. Typically, territorial tax systems have minimum tax provisions aimed at preventing companies from shifting profits to tax havens. (See, e.g., **BEAT**.)

U

unemployment insurance (or unemployment compensation). A government program that provides cash benefits to some jobless workers for limited periods. Supervised by the federal government, the state-run programs are funded by payroll taxes states impose on employers.

V

value-added tax (VAT). A form of consumption tax collected from businesses based on the value each firm adds to a product (rather than, say, gross sales). VATs are almost universal outside the United States.

vertical equity. A value judgment about whether the net tax burden on people at different levels of well-being is appropriate. (See also **horizontal equity**.)

INDEX

For the benefit of digital users, indexed terms that span two pages (e.g., 52–53) may, on occasion, appear on only one of those pages.

Page numbers followed by *b, f,* and *t* refer to boxes, figures, and tables, respectively.